LOOKING AT LOGISTICS

A Practical Introduction to Logistics, Customer Service, and Supply Chain Management

2nd edition

P.M. Price, Ph.D.

N.J. Harrison, M.Ed.

Access EDUCATION

D1210773

Table of Contents

Chapter 1

Introducing the Supply Chain

Every day, we encounter logistics. Every time we interact with a physical good, we are influenced by logistics and the supply chain the product followed to reach us. For example, we wake up in the morning to the sound of a loud but trusted and functioning alarm clock. That alarm clock functions properly and gets us up when we need to be because it was part of an effective supply chain. All of its raw materials and component parts reached the alarm clock manufacturer on time and in a good enough condition to produce a working finished product. The newly manufactured alarm clock then followed a retail store's supply chain, reaching the store safely so that it remained in working condition. Our alarm clock wakes us up each day thanks to its logistics and supply chain success!

Suppose, however, that although our trusty alarm clock still works, we decide to buy a new neon orange alarm clock to match our bedroom's new psychedelic color scheme. Our new orange clock, however, stops functioning and fails to wake us up one morning, causing us to be late for an important job interview and leaving us without an income for an additional three months! Unbeknownst to us, not all the desired component parts reached our orange alarm clock's manufacturer, causing them to use improperly fitting internal parts intended for another line of clocks. Once manufactured, our orange alarm clock was not packaged carefully and, during its truck ride from the cargo port to our local retail store, extensive jostling caused the improperly fitting parts to work loose. As a result, our new alarm clock failed to wake us up and forever changed our lives thank to its logistics and supply chain failure!

Every day, we interact with hundreds or even thousands of processed, packaged, or man-made items, from the food we eat to the clothes on our backs to the cement in the foundation of our homes. The success of our interactions with these items depends on the success of their logistics and supply chains.

A First Look at Logistics

As a discipline, **logistics** is the study or practice of how the flow of goods and corresponding information are managed and controlled from the *point of origin* (i.e., when and where they are manufactured or processed) to the *point of consumption* (i.e., when and where they are received by the end user). As we mentioned earlier, everything we see and use in our daily lives is involved in logistics, from the food on our table to the table itself.

The fact that logistics has an enormous impact on the quality of our daily lives has not gone unnoticed by the commercial world. As we will see later in this chapter, businesses that invest their time, effort, and money in examining logistics systems have found that not only will customers' experiences with their products improve, but logistics-related costs can also be reduced drastically. As such, many large corporations appoint a Vice president in charge of logistics and invest heavily in ongoing logistics research, information technology, and systems implementation. Research centers, professional organizations, and entire departments of many top universities around the world devote themselves to the study of efficient and effective logistics practices and systems. Logistics is increasingly being seen as one of the most effective means to gaining competitive advantage in an increasingly competitive global marketplace.

Is logistics and supply chain management really important to an organization's success?

During the 1999 holiday season, the new practice of online shopping, also know as e-tailing, became enormously popular overnight. The leading U.S. toy retailer, Toys-R-Us, entered into the knew world of online sales, telling customers that all orders placed by December 10th would be delivered by Christmas.

The *front end* of the logistics system (the ability to order online, process the financial transaction, and issue orders to the finished goods warehouse for picking) could easily handle the large inflow of customers' requests and the company had enough inventory on hand to fill the orders. However, the physical back end of the logistics system (picking, packaging, and transporting customers' orders) was overwhelmed. Toys-R-Us simply could not physically process and fill the orders fast enough, even though many of its employees worked tirelessly for 49 days straight!

As December 25th neared, the company had to send apologetic emails to thousands of its customers, explaining that their orders could not be filled until a week after Santa had returned to the North Pole. Many customers cancelled their orders and customer loyalty levels dropped dramatically. In 2006, *Supply Chain Digest* labeled the event as one of the world's eleven "Greatest Supply Chain Disasters."

Although burned by the logistics challenges of their first foray into e-tailing, Toys-R-Us quickly learned and adapted, handling the 2000 holiday selling season with ease. The company later outsourced its online order fulfillment to the internet powerhouse Amazon.com.

As we stated earlier, the academic discipline of **logistics** explores the management and control of the flow of goods and information. When we use the term *logistics* in the business world, however, we are focused on the function *within an organization* that handles the flow of goods and information into, within, and out from that one organization. This flow of goods and information at the core of an organization's logistics is called its **supply chain**.

The business discipline and function that focuses on the flow of goods, information, and related finance *across multiple organizations*, often as goods move and transform from a raw materials or unfinished stage to a finished product received by an end user, is called **supply chain management**. This multi-organizational flow of goods and information is also called a **demand chain** and is sometimes even called the **total value chain**.

Anything you see in front of you that is man-made was once part of a supply chain. The supply chain for Orange-U-Good, our favorite brand of orange juice, for example, would begin with oranges as they are picked and packaged for shipment in an orange grove in Florida. The Orange-U-Good supply chain would then include all the activities associated with transporting and storing the oranges until they are received by the juice manufacturer in California. Once the oranges have been squeezed dry and the juice is packaged, the supply chain then includes all the activities associated with the handling, storage, and transportation of the packaged juice until it reaches your hometown grocery store and you pick it up off the shelf.

LOGISTICS LINGO

demand chain management

When you hear the term **demand chain management** used, it is likely because great emphasis is being placed on the actual demands of the final customer or end user. When materials are *pulled* through the chain based on actual customer demand, rather than the supplier *pushing* materials through the chain according to assumed demand or other criteria, an organization can provide a high level of customer service and control the amount of inventory within its chain.

value added

In a logistics context, the phrase **value added** is related to the increase in the value of products at each stage of the supply chain, as they transform from raw materials to finished goods. In our oranges example, the grower adds value to the oranges by transporting the oranges from their fields to the orange juice producer. The juice producer adds value to the raw oranges by processing the oranges into orange juice. They add further value by transporting juice from their geographic location, where there is an abundance of juice, to Alaska, where there is a shortage of orange juice. By analyzing all the stages in the chain they can look for opportunities to add more value or reduce current costs.

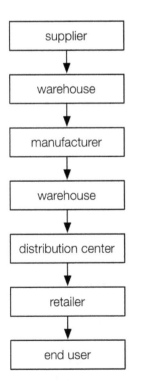

Figure 1.1 - The Simple Supply Chain

The **simple supply chain**, as shown in Figure 1.1, represents the straightforward supply chain for products such as Orange-U-Good. Spanning multiple organizations, this simple supply chain begins with the **supplier**, also known as the *vendor*, which is the company that supplies the raw materials or other goods to be used in the manufacturing process to produce the finished product. For Orange-U-Good orange juice, the supplier is the Florida orange grower.

Next within the simple supply chain are the **warehouses**. These are the locations in which goods are stored throughout the supply chain. These warehouses might be owned and operated by the supplier, the manufacturer, or the retailer or by a **third-party logistics services provider**, another company hired to provide warehouse services. Third-party logistics service providers typically specialize in a variety of logistics services, such as warehousing and transportation, and provide their services to a range of different and sometimes competing companies!

The **manufacturer** within the simple supply chain is the company that processes, manufactures, or assembles the finished product. This company takes raw materials or other unfinished component parts and transforms them into a finished product. For our orange juice example, Orange-U-Good is the manufacturer because it takes a raw material (oranges) and transforms them into a finished product (orange juice).

The **distribution center** within the simple supply chain is the location from which finished goods are sorted and shipped to various retailers or other customers. Distribution centers are relatively new to many supply chains. For many years, manufacturers' warehouses sorted and shipped finished goods. In more recent years, distribution centers have sprung up to focus on short term storage and often operate a cross docking system that minimizes the time items are within its facilities. Companies such as Walmart and Saks, Inc. have shown that using distinct distribution centers create a more efficient and effective supply chain. Like warehouses within the supply chain, a distribution center may be owned and operated by the manufacturer, retailer, or a third-party provider.

At the tail end of our simple supply chain are the retailer and the end user. The **retailer** is manufacturer's customer that sells the finished product to the end user. For the Orange-U-Good supply chain, the retailers are the many grocery stores across North America that stock their shelves with the delectable juice, including your favorite local grocer. The simple supply chain's **end user** is the customer and final consumer of the finished product. For Orange-U-Good, you and all of its other orange juice buyers and drinkers are its end users. End users are not always people who physically consume products, however. For Bright Beams, a car headlight manufacturer, its end users are the big automobile manufacturing companies that purchase and use its headlights on the automobile assembly line.

While the concepts and members of the simple supply chain are relevant across supply chain settings, the actual supply chains for most finished products are quite complex and may involve a variety of raw materials. They also typically include multiple transportation, manufacturing, warehouse, and distribution facilities in different countries around the world. To illustrate this point, let's look at the supply chain for a typical desktop computer.

A computer manufacturer's supply chain typically begins not only with raw materials, but also with a wide variety of pre-manufactured component parts. These component parts, which are typically manufactured by different companies in different locations around the world, include microprocessors, memory cards and chips, graphics cards, sound cards, network cards, USB drives, CD-ROM and DVD drives, operating software, keyboards, mice, monitors, power supplies, cooling fans, and casings. Once these component parts are assembled, the finished products, i.e., the brand new computers, are then distributed to a multitude of distribution centers, retailers, and end users around the world. In many cases, the finished products are not "finished" until they reach a country's regional warehouses and distribution centers, where language-specific keyboards, software, operating instructions, and packaging can be added. The global supply chain for a typical U.S.-based computer manufacturer is illustrated in Figures 1.2 and 1.3 below. Figure 1.2 illustrates the flow of component parts or raw materials to the manufacturing facility, or the **inbound supply chain**. Figure 1.3, conversely, illustrates the flow of finished goods to regional distribution centers, retailers, and end users, or the **outbound supply chain**.

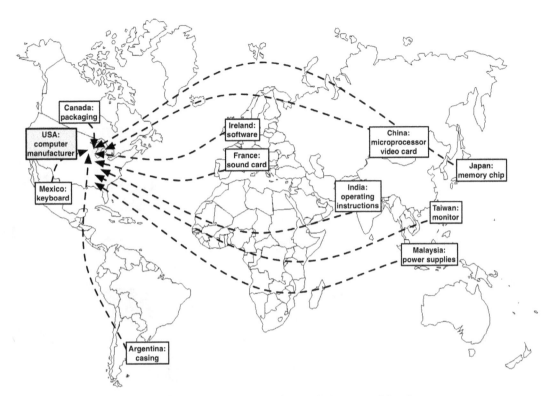

Figure 1.2 - The Inbound Supply Chain for a U.S. Computer Manufacturer

Figure 1.3 - The Outbound Supply Chain for a U.S. Computer Manufacturer

With a variety of suppliers, manufacturing facilities, retailers, warehouses, and distribution centers, our once simple supply chain now becomes a complex global supply chain. As shown in Figure 1.4, today's typical supply chain involves many members and spans multiple locations.

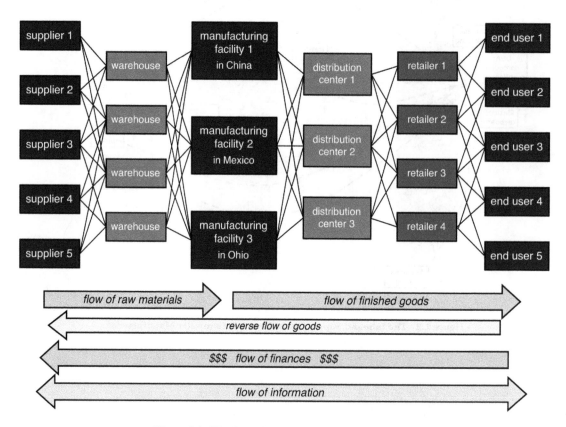

Figure 1.4 - The Complex Supply Chain of Today

Do goods flow in only one direction along a supply chain?

In Figure 1.4, goods flow in a predictable fashion from left to right (both as raw materials and finished goods) toward the direction of the end user. However, they also flow from right to left, *away from the end user*. What on earth is that about?

It is quite common for customers all along the chain to return goods to suppliers. This practice is called **reverse logistics**, a specialized aspect of logistics that concerns the flow of goods and related resources from the customer back to the supplier. Reverse logistics occurs after a product has been sold and delivered to a customer and may include product returns, damaged goods to be repaired, and items to be recycled.

Complex supply chains like the one shown in Figure 1.4 above can become pretty confusing to the average logistics manager or practitioner. To help us avoid the confusion and know exactly where we are in a complex supply chain, we refer to our own organization as the ***focal firm*** within that supply chain. We then refer to those organizations whose activities occur *before ours* within the total supply chain (i.e., to the left of our focal firm in the chart above) as being ***upstream***. Those organizations whose activities occur *after ours* within the total supply chain (i.e., to the right of our focal firm in the chart above) are referred to as being ***downstream***. For example, if our organization is distribution center 3 in the chart above, it is our *focal firm*. All the suppliers, warehouses, and manufacturing facilities are *upstream* of our focal firm while all the retailers are *downstream* of our focal firm.

INTERNAL AND EXTERNAL SUPPLY CHAINS

There are two commonly documented and analyzed types of supply chains: the *external supply chain* and the *internal supply chain*. The **external supply chain** represents the flow of goods, information, and finances when more than one company or organization is involved, typically the manufacturer and its suppliers and immediate customers, such as retailers. Both the simple and complex supply chains we have already examined are examples of external supply chains. In the case of Orange-U-Good orange juice, the external supply chain includes the flow of goods, information, and finances, beginning with orange suppliers at the orange grove and ending with the finished cartons of orange juice on your grocer's shelves.

Figure 1.5 - External Supply Chain for an Orange Juice Manufacturer

Unlike the external supply chain, the **internal supply chain** represents the flow of goods, information, and finance within only one organization. In the case of Orange-U-Good orange juice, the internal supply chain begins when the oranges reach the receiving dock at the Orange-U-Good warehouse. It ends the second the cartons of packaged orange juice leave the Orange-U-Good manufacturing facility warehouse.

A product's internal supply chain does not have to reside entirely within one building, but it does reside within only one company. Orange-U-Good, for example, may receive the fresh oranges from twenty different suppliers at its regional warehouse in Florida. It may then truck the oranges in refrigerated containers to the Orange-U-Good juicing facility in California. After the juice has been produced and packaged, Orange-U-Good may finally send container-loads of packaged juice cartons to its own regional distribution centers in Los Angeles, Newark, Detroit, Atlanta, Vancouver, and Mexico City. Although widespread, all of these logistics activities are within the Orange-U-Good orange juice internal supply chain.

The logistics department of an organization is responsible for the efficiency and effectiveness of the internal supply chain. However, for an internal supply chain to run smoothly and efficiently, many of the departments within the organization must cooperate and communicate fluidly. The success of any internal or external supply chain depends upon the cohesion of the internal

supply chain management team, which is made up of the heads of a company's core departments, including: marketing, finance, manufacturing, human resource management, and logistics. (See Figure 1.6 below.) These departments must regularly and openly share information with one another other regarding the internal flow of goods. As we will discuss in later chapters, advances in information technology systems have made this internal information sharing both easy and immediate.

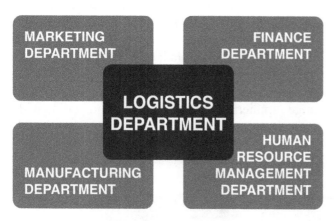

Figure 1.6 - The Supply Chain Management Team

The core of the supply chain management team is the ***logistics department***, which is responsible for the physical flow of goods and associated information into, within, and out from the organization. The logistics department bears the ultimate physical responsibility for the success of both internal and external supply chains. The head of this vital department, therefore, works closely with and depends heavily on the other members of the supply chain management team.

The ***manufacturing department*** is responsible for transforming raw or unfinished goods received into a finished or semifinished product. The head of this department depends on the other members of the supply chain management team to ensure that it has the necessary direct and indirect materials, employees, information, and finances in place to both begin the production process and to take away finished goods as they are produced to make room for more new finished products.

The ***human resources department*** is responsible for managing and meeting the needs of the workforce of the product's organization. The head of this department ensures that motivated and skilled employees are available when and where they are needed at all points within the supply chain. A shortage of skilled and motivate employees at any point within the supply chain can lead to costly delays and customer dissatisfaction.

The ***marketing department*** is responsible for the price, promotion, place, and product design of a company's products. The department's ultimate goal is to meet and exceed its customers' needs. As a member of the supply chain management team, the head of this department must work with other members of the team to help set a realistic price for products, factoring in the often substantial supply chain costs. The supply chain management team also works together to ensure that the marketing goal is met by having products in the right place at the right time in the right quantity of the right quality at a competitive price.

Finally, the ***finance department*** is responsible for financial control within the organization, including resource allocation across departments, locations, and activities. Many supply chain decisions rely heavily on information from the finance department, especially information on the amount of company resources available for supply chain activities.

THE POWER OF THE SUPPLY CHAIN

Commercial companies are responsible to their owners or stakeholders. Therefore, their primary goal of almost all companies is to generate income, i.e., make money! When supply chains are not functioning properly or if they are poorly conceived, they can lose money for a company. Imagine going to your local grocery store to buy a carton of Orange-U-Good orange juice but finding the shelves bare because your favorite brand has not yet arrived at the store. Because you must have your morning glass of orange juice, you find yourself in the precarious position of having to select an alternate brand!

But why has Orange-U-Good orange juice not yet arrived? Supply chain failure! A shortage on the dye used to print the ink on the cartons used to hold the delicious Florida orange juice caused the cartons to be delivered late to the juice manufacturer, which led to a delay in juice production, which led to a late delivery to juice retailers, such as your local supermarket. This delay not only loses the orange juice company immediate sales, but it also decreases customer satisfaction and may reduce customers' brand loyalty. This delay let customers such as you experience a wide variety of different brands of orange juice, some of which you might like more and choose in the future! Therefore, a study of products' supply chains and the disciplines of logistics and supply chain management are critical for commercial survival and success in today's increasingly competitive global marketplace.

Companies can make or lose more money or gain or lose competitive advantage based on the efficiency and effectiveness of their supply chains. For example, after World War II, when most of Europe had been exposed to Hershey's chocolate from the ration packs of American GIs, the American-based Hershey company chose not to extend its supply chain into Europe. Its primary competitor, Mars, did choose to extend its chocolate supply chain into Europe. These decisions had significant and long-lasting impacts for both companies. Mars is the world's largest-selling chocolate manufacturer and Hershey is not even in second place.

If a supply chain is efficient in its design and operation, it is streamlined and uses the most cost-effective practices for the company, thus saving the company money. For example, Walmart was one of the first national retailers to use the streamlined logistics practice of cross-docking at its regional distribution centers. ***Cross-docking*** is the supply chain practice in which finished goods from a variety of suppliers or locations are received at one end of a warehouse facility or distribution center. The goods are immediately broken down, sorted, and placed into trucks or containers at the other end of the facility for immediate shipping. This practice allows finished goods to get to end users quicker and provides significant savings in warehouse costs.

Finally, when a supply chain is effective in its design and operation, it not only flows smoothly, but, to be competitive, it also adds value to the product that customers and end users desire. For example, Dell, Inc. was one of the first computer manufacturers to eliminate retailers from its supply chain and engage in the logistics practice of postponement. ***Postponement*** is the supply chain practice in which final manufacturing activities such as packaging and assembly are delayed as far into the distribution process as possible. With companies like Dell, adding specific end-user requirements to computers, such as upgraded memory chips or video cards, are postponed until immediately prior to shipment to the end user. As a result of practicing postponement, Dell has a worldwide reputation for being highly responsive to end users' needs.

CHAPTER 1 REVIEW QUESTIONS

1. *Logistics* focuses on the flow of goods between which two points?

2. What are *warehouses* and *distribution centers*? How are they different?

3. Provide one example of an *inbound supply chain*.

4. Now provide one example of an *outbound supply chain*.

5. Which type of supply chain is representative of the majority of supply chains today – the *simple supply chain* shown in Figure 1.1 or the *complex supply chain* shown in Figure 1.4? Why do you think this is true?

6. Explain how one company can be a part of both *internal* and *external supply chains*.

7. Why is the Human Resources Manager a critical part of the internal supply chain management team?

8. What might happen if the Marketing Manger did not work with other members of the supply chain management team?

9. What two practices do each Walmart and Dell use to make their supply chains more efficient? What benefits do these practices provide?

10. Why do you believe the discipline of logistics is important for business operations in the 21st century?

CHAPTER 1 CASE STUDY

A Supply Chain Fairytale

Once upon a time...

Once upon a time in the not too distant present in a kingdom called "the Company," there was an evil stepmother called "the CEO," whose only concern was keeping the Shareholders happy with good dividend returns. She had two ugly daughters. One was called "Finance" and the other was called "Marketing." Unlike the other evil stepmother of childhood fairytales, our "CEO" also had an ugly son called "Manufacturing."

The ugly sister "Marketing" was preoccupied only with the handsome "Customer." Nothing mattered to Marketing except getting goods delivered and keeping the "Customer" happy, no matter what the cost. Marketing didn't care if she made "the Company" poor because she desperately wanted to please the handsome "Customer" and she would often send him what he needed by an expensive golden airplane instead of sending items by the more affordable horse-powered trucks.

The other ugly sister, "Finance," had no time for handsome customers. Her true love was money and she wanted to hold onto every penny "the Company" had. Finance insisted that "the Company" should do everything at the lowest cost possible. The stingy Finance often fought with her frivolous sister, screaming, "We must protect the Company and reduce all costs!" to which Marketing would cry, "But we need to keep the Customer happy! I want to live happily ever after with him!" Both sisters naively thought that reducing costs and maximizing customer service were mutually exclusive.

Adding to the family chaos was the ugly and very demanding brother, "Manufacturing." He liked to build and build and build for "the Company," but he thought that he was the fairest of them all and demanded that everything he needed to build should be supplied immediately and on a silver platter. Manufacturing and Finance fought long and often because the demanding brother wanted lots of extra materials to be on hand "just in case" the Company needed more things to be built, while his stingy sister never wanted him to order more materials than he absolutely needed and insisted that he order the cheapest materials available, regardless of their quality. When Manufacturing got his way and won these heated arguments, the Company's royal warehouses were overflowing with extra goods, resulting in increased inventory holding costs and a very angry evil stepmother CEO. When Finance got her way, there were never any extra materials ordered and the royal warehouses remained almost empty. This pleased the CEO (because there were no extra inventory holding costs) until the handsome Customer told the CEO that he needed an extra 500,000 widgets built immediately. Because there were no extra materials available, Manufacturing could not begin building widgets for the Customer until after the holiday weekend. This displeased the evil CEO stepmother greatly.

Manufacturing grew tired of arguing with his stingy sister, Finance, and decided to reduce his costs and please the evil stepmother CEO by engaging in long production runs, building millions and millions of widgets at a time. While this did reduce production costs, Manufacturing naively believed that this would also keep the Customer happy by having so many widgets immediately available. However, these millions of widgets were royal blue. The handsome Customer told Marketing that he was growing weary of royal blue and now wanted all widgets to be awe-inspiring platinum. When Marketing told her brother that the next order for the handsome Customer must be changed to awe-inspiring platinum, Manufacturing flew into a rage, screaming, "We have just started our production run of five million royal blue widgets! I will not change it just because some pretty boy customer has changed his mind! It will cost the Company and my sub-realm too much money!" Marketing grew even angrier at her demanding and resistant bother, grabbing him the collar and bellowing into his face, "You WILL change the order to awe-inspiring platinum! If you do not, the handsome Customer might leave us for another kingdom and WE CAN'T HAVE THAT!"

Thus, all was not rosy in the family of our evil stepmother CEO. Now enters the poor Cinderella stepsister of our story, the stepsister with the mellifluous name of "Logistics." Logistics was hardworking and fair and kind and just and, well, an all-around perfect person. She knew that the verdant and rich Company would shrivel up into a wasteland of hopelessness and despair if her siblings did not stop fighting. She knew what needed to be done, so she rolled up her sleeves and got to work. She decided that, although they were ugly (and frivolous, stingy, and demanding), Marketing, Finance, and Manufacturing were all important to the Company's prosperity. She knew that they all had important needs and concerns, so she decided to put aside family differences and work with them all.

Logistics worked with Marketing to ensure that all widgets were picked, packed, and transported to the handsome Customer to ensure that what he wanted arrived in the right quantity, of the right quality, at the right time, and at the right place, while also being mindful of keeping costs as low as possible. Logistics also worked with Manufacturing to ensure that he had the exact building materials he needed in the right quantity, of the right quality, at the right time, and at the right place, while still being mindful of keeping costs as low as possible. Finally, Logistics worked with Finance to minimize inventory holding costs through inventory management.

Through her challenging work with her equally challenging siblings, Logistics learned an important lesson of logistics management: minimize all costs associated with all the activities of internal customers (finance, marketing, and manufacturing) while ensuring the right quantity of goods of the right quality are delivered to the external customer at the right time and to the right place with minimum costs and maximum level of service.

The hardworking Cinderella of our story, Logistics, accomplished all of this by listening to her siblings' needs and getting down to work. And she did all of this without the help of a fairy godmother or some random prince to come to her rescue! She also learned that Marketing, Finance, and Manufacturing weren't so ugly after all when someone finally listened to them and the evil stepmother CEO wasn't even evil when her headache subsided after all her step-kids stopped arguing.

And they all lived happily ever after...

The End?

Chapter 2
Logistics & Supply Chain Management

The History and Development of Logistics

The term *logistics* was first used in 1670 by French military circles to describe the specific practical problems of supporting armies on the move. Over the past 50 to 60 years, logistics as a discipline has entered the commercial world. The discipline of logistics has evolved through the following four distinct stages.

Stage 1: Fragmentation. Before 1950, supply chains were fragmented and businesses typically performed what are now considered logistics tasks across different departments of an organization. These tasks were performed in isolation from each other because departments in the same organization rarely shared information and even saw each other as competitors.

Stage 2: Evolving Integration. During the oil crisis of the 1970s, costs spiraled and international competition threatened formerly secure domestic companies. The supply chain began to come under scrutiny as a possible means of reducing an organization's operating costs. Companies began to integrate their logistics/supply chain tasks into two functional areas: materials management and physical distribution. ***Materials management*** is the function that provides support to the manufacturing process and focuses on the planning and control of the flow of raw materials and component parts from the supplier to the end of the production process. ***Physical distribution management*** focuses on the activities surrounding the movement of finished goods.

Stage 3: Internal Integration. In the 1980s and 1990s, companies continued to focus the supply chain. Logistics and supply chain tasks were no longer viewed as a cost of doing business, but instead, as a means of increasing efficiency and reducing operating costs. As shown in the

Stage 3 and 4 organization chart in Figure 2.1 below, logistics tasks began to become integrated under one Logistics department or manager, including the three Stage 2 functional areas of procurement, materials management, and physical distribution.

Stage 4: External Integration. From the 1990s through today, as companies integrate their internal logistics and supply chain tasks under one department or manager, companies have begun to integrate supply chains externally with suppliers and customers. With rapidly developments of information technology, information sharing among the internal and external members of a product's supply chain is not only possible, but is usually the most cost-effective means of doing business. Despite its efficiency and effectiveness, not all companies have reached Stage 4 in the evolution of their logistics and supply chain functions.

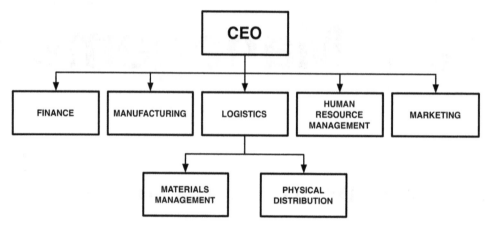

Figure 2.1 - The Organization Chart of a Logistics Stage 3 or 4 Organization

DEFINING LOGISTICS AND SUPPLY CHAIN MANAGEMENT

As we stated in Chapter 1, within a business setting, the term *logistics* refers to the function and associated activities within an organization that handles the flow of goods and information into, within, and out from that one organization. Two core logistics-related activities in which organizations are engaged are *logistics management* and *supply chain management*.

According to the website of one of the premier professional organizations of logistics professionals, the Council of Supply Chain Management Professionals (CSCMP), **logistics management** is "that part of supply chain management that plans, implements, and controls the efficient, effective forward and reverse flow and storage of goods, services and related information between the point of origin [a focal firm's suppliers] and the point of consumption [a focal firm's customers] in order to meet customers' requirements." CSCMP further adds that logistics management is "an integrating function, which coordinates and optimizes all logistics activities, as well as integrates logistics activities with other functions [departments within an organization]." While this definition sounds like quite a mouthful, logistics management is essentially the management of the flow and storage of goods and related information into, within, and out from an organization, spanning and coordinating multiple departments and functions within that organization which engage in logistics-related activities.

But what are these activities central to logistics? All the logistics activities occurring within a company can fit into one of three categories: inbound processes, internal processes, and outbound processes. ***Inbound processes*** are those logistics activities that take place at the beginning of the company's internal supply chain before goods are received from the supplier, such as purchasing and supply management. ***Internal processes*** include logistics activities such as internal warehouse management, materials handling, and inventory management, that support the production process as a company transforms raw goods or component parts into finished goods. Both the inbound process of purchasing and the internal process of internal warehouse management together form the previously described function called ***materials management***. Finally, ***outbound processes*** are those logistics activities that take place after the organization has produced its finished product and include finished goods warehouse management, transportation, and external distribution center management. Together, these three activities form the practice called ***physical distribution management***.

Related to logistics management but taking it a step further is ***supply chain management***. According to their website, the CSCMP defines supply chain management as "all of the planning and management of all activities involved in the sourcing and procurement, conversion, and all

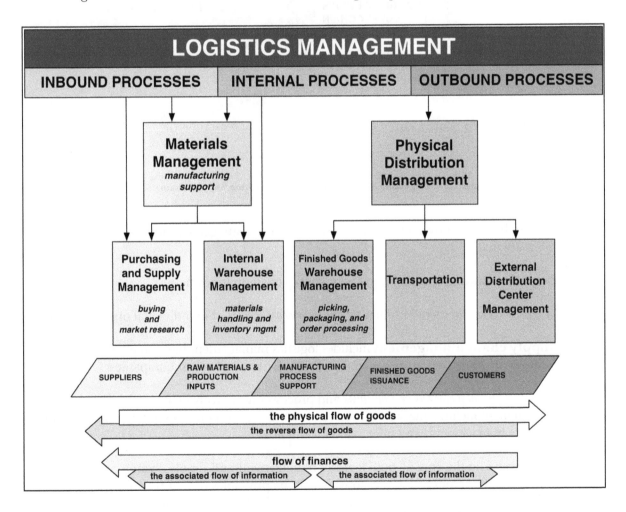

Figure 2.2 - A Map of Logistics Management Processes

Logistics Management activities." Making it distinct from logistics management, they add that supply chain management "includes coordination and collaboration with channel partners, which can be suppliers, intermediaries, third-party service providers, and customers. In essence, [it] integrates supply and demand management within and across companies." As shown in Figure 2.3 below, supply chain management attempts to integrate the supply chains of individual organizations to meet the demands of the end user of their collectively manufactured product or service.

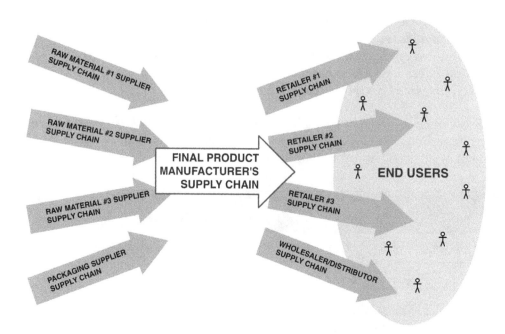

Figure 2.3 - Integrating Multiple Supply Chains within Supply Chain

The primary differences between the disciplines of logistics management and supply chain management are that:

- **Logistics management** is a *subset* of supply chain management.

- "Logistics Management" is often a *function or department* within individual organizations.

- **Supply chain management** includes logistics management but also involves the major business functions, departments, and processes within and across companies.

- Those *additional major business functions* and processes also involved in supply chain management include: marketing, sales, product design, finance, manufacturing, human resource management, and information technology.

Logistics, however, is at the core of both logistics management and supply chain management. In addition, there are four types of logistics to which all the principles of logistics management and supply chain management covered in this text would apply. These four types of logistics, which are based on the supply chain setting, are:

- *Business logistics*, for which the focus is the efficient and cost effective flow of goods or services within a commercial organization;

- *Military logistics*, for which the focus is the movement of military resources to troops and bases at exactly the right time to exactly the right place;

- *Production logistics*, for which the focus is the efficient flow of materials to workstations and machines within the manufacturing environment; and

- *Event logistics*, for which the focus is getting materials to, setting up, running, and taking materials down from specific events, such as concerts or sports competitions.

CREATING VALUE THROUGH LOGISTICS

As logistics developed as a discipline and its corresponding logistics systems took advantage of rapid advances in information technology, companies found that operating costs could decline and customers could become more satisfied. For example, over the past twenty years, many companies found that inventory control costs were cut substantially as they implemented the use of bar codes and scanning equipment. During the same time, advances in cargo port container handling systems allowed many global companies to provide the invaluable added customer service of drastically reduced delivery times. As a result, the **core objectives of logistics management** within a commercial organization today are to:

- Significantly *reduce* a supply chain's operating *costs*; and

- *Increase customer service* provided to the organization's customers, including not only the immediate external customers, but also the internal customers and the product's end users.

Most of the time, the objectives of logistics management within an organization are at odds. To increase customer service levels, costs invariably have to be raised. Conversely, to reduce costs, customer service levels may have to be minimized. Logistics managers use the **tradeoff principle** when making logistics decisions in which the advantages and disadvantages of decisions are considered and weighed based on the degree to which they provide: maximization of cost savings, resource use, and customer service level increases.

In addition to minimizing cost and maximizing customer service, logistics and supply chain management create substantial **value** for all involved (i.e., the organization and its customers, suppliers, and owners/stakeholders). This value is often called **utility**, an economics term referring to the satisfaction or happiness customers experience when they consume an organization's goods or services. There are four primary types of utility: *form, time, place,* and *possession*.

Form utility is the value added to products as their form changes, for example, as raw materials are transformed or manufactured into finished goods. Form utility is created by the manufacturing department within an organization.

Place utility is the value added to products when they are at the right place within the supply chain, from the receipt of raw materials from suppliers to distribution of finished goods to external customers, i.e., when they are where both internal and external customers want them. Place utility is created by the logistics department, which helps get products exactly to customers' desired locations and also helps companies use geographically distant or dispersed suppliers, whose products may be desired because they are cheaper or of a better quality.

Time utility is the value added to products when they are available at the time (i.e., when) both internal and external customers desire them. Time utility is created by the logistics department, which helps get products to customers exactly when they want them.

Possession utility is the value added to products when a desire to possess them has been created in the minds of the consumers. Possession utility is created by the marketing department, which promotes products both directly and indirectly to the organization's customers.

Of the four types of utility, two types – time utility and place utility – are added by logistics and supply chain management activities. Again, logistics adds time value by getting products to customers exactly when they want them. Best Buy and Toys-R-Us, for example, use logistics management to ensure that the newest Nintendo, X-Box, and Playstation game systems arrive into all of their stores within the U.S. from manufacturers in Asia in time for the busy Christmas shopping season. Logistics also adds place value by getting products exactly to customers' desired locations or by getting products from distant or dispersed desired suppliers. Starbucks strives hard to offer place value, for example, by making sure that the same exact coffee products and cups are found in all of their store locations worldwide so that your seasonally offered Grande Skinny Gingerbread Latte will look and taste exactly the same in New York City; Anchorage, Alaska; Dublin, Ireland; and Shanghai, China!

LOGISTICS LINGO

value chain

The two primary objectives of logistics within an organization are to reduce cost and maximize customer service/value. Companies analyze and modify their supply chains in order to achieve these objectives. Therefore, the supply chain is called the **value chain** when it is outlined and examined in terms of value added throughout each of the chain's stages.

Every stage of the supply chain adds value to an organization's product. The true value of the product is the customers' perception of it, i.e., what they are willing to pay for it. When analyzing the value of the product, an organization checks to see if any parts of the supply chain could add more value. E-commerce, for example, has allowed manufacturing companies to sell directly to customers, eliminating wholesalers and retailers. The resulting value-added cost savings can be shared directly with customers.

As logistics and supply chain management both attempt to decrease an organization's costs and increase its customer service levels, the degree to which they can achieve these objectives and create optimum value are influenced by a variety of factors in the external business operating environment. These influential and supply chain-shaping factors are:

- **Information technology.** With the increase of logistics lean supply chain and immediate delivery practices such as Just-in-Time, substituting information for inventory has become standard practice.

- **Global complexity.** Global markets are becoming increasingly open and accessible for both suppliers and customers.

- **Customer demands.** With increasing market competition, customers are demanding more frequent deliveries, smaller quantities, and increased customer service, all at a lower cost.

- **E-commerce.** Logistics must now provide physical support for the ever-growing world of electronic transactions such as e-commerce.

- **Competitive advantage-seeking.** As products become more homogeneous, organizations are looking to logistics practices to add value to products and gain advantage over competitors.

- **Transportation deregulation.** Since transportation has been deregulated, organizations are now able to negotiate transportation rates.

CHAPTER 2 REVIEW QUESTIONS

1. In the 1970s, companies began to integrate supply chain tasks into which three functional areas?

2. Why did companies begin to integrate supply chain tasks at that time?

3. At what point did supply chain tasks begin to become integrated under one logistics manager?

4. Which business activities most commonly fall within the scope of a logistics manager's responsibility?

5. What is materials management? Is it an inbound, internal, or outbound process of logistics management?

6. Which activities of logistics management internal and outbound processes are similar?

7. Describe one way in which logistics management and supply chain management are different.

8. Within a commercial enterprise, what are the core objectives of logistics management?

9. Please provide an original example of how supply chain management offers each time and place utility.

10. Why might a supply chain be called a value chain?

CHAPTER 2 CASE STUDY

The Apple Supply Chain

Not too long ago, we read newspapers, called a free telephone number to get the day's local weather, and played board games with our families. Thanks to Apple and the introduction of the iPad in 2010, we now rely on tablet computers to get news and opinions from around the world, see satellite images of local weather systems, and pass our time flinging birds to kill armies of holiday pigs. In one short year, the iPad became a necessary fixture for many American, European, and Asian households. During this time, competitors offered up a variety or cool devices with comparable and sometimes even superior features, but Apple was able to fend them all off and claim ultimate victory over the tablet computing market. Apple was able to maintain market dominance thanks to something not normally part of Apple's cadre of competitive advantages: low prices.

Apple introduced its entry level iPad to the world for a mere $499. As the iPad became thinner, sleeker, and faster, Apple kept its entry level iPad 2 at $499. Throughout the tablet market's nascent years of 2010 and 2011, other tablet computers could not come close to the $500 mark. Even Motorola's much awaited XOOM tablet, with beefier technical specs than Apple's iPad, could not compete because it entered the market at $800, 60% above the $500 that consumers came to expect to pay for a tablet computer.

Not typically known for its low prices, Apple has been able to keep iPad prices low and will continue to do so for the foreseeable future. How on earth can the company known for high end, high price computers achieve competitive advantage with low prices? With supply chain management, of course! Apple has streamlined its offering to include only five devices (iPod, iPad, iPhone, Mac, and AppleTV) with a total of fifteen variations of these devices combined. Most of this limited range of devices shares common component parts. As a result, Apple can achieve economies of scale by placing staggeringly large pre-orders of 10,000,000+ parts from its suppliers. In 2010, semiconductor research firm iSuppli found that Apple was the second largest purchaser of semiconductor components and predicted that the company would pull into first place in 2012, ahead of Hewlett-Packard and the current leader, Samsung.

Over the past decade, Apple has honed the art of large pre-orders from suppliers, beginning with the introduction of the iPod in 2011. Over the years, this practice has provided Apple with pricing discounts and stock guarantees from its suppliers. For example, when earthquakes and tsunamis devastated Japan in March 2011, Apple was able to continue to rely on components from its Japanese suppliers and keep its iPad prices low, even though the same suppliers could not fill the orders of Apple's many competitors. During this quarter, which was devastating to most of the computer market, Apple was able to sell a hefty 4.7 million iPads and 18.7 million iPhones. As is typical of any situation in which there are shortages, suppliers take care of their biggest customers first. Because its streamlined line of products requires vast quantities of a limited range of components, Apple remains the biggest customer for most of its Japanese suppliers, placing it in the fortunate position of supply chain dominance.

References

Goldman, D. (2011, April 22) How Apple blocks its competition. *CNNMoney.com*. Retrieved from http://money.cnn.com/fdcp?unique=1305163847955.

Kane, Y.I. (2011, April 21) Apple: no disruptions from Japan. *The Wall Street Journal Blogs*. Retrieved from http://blogs.wsj.com/digits/2011/04/21/apple-no-disruptions-from-japan/.

Ong, J. (2011, April 21) Wall Street: Apple is a "magical growth story" in tech, defies gravity. *Apple Insider*. Retrieved from http://www.appleinsider.com/articles/11/04/21/wall_street_apple_is_magical_growth_story_in_tech_defies_gravity.html.

Perlow, J. (2010, February 7) Apple's secret iPad advantage: The Supply Chain. *zdnet.com*. Retrieved from http://www.zdnet.com/blog/perlow/apples-secret-ipad-advantage-the-supply-chain/15813.

CASE STUDY

Case Study Questions

1. At which stage of development might Apple's supply chain be? Why?

2. How did Apple create value through its logistics practices?

3. After the devastating 2011 earthquakes in Japan, how did Apple achieve time utility?

4. Which supply chain shaping factors does the case study demonstrate?

Chapter 3

The Physical Side of Materials Management

Over the past ten to twenty years, logistics academics and practitioners have divided the world of logistics management systems into two primary areas: *inbound logistics* and *outbound logistics*. In Chapter 2, we defined inbound logistics processes as those logistics activities that take place at the beginning of the inbound supply chain until goods are received from the supplier. Outbound logistics was defined as those logistics processes that take place after the organization has produced its finished product.

In this chapter, we will explore one area of inbound logistics: the physical side of materials management. Remember our model of logistics management from way, way back in Chapter 2? Our model also includes internal processes, which are usually divided among and included within the realms of either inbound or outbound logistics.

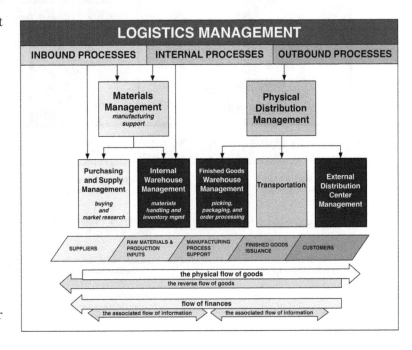

INBOUND LOGISTICS AND MATERIALS MANAGEMENT

Inbound logistics includes all the logistics activities that occur at the beginning of a company's internal supply chain, from the moment an order for goods is placed with the supplier until the organization receives the goods from the supplier. Inbound logistics includes both financial (purchasing) and physical (warehouse management) activities. ***Outbound logistics*** includes all the logistics activities that occur at the end of an organization's logistics chain, from the moment an organization has produced its finished product until the product is received by its immediate user. Outbound logistics includes both distribution center/finished goods warehouse management and transportation activities.

Inbound and outbound logistics processes occur throughout a product's total supply chain. Each individual member (i.e., company) of a product's total supply chain engages in both inbound and outbound logistics. For example, as shown in Figure 3.1 below, the supply chain for our favorite orange juice includes four members: *the raw materials supplier* (the orange grove); *the manufacturer* (Orange-U-Good juice company); *the distribution center* (a 3rd-party service provider); and *the retailer* (your local grocery store). As Figure 1 illustrates, each of these members of the juice supply chain are engaged in both inbound and outbound logistics activities. For example, inbound logistics activities for the orange grove include receipt of supplies for the orange growing process while their outbound logistics activities include delivering their finished product (oranges) to the immediate user (the Orange-U-Good juice factory).

SUPPLY CHAIN MEMBER		INBOUND LOGISTICS	OUTBOUND LOGISTICS
RAW MATERIALS EXTRACTOR/SUPPLIER	Orange growers in Florida orange tree grove	Receiving fertilizer and orange picking supplies from suppliers	Delivering oranges to manufacturing facility in right quantity at right time and place
MANUFACTURER	Orange-U-Good juice manufacturing facility	Receiving, inspecting, and holding oranges for juicing	Packaging juice and delivering right quantity of juice to distribution center at right time and place
DISTRIBUTION CENTER/WAREHOUSE	3rd party regional distribution center	Receiving, inspecting, and holding/storing juice	Sorting and delivering right quantity of juice to right retail location at right time
RETAILER	Your favorite local grocer	Receiving, inspecting, and holding/storing juice for store shelf placement	Distributing juice to paying customer

Figure 3.1 - Inbound & Outbound Logistics of Orange-U-Good Orange Juice

In the supply chain management industry, the coordination of inbound logistics systems and processes is called *materials management*. The coordination of outbound logistics systems and processes is called *physical distribution*. In Chapters 5 and 6 to follow, we will take a deeper look at the world of physical distribution. In Chapter 4, we will explore purchasing, the financial side of materials management. This chapter, however, we devote entirely to the physical side of materials management.

Materials management has inbound logistics at its core and has traditionally been associated with the inbound activities surrounding manufacturing or production. Inbound logistics activities occur throughout a product's supply chain, however. Remember our Orange-U-Good orange juice? All the members of its supply chain engaged in inbound logistics activities, even after the production of the orange juice. For example, both the third party distribution center and the retailer received, inspected, and stored the juice, which had already been produced by the manufacturer. Therefore, our definition of **materials management** is: the coordination of inbound logistics systems and processes (i.e., the functions associated with receiving goods into an organization).

Materials management focuses on two distinct types of activities: *financial activities* and *physical activities*. The financial components of materials management are: purchasing and supply management, which will be covered in the next chapter. The physical side of materials management includes three primary components: **warehousing**, **materials handling**, and **inventory management**.

WAREHOUSING

A **warehouse** is a facility or area within a facility in which an organization receives, inspects, stores, selects, packs, and issues any of a variety of materials needed for an organization's operations. These incoming and stored materials might include: raw materials for manufacturing; equipment, tools, spare parts, or supplies for distribution and maintenance operations; or packaging materials for both finished goods packaging and product distribution. Warehouses are found throughout a product's supply chain and are a part of both inbound and outbound logistics activities. Looking at an example of an ice cream supply chain in Figure 3.2 below, warehousing facilities and activities are found not only in the product's official distribution center warehouse, but also in in-house storerooms and warehouse facilities within the supplier's, manufacturer's, and retailer's facilities.

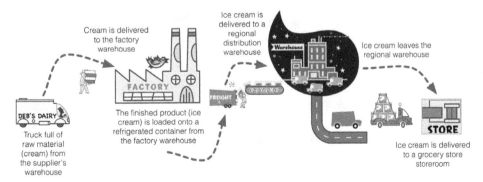

Figure 3.2 - Warehouses in the Ice Cream Supply Chain

When we think of a warehouse, many of us think of a big, old, deserted dusty building with shelves piled high with even dustier boxes. Warehouses, however, are actually very dynamic facilities, with people, equipment, and materials in constant movement as goods rapidly flow in and out as need demands. While our antiquated visions conjure up only the notion of a storage facility, a warehouse is so much more. Its four core operational functions are:

1. *Receive and inspect inbound goods;*

2. *Store goods, materials, and equipment safely and securely;*

3. *Select/pick goods against users' demands; and*

4. *Package and issue goods for manufacturing and/or distribution.*

Warehousing Functions at Ben & Jerry's Ice Cream

According to the Ben & Jerry's web site (www.benjerry.com), warehouses play an integral part of its ice cream supply chain. First, the warehouses within its three ice cream manufacturing facilities in Vermont receive pasteurized and cooled milk from the St. Alban's Dairy Co-op. The milk is kept here until it is needed for the ice cream production process.

After the delightfully delectable ice cream has been manufactured and individually packaged, it heads to the facility's freezer warehouse. As they head to the warehouse, all individual pints of ice cream are visually inspected and randomly selected ones are tested by the Quality Assurance department. (Those with the enviable job of professional tasters get to take a bite from the center of each pint selected!)

After meeting the stringent standards of the Quality Assurance folks, Ben & Jerry's ice cream then undergoes a unique packaging process at each facility's freezer warehouse. As they flow along a conveyor belt, every other pint of ice cream is turned upside down by a device called the "Invertor." The pints are then sent to the "Bundler" where they are placed in groups of eight into a plastic "Sleeve," which is then briefly heated, thus forming nice, tight packages for shipping. These "Sleeves" of ice cream are then placed by hand onto pallets and again shrink-wrapped after the pallet has been filled with Sleeves.

The shrink-wrapped pallets of ice cream are then sent to the central Ben & Jerry's freezer warehouse and distribution center in Rockingham, Vermont. At this central facility, ice cream is received in a temperature-controlled setting; stored safely and securely; and then picked, issued, and perhaps repalletized for distribution to retailers and happy customers around the world!

Along with these core operational functions, warehouses also play a highly strategic role within supply chain management. Warehouses and warehouse operations can both reduce overall supply chain costs and increase supply chain speed and effectiveness through efficient warehousing practices. To achieve efficient practices, organizations must:

- Select the **most efficient type of warehouse** and

- Design the **most efficient warehouse layout**.

When it comes to selecting a type of warehouse, organizations must consider the following type categories:

Single-Story versus Multi-Story Buildings. Single-story warehouse buildings are generally cheaper to construct, maintain, and operate. A single-story design also lends itself to a more efficient flow of goods through a warehouse. Organizations must sometimes consider multi-story warehouse buildings, however, when land is scarce and land costs are prohibitively high. For example in New York and Tokyo, an organization may find that installing elevator and complex conveyor systems in a multi-story facility is actually less expensive than buying enough inner-city land to construct a single-story facility.

Purpose-Built versus Converted Buildings. A *purpose-built warehouse* is a warehouse building that has been designed and constructed according to an organization's individual needs and operational requirements. A *converted warehouse* is a building that had originally been designed for another purpose but had since been converted to a warehouse. With a purpose-built warehouse, organizations can get the exact type and style of warehouse exactly where they want it. When organizations don't have the capital required for expensive new construction, converted warehouses can offer a beneficial option.

Third Party Facilities. Situations arise in which an organization may not want to build or convert a warehouse building. For example, it may: lack the financial resources to build or convert a warehouse; experience frequent changes in demand, translating to frequent changes in warehouse space needed; or be entering a new market and be unsure of future demand and warehousing needs. In these situations, an organization would consider renting a third-party warehouse facility.

Bonded Warehouses. When moving goods internationally, most organizations consider the option of a bonded warehouse. When goods arrive from another country, the company receiving the goods must immediately pay excise taxes and customs duties. If a company secures a bond for potential taxes and duties of future incoming goods, it may them temporarily store foreign inbound goods in a *bonded warehouse*. The company may then legally defer the payment of taxes or duties until the goods are removed from the bonded warehouse. In addition, not only can goods be stored in a bonded warehouse, but they may also be assembled or partially assembled there.

External Inventory Yards. As an addition or alternative to using a warehouse building, many organizations also use an *external inventory yard*, an open, outside warehousing area used for storing a variety of nonperishable goods. External inventory yards are often used for storing: stoneware; heavy iron and steel castings; heavy duty electrical cable; outdoor machinery; scrap and waste materials; coal, coke, and other fuels; and garden materials and supplies.

Regardless of the type of warehouse used, organizations are all concerned with designing the most efficient warehouse layout possible. The ultimate goal of warehouse layout design is to achieve efficient overall warehouse and logistics operations. A warehouse with a poor design can lead to both increased cost for an organization and unsafe working conditions for its employees. For example, a company in Nebraska purchased a grain warehouse in the 1980s to convert it into a warehouse for storing U.S. government powdered milk. During the warehouse layout conversion process, the upper levels of the warehouse were not considered or modified, leading to disastrously fatal consequences. In 2004, when trying to access these upper levels, a warehouse manager fell 40 feet to her death after a rung in a wooden ladder gave out. Poor warehouse layout and design regularly cause fatalities around the world, with many now occurring in warehouse-style superstores where shoppers neither wear hardhats nor are trained in warehouse picking procedures.

Before considering the important subject of warehouse layout, we must first become acquainted with the sections of a warehouse. Most warehouses include:

- **Goods-In Bays**. These are the external docks where goods are initially received into the warehouse.

- **Receiving Area**. Goods are temporarily held here while the incoming order is checked, inspected, and coded/labeled for subsequent storage.

- **Storage Area**. This is the area in which goods are held by an organization until an order for them is received.

- **Order-Picking Area**. In this area, goods are selected after an order has been received. The order picking and storage areas may be: 1) exactly the same areas; 2) opposite aisles flanking the same row of goods; or 3) separate areas of the warehouse, especially in the case of automated or live storage systems.

- **Packaging and Unitization Area**. Goods to be issued are packaged here and placed into unit loads, such as within pallet loads or containers.

- **Staging Area**. This is the area in which packaged and/or unitized goods are labeled for issuance and held until transportation arrives.

- **Loading Bays**. These are the external docks where packaged and unitized goods are transferred from the warehouse to a transportation vehicle, such as a truck or train.

When designing a safe, efficient, and effective warehouse layout, organizations place the location of these sections to achieve a logical, sequential, linear flow of goods. In larger warehouses, as shown in Figure 3.3 on the right, the goods-in bays and loading bays are often located at opposite ends of the facility.

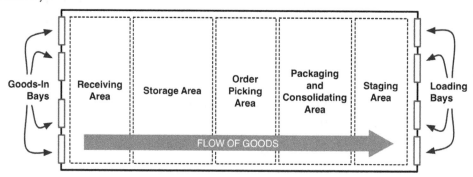

Figure 3.3 - Warehouse Layout and Flow

Besides the location of the sections of a warehouse, an organization must also consider the goods flowing into and out of the warehouse to design an effective and efficient layout. The size, weight, and handling requirements of goods to be held have a significant impact on warehouse layout. For example, large and heavy goods will need to be stored in areas with wide aisles that allow plenty of maneuvering room for special handling equipment. In addition, the frequency with which goods are issued has a significant impact on warehouse layout and where goods are placed within a warehouse. For example, in smaller warehouses, goods-in bays and loading bays may need to be placed on the same side of the warehouse building when only one side of the building has road access. In such cases, as shown in Figure 3.4, goods are placed in shelves closer to the goods-in/loading bay side of the building when they are issued more frequently.

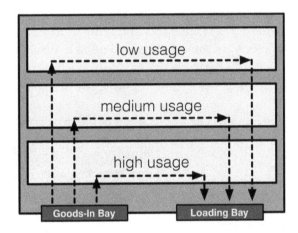

Figure 3.4 - Warehouse Layout & Goods Placement by Issue Frequency

MATERIALS HANDLING

Now that you have been introduced to warehousing, the second of the three physical components of materials management is materials handling. As defined by the Materials Handling Industry of America (MHIA), materials handling is "the art and science associated with the movement, storage, control, and protection of goods and materials throughout the process of their manufacture, distribution, consumption, and disposal." In simpler terms, ***materials handling*** is the focus on materials (physical goods in raw, semifinished, and finished states) and how they are handled (moved short distances and stored). Both materials handling and transportation focus on the movement of goods, but materials handling focuses on the short-distance movements of goods within a warehouse or other facility and transportation focuses on the long-distance movement of goods between facilities.

Well, even to those of us most unacquainted with supply chain management, it's quite obvious that materials must be handled as they flow along the supply chain. Those pints of ice cream don't grow little legs and walk themselves from the factory warehouse to the grocery store! Why then, is it important to study or focus on this handling of goods? In three words – **space**, **labor**, and **service**!

Materials handling can be used to maximize the space available so more goods can be stored in the same space or it can reduce the space needed for storage and handling of goods, creating a more efficient warehouse layout and design. Materials handling can also reduce the amount of labor involved in handling goods and can create a safer working environment for those handling the goods. Finally, materials handling can enhance service provided to immediate customers and end users by both minimizing product damage and improving the speed of distribution.

Warehouse and supply chain managers can achieve the benefits of space, labor, and service by practicing two key principles of materials handling: the principles of **product flow** and **the unit load**. First, to attain supply chain efficiency, materials handling experts examine the flow of products or materials through the organization. For example, they analyze whether it is more efficient to handle goods manually or mechanically at different points within a warehouse. With *manual handling*, goods are moved and lifted by hand or by using hand-operated devices. With *mechanical handling*, goods are moved and lifted using a mechanized device.

Charting the Way!

Materials handling experts often rely on one critical skill to examine the flow of goods through an organization or even a single facility: charting. A *flow process chart* is used to document the current flow of a product through an organization or facility. This chart is then analyzed to see if any steps can be combined, changed, or eliminated for greater efficiency in product flow. A new flow process chart is the drafted reflecting a proposed and potentially more efficient product flow.

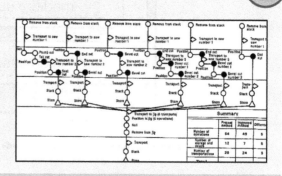

Materials handling experts often determine that it is most efficient to handle the same goods both manually and mechanically at different points of handling within the warehouse. At the Ben & Jerry's ice cream factory, pints of frozen ice cream are handled mechanically as they travel by conveyor to the freezer warehouse and into multiple-pint sleeves for shrink-wrapping. The shrink-wrapped pints within the sleeves are then stacked manually (by hand) onto pallets for additional shrink-wrapping in preparation for shipping. In this process, it is much quicker (and thus more efficient) for the many pints of ice cream coming from the factory to be handled mechanically by conveyor. After the pints have been shrink-wrapped into unit of eight, manual handling becomes more effective than mechanical handling. Units of packaged ice cream must be stacked firmly and evenly onto pallets and undergo a final visual inspection to ensure that there are no product defects before leaving the warehouse.

Now that you understand product flow, the second key principle of materials handling is the unit load. A *unit load* is any quantity of a material assembled and restrained so that it can be handled, moved, stored, and stacked as a single object. In our Ben & Jerry's example, eight individual pint containers of ice cream were placed into a plastic sleeve and shrink-wrapped so that they could be handled as a single unit or a unit load, thus enabling eight shrink-wrapped pints of ice cream to be handled eight times quicker than eight individual pint containers of ice cream.

The two core structures of the unit load within materials management are the *pallet* and the *container*. A ***pallet*** is a flat, unit load structure used to support materials for stable transportation and storage. Goods are shrink-wrapped, stretch-wrapped, or strapped onto a pallet to form a secure load. The main function of the pallet at the base of the load is to maintain a gap between the floor and the load so that a lifting device can place its "forks" under it without affecting the load's stability or security. The majority of pallets are made of wood, but alternatives include: *plastic pallets*, for messy, perishable items; *metal pallets*, for heavy items; and *paper pallets*, for lightweight, disposable applications.

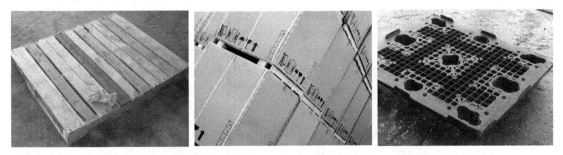

Figure 3.5 - Wood Pallet, Boxes Strapped onto Wood Pallets, and Plastic Pallet

The second core structure of the unit load within materials handling is the ***container***, essentially a large, rectangular metal box, typically 8 feet wide by 8 feet 6 inches high by 10, 20, 40, 48, or 53 feet long. These quite ordinary looking large boxes, however, have accomplished the extraordinary feat of revolutionizing the shipping industry. The standard size and style of the container allows international, intermodal transport of goods. ***Intermodal transport*** is the transportation of goods using more than one form of conveyance, such as road and rail or air and water. Therefore, a factory in Shanghai, China producing toys for an upcoming family film about wizards, hobbits, or superheroes can fill an entire container with tens of thousands of action figures. This container can then travel by rail from the factory to the Port of Shanghai. The container can then journey across the Pacific Ocean to the Port of Los Angeles, where it can be unloaded and then travel by rail to Pittsburg, Pennsylvania. At this point, the container of much-awaited action figures can be unloaded from the rail tracks and loaded immediately onto a tractor-trailer frame. It can now travel by truck 20 miles to a popular retail chain's distribution center where the container can now be opened and its precious contents distributed to multiple stores in the tristate area.

Figure 3.6 - Three 48' Containers Stacked in the Port of St. John's, Newfoundland and a 20' Container Rolling Down the Streets of Downtown Boston

Throughout this entire process, using a container has allowed the thousands and thousands of highly desired new action figures to be handled as a single unit. This not only increased the speed and ease of handling, but, because the container was sealed, it significantly reduced the risk of damage and theft. Finally, because of its standard size, the container could be stacked when it was awaiting further transportation at the cargo and rail ports, thus maximizing the storage space at multiple container ports in this outbound chain from the factory to the retailer.

Unless you are part-superhero, items formed into pallet or container unit loads generally become too heavy or too large to handle. It's now time to bring in the big guns: materials handling equipment. ***Materials handling equipment*** is a manual or mechanical device used to move, store, or lift unit loads or individual items during any segment of the logistics chain. Using such equipment can speed up operations, reduce costs, and often reduce the risk of back injuries to warehouse personnel. There are probably almost as many types of materials handling equipment as there are materials to be handled, but there are five distinct categories of materials handling equipment:

- ***Transport equipment*** is used to move goods and unit loads from one place to another, typically within a warehouse or external inventory yard facility. This category of materials handling equipment includes: industrial truck, such as forklift trucks; cranes, such as the large cranes found at cargo ports used to move containers from ships to rail or truck frames; and conveyors, such as those used to move pints of Ben & Jerry's ice cream from the factory to the freezer warehouse.

Figure 3.7 - Examples of Automatic Identification, Transport, and Storage Equipment: bar code scanner, conveyor, and movable racking

- ***Positioning equipment*** is used to reposition goods into place for subsequent handling. At the Ben & Jerry's factory warehouse, an "Invertor" is used to turn every other pint of ice cream upside down for subsequent handling and packaging.

- ***Unit load formation equipment*** is used to restrain goods and form them into a single unit load. Shrink-wrapping, stretch-wrapping, and strapping equipment used to secure goods onto pallets are all examples of unit load formation equipment.

- ***Storage equipment*** is used to hold materials in warehouse and external inventory yard facilities for both short and long-term timeframes. Examples include the shelving and racking systems common in most warehouses and storerooms.

- *Automatic identification and communication equipment* is used to identify goods to assist with inventory control and materials flow. RFID tags and readers, bar code printers and readers, and other optical reading systems are examples of automatic identification and communication equipment.

INVENTORY MANAGEMENT

As we have explored the physical side of materials management throughout this chapter, we first examined warehousing and explored where materials are held. We then looked at materials handling and delved into how materials are handled within a warehouse or storage facility. We are now ready for the more theoretical third and final component of the physical side of materials management: inventory management.

Inventory is the collection of goods, materials, and physical resources held by an organization, typically in warehouse facilities, distribution centers, external inventory yards, and in transit. Basically, if it is a tangible item and an organization holds it for any length of time, from minutes to months, it is likely to be inventory. Under this definition, a broad range of items within an organization can be considered inventory. Inventory within a typical manufacturing organization can be further classified, however, into the following four categories:

- *raw materials*, which are all goods used to assemble or produce a finished product;

- *work-in-process*, which are partially finished goods which are likely to be finished at a later point in the supply chain;

- *finished goods*, which are the fully assembled, produced, or manufactured goods to be delivered to the customer; and

- *maintenance, repair, and operating (MRO) supplies*, which are those goods essential to the operations of an organization but not used to become part of the finished product.

These four categories of inventory can be found throughout a product's entire supply chain, from the suppliers of the raw materials to the finished goods delivered to the final customer. Given that inventory is critical to an organization's operations and that it can be found in so many forms in so many places throughout the supply chain, the process of managing and administering this inventory to ensure that it is available where and when it needs to be becomes very important. This process is called *inventory management*. Along with ensuring and managing inventory availability, the process of inventory management is also used by many organizations to enhance customer service, increased operational efficiency, and reduce operating and supply chain costs. Within the world of inventory management, there are four key practices that have an impact on inbound logistics and materials management: *inventory receipt, inventory coding, inventory control,* and *physical inventory checking*.

Inventory Receipt

Inventory receipt is the process of preparing for and receiving inventory into an organization's warehouse facility and inventory management system. Its ultimate goal is to make this process as efficient and effective as possible. One vital element of the inventory receipt process is documentation. Organizations use a comprehensive set of documents to facilitate the control of inventory received. Some of these documents, such as the Need to Reorder Notification and the Purchasing Order, are generated by the organization itself while other documents, such as the Advice Note of Intended Delivery and the Internal Packing note, are generated by the supplier and other parties.

In addition to documentation, another vital element of the inventory receipt process is inspection. When inventory is received into a warehouse area or facility, it is inspected against predetermined levels of acceptability. Two common methods of inspection are the 100% Method, in which an organization tests all the items received, and the Sampling Method, in which an organization tests only a sample of each batch of items delivered.

Inventory Coding

When inventory arrives into a warehouse, it is accompanied by a significant amount of information about: the name and location of the supplier; the inventory item itself, including the size, quantity, type, and color of the items; the storage conditions needed; and the warehouse storage location for the inventory. To simplify how all of this information about inventory received is represented, inventory codes are used.

An inventory code is a condensed series of numbers and/or letters used to convey information about inventory. These codes are assigned using a uniform coding system, which can be understood across an organization or even across multiple organizations in a supply chain. The practice of assigning and using inventory codes, or inventory coding, provides the following three benefits:

- *Increased efficiency.* Long and complex descriptions of orders are no longer required when inventory codes are used! In addition, both verbal and IT-based communication about inventory is much quicker when codes are used. Time yourself as you say the following two requests for the same item aloud: "Could I please have a 28"x36" replacement carbon filter manufactured by High-Q Air Systems that fits in the air filter vent slots above the donut boiler in Factory Zone 3B?" and "Could I please have a 28-HQ-3B?"

- *Improved accuracy.* When using inventory codes, a large amount of information about inventory can be conveyed, providing highly detailed and accurate item descriptions.

- *Reduced errors.* Finally, when inventory codes are used, far fewer words must be said or typed. This greatly reduces the chances of human error in both conveying and interpreting information about the inventory.

Inventory Control

The essential objective of inventory management is ensuring that the right inventory of the right quantity and quality is available at the right time and place. A system that controls inventory and its levels held to achieve these objectives for an organization is its inventory control system. In a nutshell, inventory control is all about how much inventory to hold and where to hold it.

Holding inventory can be very expensive for an organization. Not only does inventory occupy costly warehouse space, but it also incurs related handling, management, and administration expenses. Despite these expenses, it can be advantageous for a warehouse to hold inventory, especially when:

- inventory deliveries are unreliable,

- an organization wants to take advantage of seasonal and bulk discounts from the supplier,

- an organization must reduce the risk of halting manufacturing operations in case raw materials inventory runs out, and

- manufacturing output flexibility is needed so that finished goods can be produced in varying quantities to adjust to fluctuating customer demand.

Inventory control systems help an efficiency-minded organization manage the cost of inventory holding by determining the most efficient and effective inventory levels needed for individual items. To manage and control these inventory levels, organizations must determine two key factors: *how much* to order/reorder and *when* to order/reorder. This information determined helps organizations supply a constant flow of inventory to its operations.

Inventory control systems are usually computer-based and rely on a series of mathematical formulae and techniques. The most common inventory control techniques and systems include:

- *Economic Order Quantity (EOQ)*, an inventory model that determines how much inventory to order by determining the inventory holding level (amount) that will meet customer service levels while minimizing ordering and holding costs.

- *Just-in-Time (JIT)*, an inventory control system developed by the Japanese auto industry that controls material flow into assembly and manufacturing plants by coordinating demand and supply to the point where desired materials arrive just in time for use. This system typically involves holding very little inventory.

- *Materials Requirement Planning (MRP)*, a decision-making methodology used to determine the timing and quantities of materials to purchase.

- *Manufacturing Resource Planning (MRP II)*, a decision-making methodology which integrates systemwide manufacturing, inventory, and finance operations to achieve optimum financial results in inventory and manufacturing resource control.

- **Distribution Resource Planning (DRP II)**, a system focused on receiving, warehousing, and holding goods at the lowest possible cost within the distribution system while still meeting customers' inventory needs through efficient distribution activities.

- **ABC analysis**, a classification system used to help organizations place its range of inventory into categories based on which items are used and issued most frequently.

Physical Inventory Checking

Inventory represents a substantial financial asset on an organization's balance sheet. It is critical for an inventory manager to ensure that the actual inventory held corresponds to the inventory represented within the organization's computerized inventory control system. For most organizations, a full **physical inventory check** must be carried out at least once a year to provide validated figures for the organization's annual final accounts. Common forms of physical inventory checking include:

- **Periodic inventory checking**, in which a complete physical inventory check performed at timed intervals. Typically, these intervals occur quarterly or at the end of the fiscal year. A periodic inventory check must be carried out on a non-working day because the warehouse must be closed to allow inventory checkers the time and space to count carefully and check discrepancies.

- **Continuous inventory checking**, in which a section of items within a warehouse is checked every week throughout a twelve-month period. This form of inventory checking allows a warehouse to continue operating 365 days a year.

- **Spot-checking**, which is designed to verify portions of the inventory held, without prior notification to warehouse staff. Spot-checking is used primarily as a security and antitheft measure, not for final annual inventory calculations. Therefore, it is typically used in combination with one of the previous two forms of physical inventory checking.

CHAPTER 3 REVIEW QUESTIONS

1. What types of inbound logistics activities might occur at a national retailer's regional distribution center?

2. What types of outbound logistics activities might occur at the same distribution center?

3. Along with purchasing, what is the other half of materials management? What are its primary components?

4. When might a company use a bonded warehouse?

5. When designing a warehouse layout, why might it be important to place a staging area near loading bays?

6. What benefits does materials handling provide?

7. What are the two core structures of the unit load? In what types of situations would each be used?

8. Please list the four categories of inventory and provide at least two examples of each.

9. What role do computers and information technology play in inventory control?

10. Which provides a more accurate account of an entire warehouse's inventory levels – periodic inventory checking or spot-checking? Please explain.

CHAPTER 3 CASE STUDY

AccuBar and Beverage Inventory Management

When we think inventory management, we tend to think of massive warehouses or even acres of external inventory yards. Although there is nary a warehouse nor external inventory yard in sight, restaurants carry a significant amount of inventory that must be processed and managed. Not only are there food ingredients to manage, there are also plates, glasses, menus, bathroom supplies, and thousands of gallons of beverages that customers consume every day. Restaurants that offer even a standard variety of alcoholic beverages bring a further level of complexity to the inventory that must be maintained. There are many types of alcoholic beverages with a dazzling degree of variegation within each type, which includes factors such as brand, age, and price. Restaurants and bars that offer a range of wines must maintain an even more complicating degree of variety within their alcohol inventory because they may stock hundreds of different wines, varying in price, rating, type, winery, and region and year of production.

You might think that maintaining an inventory of alcohol would be as simple as placing a bottle on a shelf and pouring from it as needed. However, with hundreds of bottles to maintain, how can a bartender know where to find each bottle needed? How can a restaurant manager know when stock is running low on specific wines or liquors or if certain alcohols are just not selling? Worse yet, how can a restaurant owner know when money is being lost because bartenders are offering free drinks to friends or bottles of champagne are finding their way into employees' rucksacks?

One way in which restaurant and bar managers can manage a complex inventory of hundreds of wines, liquors, and beers is to use a beverage management system. One such system popular with many American restaurants and bars is AccuBar, a Windows-based system that utilizes handheld scanning devices that link wirelessly to a computer-based inventory system. The system can then be used to manage inventory, process incoming orders from suppliers, establish automatic reorder points, and identify slow moving stock. All of this can be done paperlessly, too, without harming a single tree!

AccuBar is based on a simple bar code scanning system. For example, when wine orders are received from suppliers, a restaurant simply scans in the bar code of each bottle of wine using the handheld scanner. This allows the incoming inventory to be checked for discrepancies or breakage before the supplier's driver even thinks about hopping back into the truck and driving away. For bottles that do not have barcodes, AccuBar can assign bar codes and create labels to print and affix to these items as they arrive. To make inventory management even simpler, AccuBar creates bar coded neck tags that can be affixed to bottles with or without bar codes to make scanning easier so that bartenders don't have to search for elusive bar codes in dimly lit bars. With bar code labels or neck tags firmly in place, handheld devices are then used to scan bottles as they are taken from inventory (such as when you have decided at long last to buy that bottle of Dom Perignon) or as inventory is checked.

As bar codes are scanned, the handheld device sends information wirelessly to a computer that stores this information in its beverage management system. This computer-based system can be used to generate instant reports on inventory held and can also connect to a restaurant's POS (point of sale) system. Establishments using the AccuBar system have found that they have increased the efficiency and accuracy of their inventory management, reduced their long-term IT costs, and improved loss prevention because it is must harder to steal or misuse alcohol when someone can easily find out if it's missing.

A recent feature added to AccuBar is the iPad wine list. Establishments using the beverage management system can offer their customers an iPad, iPhone, Android tablet, or other smart handheld device with an accurate and complete wine list. Customers can then use this device to search through hundreds of wines using criteria including winery, type, region, price, ratings, and year. Some restaurants and bars using the new iPad wine list have reported a 10 to 20% increase in wine sales, perhaps because people are more apt to experiment or go outside their price range when they have more information. As one wine steward explained, people seems more likely to trust the device than to trust the waiters.

References

Accubar (2011) Inventory so easy, you'll actually do it. *Accubar* website. Retrieved from http://www.accubar.com/.

Beverage World. (2011, May 11) iPad wine lists take step forward with established hospitality system. *Beverage World*. Retrieved from http://www.beverageworld.com/index.php?option=com_content&view=article&id=39200:-ipad-wine-lists-take-step-forward-with-established-hospitality-system&catid=3:daily-headlines&Itemid=173.

Sheen, R. (2011, May 1) Why inventory management is crucial for small businesses. *Financial Post*. Retrieved from http://www.financialpost.com/entrepreneur/without-borders/inventory+management+crucial+small+businesses/4706464/story.html.

Case Study Questions

1. How might AccuBar be involved in a restaurant's three primary components of materials management: warehousing, materials handling, and inventory management?

2. Which of the four categories of inventory does the AccuBar system manage? (Hint: there may be more than one correct answer!)

3. In what way is AccuBar a perfect example of an inventory management system?

4. How is AccuBar involved in all four key inventory management practices?

Chapter 4
Inbound Logistics and Purchasing

Just like the global supply chain, purchasing touches almost every aspect of our daily work and home lives. For example, take a look around you right now. Make a mental list of all the items surrounding you, such as a desk, chairs, carpeting, clock, etc. Did the items on your mental list magically appear one day or grow up from the ground around your feet? Unless you happen to be a true Emersonian transcendentalist sitting in the middle of the woods with no clothes on, chances are that almost all the items on your list were once part of a supply chain and were purchased by someone. Even the walls around you were once sheetrock, plaster, and paint that were purchased by a builder.

Of all the activities within the world of logistics management, *purchasing* is perhaps the one that we already know the most about. Most of us, unless we happen to be lucky enough to have more money than sense, are highly proficient purchasers. We take the activity of purchasing seriously because wise purchases leave us with more expendable cash for even more purchases.

In this chapter, we will explore purchasing within the world of logistics and supply chain management. We will examine the stages of the purchasing process and see that you already engage in these stages on a regular basis and may even be in the middle of one right now! Finally, we will introduce the growing world of internet purchasing and e-Procurement and its effect on the global supply chain.

INTRODUCTION TO PURCHASING

In Chapter 3, we introduced inbound logistics and defined their processes as "those logistics activities that take place at the beginning of the internal supply chain until goods are received from the supplier." We further defined the coordination of inbound logistics systems and process as materials management. As shown in Figure 4.1 below, the segment of materials management whose activities occur entirely within inbound logistics processes is that of purchasing and supply management.

Before we explore purchasing in depth, we must first examine supply management.

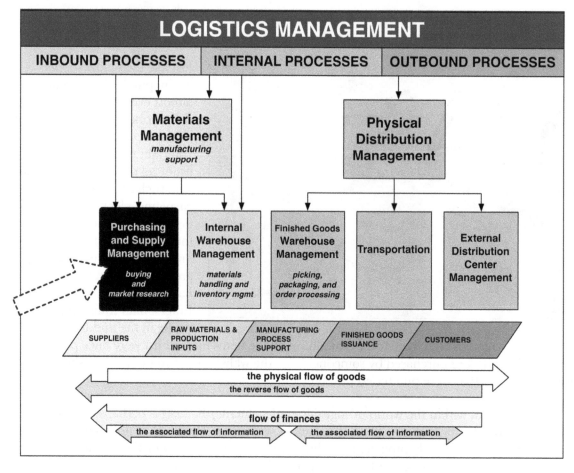

Figure 4.1 - Purchasing and Supply Management within Logistics Management

Supply Management versus Purchasing

The purchasing component of logistics ensures that the materials and service needs of an organization are met by acquiring goods and services in the right quantity of the right quality, delivered to the right place at the right time, while maximizing service to internal customers and minimizing the total cost to the organization. The short-term goal of this initial inbound logistics management process is the immediate acquisition of goods or services, which falls under the umbrella of ***purchasing***. The longer term goal of inbound logistics is a strategic one: working closely with suppliers of needed goods and services to ensure their long-term availability. For example, what good is only 5000 gallons of screamin' streamin' yellow paint for your new line of sports cars if the paint manufacturer will be ceasing production of screamin' streamin' yellow in six months due to the rising cost of one of its ingredients, yellow dye number 6.   This longer term strategic approach to purchasing and supplier relations is called ***supply management***.

When referring to a department or function, many organizations use the term purchasing, while others use the terms ***procurement*** and ***acquisition*** to refer to the same thing. Some organizations even use all three words interchangeably! Generally, all three terms relate to the buying of goods and services for an organization. When supplier relations are involved and the buying of goods is planned strategically over the long term, organizations typically refer to this approach as supply management, ***supplier relationship management***, or ***strategic sourcing***.

As shrewd consumers in today's highly competitive marketplace, we want to make wise purchasing decisions by buying a quality product while saving ourselves money. Therefore, as individual consumers, we often view our suppliers and their salespeople through world-weary eyes as competitors and adversaries, trying to get our business while increasing their own profits. With the supply management approach, however, suppliers are not viewed as competitors or adversaries. They are instead viewed by today's organizations as important counterparts in their products' supply chains. Organizations work with their suppliers to develop long-term relationships not only to ensure long-term supply availability, but also to streamline the product or service acquisition process to make for faster and more effective inbound logistics management processes.

Using the supply management approach, an organization's purchasing department works together with its suppliers, but also with its peers in production, engineering, finance, marketing, and quality assurance in a cross-functional team. This supply management team engages in many strategic, long-term activities related to purchasing or acquiring goods, including:

- *internal analysis*, in which organizations look inward and examine their own spending or purchasing processes to make them more efficient;

- *market research*, in which organizations look not only at customer demand forecasts, but also at the long-term supply availability and cost increases to make long-term production decisions;

- *strategic sourcing*, in which an organization works to identify, develop, and manage key suppliers to build supply chain relationships that outperform those of its competitors; and

- *negotiating contracts*, in which an organization works with suppliers to agree on long-term supply contracts.

The Five "W"s of Purchasing

The term purchasing refers to both a functional activity and a functional department within an organization. As an activity, purchasing is the short-term to medium-term acquisition of goods and services in the right quantity of the right quality, delivered to the right place at the right time, while maximizing internal customer service and minimizing cost to the organization.

As we plunge ahead into the wild and exciting world of purchasing, let's begin by asking and answering who, what, where, and why questions to become acquainted with this important field.

First, **who does the purchasing?** Most organizations have a ***Purchasing Manager*** or Purchasing Officer who is responsible for directly acquiring or approving the acquisition of purchases from suppliers. In larger companies, the Purchasing Manager may oversee a range of Buyers or Purchasing Agents, who investigate suppliers, negotiate contracts, complete the hands-on purchasing activities, and plan for product deliveries with the Warehouse Manager. In smaller companies, however, the Purchasing Manager may be the organization's sole Buyer or Purchasing Agent and conduct all purchasing-related activities him/herself.

Second, **what is purchased?** We mentioned earlier that, in purchasing, "goods and services" are acquired, but what exactly does this mean? Basically, whatever an organization may need to function but does not produce itself are the goods and services to be purchased. Goods purchased may include raw materials, semifinished goods, and finished goods used to produce the organization's final product. For example, a bicycle manufacturer purchases aluminum sheeting for bike fenders, inner tubing for the tires, handlebar baskets, and colorful cardboard packaging. In addition, some product purchase may be custom-made, while others are ***off the shelf products*** that are purchased as they are without customization.

Goods purchased also include maintenance, repair, and operating (MRO) supplies and capital goods. ***MRO supplies*** are the goods not used to become part of a finished product but are instead essential to the operation of an organization. For example, the light bulbs, copier paper, and machine oil for our bicycle manufacturer are all MRO supplies to be purchased. ***Capital goods*** are manufactured, finished products used to produce other goods. Examples of capital goods include tools, machinery, and buildings.

Unlike goods, services purchased are not tangible products, but are instead any action or activity that an organization needs but cannot or has decided not to complete itself. For example, our bicycle manufacturer may purchase a wide range of third-party services, from office janitorial service to rate negotiation assistance on international freight shipments.

Third, **where is purchasing done?** Much to the dismay of the neat-freak portion of the logistics management population, purchasing is not completed in a neat, orderly, predictable environment. It is instead conducted within the growing, messy, chaotic world of the global market. This messy, massive global market, however, makes for an environment of perfect competition.

When there are only a few suppliers or buyers for a product, imperfect market conditions result, allowing for one side to have more power and control over the market price of the goods. For example, if just one supplier were to have a monopoly on the toothpaste market, it might cruelly and impersonally determine the maximum amount consumers would be willing and able to pay for this much-needed product. The result might be a $20 tube of minty freshness instead of today's $2 tube.

Large numbers of buyers and suppliers, however, make for a more ideal purchasing environment. When the buyers and suppliers of an item exist in large numbers, there is more open information sharing of prices and product availability and it is much easier for buyers and suppliers to both enter and exit the market. Thus, when efficient and cost effective supply chains are desired, organizations seek to purchase goods and services within these more competitive market conditions.

When purchasing decisions and activities are controlled from one central location within an organization, it is called **centralized buying** or *purchasing within a centralized organization*. When purchasing decisions and activities are controlled from different locations or divisional levels within an organization, it is called **decentralized buying** or *purchasing within a decentralized organization*.

When purchasing is centralized, larger volumes are purchased from a single supplier, who can offer lower prices, volume discounts, and better payment terms. Within the organization, purchasing is consolidated, efficiencies are increased, and purchasing operational costs are lowered.

The disadvantage of centralized buying is the lack of control it offers divisional and local managers within an organization. When purchasing is decentralized, divisional and local managers have greater control over those element of the purchasing process that directly impact their departments and they feel a greater sense of ownership of the process. They can also plan for product deliveries that best suite their own time and place needs, instead of those of the organization as a whole.

Most organizations engage in both centralized and decentralized buying strategies, in which products and services are purchased either centrally or locally, depending on amounts to be purchased, the organization's overall strategy, purchasing timeframes, etc.

Fourth, **when are purchasing activities conducted?** Purchasing is an ongoing activity and is typically a continuous cycle of evaluating needs, evaluating potential suppliers, issuing purchase orders, evaluating supplier performance, and, again, evaluating new needs. When examining how a company orders individual products from individual suppliers, however, purchase orders can be placed with varying degrees of frequency.

A **one-off purchase** is a one-time purchase for a specific project that will not be repeated, such as your hot tub purchase for Dad or the U.S. government's acquisition for a replacement for the President's plane, Air Force One.

Automatic inventory replacement is the technique of automatically ordering goods when inventory reaches a specific level. The goal of automatic inventory replacement is to maintain predetermined levels of stock within an organization so that inventory will not run out, causing costly manufacturing delays. For example, a manufacturer would have an automatic inventory replacement agreement with all of its critical parts' suppliers to ensure that it can continue its manufacturing operations without a Purchasing Manager having to take the time to determine a need and place an order with the supplier.

Finally, *forward buying* is the practice of purchasing goods in advance of requirements. This practice is used to avoid supply shortages and ensure a constant supply of goods for production and other operations. When storage space is available, forward buying is also used to acquire goods at a lower fixed price when it is anticipated that prices will soon rise. A computer manufacturer might use forward buying with a processor chip supplier to compensate for both.

Fifth and finally, **why is purchasing important?** Obviously, in order for companies to function, they need goods and services. In today's competitive global environment, it is neither cost effective nor efficient for a company to produce all the goods and services it might need. Imagine automobile manufacturers creating every single part of each car manufactured themselves, from the rubber in the tires to the entire satellite radio system! Even the smallest cottage industries rely on purchasing some amount of raw materials and packaging. For example, a local honey producer, Honey-Bee-Good, will not need to purchase as many goods and services as an automobile manufacturer, but it will need to purchase beekeeping equipment, glass jars and printed labels for finished honey, and advertising agency services to come up with a catchy Honey-Bee-Good jingle for a local radio ad.

Along with being a necessary corporate function, effective and efficient purchasing can be used to save money and have an impact on a company's bottom line. Consider the impact a new Purchasing Manager had on Honey-Bee-Good's bottom line…

As a new small business, Honey-Bee-Good did not need department managers. The company owner and various members of her family did whatever company functions were necessary when they were necessary. For example, the company purchased its jars and labels from one packaging provider in small quantities, as they were needed. As the company grew, it placed larger orders for jars and labels, but continued to pay the original rates. After five years of steady growth, the Honey-Bee-Good owner and CEO decided that it was time to hire a Purchasing Manager because she was spending at least 60% of her time in purchasing-related activities. On his first day of work, the new Purchasing Manager looked at Honey-Bee-Good's purchasing records and gasped in horror. He immediately got bulk purchase bids from three different jar and label producers, including their current provider. The Purchasing Manager then negotiated a two-year contract with the company providing the best offer for Honey-Bee-Good, which, interestingly, happened to be the same company they had been using! Under the new contract, however, Honey-Bee-Good was given a 15% discount on all orders over $500. So what effect would this have on Honey-Bee-Good's bottom line in the first year of this new purchasing contract?

From simply renegotiating a packaging contract, Honey-Bee-Good is now $30,000 richer each year! This simple act of good purchasing, which took the Purchasing Manager only two days to complete, resulted in a 30% increase in the company's profits! Honey-Bee-Good's Purchasing Manager won't stop here, however. He can continue to look for ways to improve the efficiency and cost of all corporate purchasing, from the negotiating better purchasing contracts with bee keeping equipment providers to finding discount office supply wholesalers that offer free delivery.

	Before Discount	After 15% Discount
Production Labor Cost per Jar of Honey	$1.50	$1.50
Packaging Cost per Jar	$2.00	$1.70
Corporate Overhead Allocation per Jar	$0.50	$0.50
Total Cost of Jar Produced	$4.00	$3.70
Selling Price per Jar	$5.00	5.00
Profit per Jar	$1.00	$1.30
Profit per 100,000 Jars (annual production)	$100,000.00	$130,000.00

Figure 4.2 - Honey-Bee-Good Cost and Profit Structure

Other purchasing practices, such as *reciprocity* and *forward buying*, can provide a competitive advantage to motivated companies like Honey-Bee-Good. **Reciprocity** is a mutually beneficial practice between two companies in which they agree to buy each other's products or services. Honey-Bee-Good, for example, could form reciprocal buying arrangements with its jar supplier, Jersey Jars, in which Honey-Bee-Good purchases only from Jersey Jars and its products are the sole "honey of choice" in the lunchrooms of all Jersey Jars manufacturing facilities worldwide.

As previously stated, ***forward buying*** is the practice of purchasing goods in advance of requirements. This practice is used to avoid supply shortages and ensure a constant supply of goods for production and other operations. When storage space is available, forward buying is also used to acquire goods at a lower fixed price when it is anticipated that prices will soon rise. For example, Honey-Bee-Good decided to use forward buying with Jersey Jars to ensure that it could avoid the fiasco of its competitor, Busy Bee Honey, who lost a month of sales because the manufacturing facilities of its jar supplier, Midwestern Packaging, were ravaged by tornadoes and could not produce honey jars for a month.

The rewards reaped from efficient and effective purchasing practices can allow companies like Honey-Bee-Good to have extra financial resources to: provide increased customer service; invest in marketing to attract new customers; construct new production and distribution facilities to expand the product's geographic reach; reinvest in product research and development to improve products and develop new product lines; attract and retain top quality employees; and provide greater returns to shareholders.

THE PURCHASING PROCESS

After companies have negotiated great savings or found world-class suppliers at affordable rates, they do not rest on their past glorious achievements of great savings. Instead, they strive for continuous improvement in their purchasing practices. No matter how great a new contract with a supplier may appear, it is of little use if the desired products are delivered at the wrong time or in incorrect quantities. Purchasing Managers monitor and manage the entire process of purchasing a good or service, from the moment the company expresses a need for a particular product to the moment the product is received and the purchasing order is closed out. This section of the chapter will introduce the seven stages of this very important purchasing process.

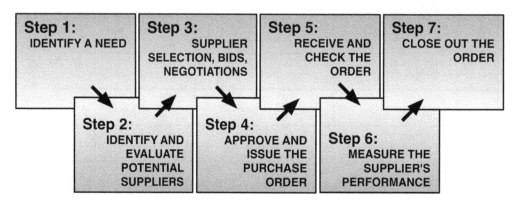

Figure 4.3 - The Seven Steps of the Purchasing Process

To help us as we explore the stages of the purchasing process, let's use a scenario that may be more familiar to many of us… Grandma's 80th birthday party is rolling around in the next few weeks. Everyone in the family has decided to pool their resources to buy Grandma one magnificent, expensive, extravagant gift – a 52" plasma, flat screen television. Because you are studying purchasing, you have been elected as the family's Purchasing Officer. (Lucky you!) Let's consider how your own purchasing process is similar to that of Purchasing Managers from large and small companies alike.

Step 1 - Identify a Need

Before Grandma's birthday, the family held a meeting to determine what Grandma needed most for her amazingly, awesome birthday present. When the family decided what was needed (i.e., a very large television), they informed you, the family Purchasing Officer so that you could, in the words of Aunt Tillie, "Take care of it."

In most mid-size to large-size companies, when an individual or a department within an organization, experiences or anticipates a need for a good or service, they typically do not go out and acquire it themselves. If they did, like Honey-Bee-Good in its early days, they would not achieve economies of scale and reduced prices for larger orders. Instead, they let the Purchasing Manager or department know what is needed, in what quantity, with what quality, where, and at what time.

In most mid-size to large-size organizations, when a need for a good or service is determined, the Purchasing Manager is informed. Typically, the individual or department needing specific goods sends a **purchase requisition** to the Purchasing Manager. This purchase requisition is not an actual order for the goods; it is a request for the Purchasing Manager to purchase these goods.

Purchase requisition forms differ from organization to organization. However, most commonly contain: the specific details of the items requested, also known as specifications; the preferred vendors or suppliers; the quantity of items needed; the date of the requisition; the desired date of receipt; the estimated unit cost of each item; the internal department or account to be charged; and the signature or details of a company official authorizing the purchase. While purchase requisitions have traditionally been paper-based forms filled out by the requestor and hand delivered, mailed, or faxed to the Purchasing Manager, they are increasing becoming computerized for instant information transmission.

When goods are requested, a **purchase requisition form** is used. When services are requested, however, a **statement of work (SOW)** is used. The SOW describes the services needed, where and when they are needed, and the type of vendor needed. It may also include specific personnel requirement, performance, and assessment details and the terms and conditions of payment. The Purchasing Manager then uses the SOW in soliciting bids from potential suppliers. After a supplier has been selected and a contract has been awarded, the statement of work becomes part of the contractual agreement. It is used as a basis for evaluating whether or not the supplier is provided the needed service when, where, and how needed.

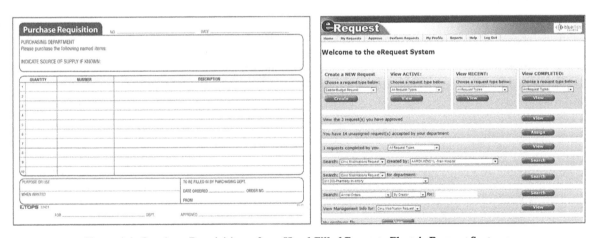

**Figure 4.4 - Purchase Requisitions, from Hand-Filled Forms to Electric Request Systems.
The eRequest software system handles purchase requisitions, as well as finance, human resources, and hiring needs requests. It was developed by Bluefish Systems, a growing national IT firm that sprang up fifteen years ago from the needs of its local health care community in Arkansas.**

Before we move on through the rest of the purchasing process, we must consider whether an organization has existing contracts or other relationships with **preferred suppliers** for the goods or services requested. This situation occurs when suppliers and their products have been tried and tested. The organization feels comfortable with a specific supplier for a specific product or range of products. When this occurs, an organization does not need to complete Steps 2 and 3 of the purchasing process, i.e., selecting potential suppliers, obtaining bids, and negotiating contracts. For example, after Honey-Bee-Good negotiated a new two-year contract with their existing jar and label supplier, Paxton Packaging, the Production Department could then send a purchasing requisition for needed jars to the Purchasing Manager (step 1), who would then send a purchase order directly to Paxton Packaging (step 4), completely bypassing the supplier identification, selection, and negotiation processes (steps 2 and 3).

After step 1, when a purchase requisition has been received for new goods or services, some companies also consider a **make or buy decision**. Companies consider whether it would be more efficient and cost effective to buy the goods or services from suppliers or to make the goods (or complete the services) themselves.

Companies may elect to make their own product or service if: it has the equipment and resources to produce the product or perform the service; it can be accomplished at a significantly lower cost than buying it; a skilled supplier cannot be found who meets the necessary product quantity, quality, and delivery time and place criteria; or staff and equipment are readily available in-house that might go unused otherwise.

Conversely, companies may elect to buy goods from outside suppliers or outsource desired services to a third party if they don't have the equipment or staff necessary. Even when companies have the needed equipment and resources, may still make a buy decision if: it is not cost effective to make the goods or perform the services, as in the case of a **one-off purchase**, a one-time purchase that will not be repeated; the quality of the supplier's goods or services cannot be matched internally; suppliers hold a patent or trademark that doesn't allow other companies to produce the goods; or the organization wishes to have suppliers available as part of a global multi-sourcing strategy. In today's competitive global marketplace, many organizations are finding that it is far more cost effective to outsource a large portion of desired goods and services.

When companies decide to buy, the Purchasing Manager typically deals with only a small number of suppliers for each good or service - sometimes only one! When companies decide to make required goods, the Purchasing Manager's job becomes considerably more complex. For each good made, the Purchasing Manager will have to select suppliers and negotiate purchasing contracts for each part of the item to be produced, which might include a variety of raw materials, partially finished goods, and completed parts. As a result, for a single requisitioned item to be produced, the Purchasing Manager may need to deal with as many as fifty suppliers!

Step 2 - Identify & Evaluate Potential Suppliers

Thinking back to Grandma and her big screen TV, would you, as your family's trusted Purchasing Officer, simply walk into a store and purchase the first 52" flat screen you see? Unless you want the wrath of Aunt Tillie and Uncle Bingo plagued upon you, you are likely to want to spend the family money wisely. Therefore, you will probably investigate different televisions and their prices and service agreements at different retail stores.

Similarly, when Purchasing Managers receive a purchasing requisition for a new good or service, they do not pounce on the first supplier who waves in their direction. Some may have the luxury of using **insourcing**, which occurs when a department, organization, branch, or subsidiary within a large company decides to acquire a desired good or service from a location within the company itself. Most, however, must use **outsourcing**, in which they instead search for and compare multiple suppliers that could provide the needed product. The Purchasing Manager first sends an *RFI (request for information)* to a wide range of potential suppliers, asking them to provide information about the desired product, the organization itself, its locations, and its capabilities. Considering the information obtained from suppliers responding to the RFI, the Purchasing Manager then issues an *RFP (request for proposal)* or an *RFQ (request for quotation)* to potential suppliers as an invitation to submit a bid for a contract to provide the needed goods or services. The RFP or RFQ sent would outline the quantity, quality, time, and place goods or services are needed. It would also contain a deadline for suppliers' proposal or quotation submissions and ask suppliers to outline the overall cost for the proposed purchase. Finally, it might contain information about their expectations of the selected supplier, its performance, and the product. When the organization receives proposals and quotations from potential suppliers, it is ready to move on to Step 3, the bidding, selection, and negotiation process.

The amount of energy and time a Purchasing Manager invests in preparing RFIs, RFPs, and RFQs in Step 2 depends on the importance and size of the completed product for which the requested good or service is needed. The intensity of the supplier search will also be influenced by relationships with existing suppliers. Four types of purchasing situations, in order of increasing intensity according to supplier relationships and strategic importance of products purchased, are:

- **straight repurchase**, in which there is a contract for the good or service with an existing supplier at a set price. In this situation, no RFIs, RFPs, or RFQs would be needed and Step 2 would be skipped entirely. For example, Honey-Bee-Good would have a straight repurchase of its honey jars and labels after signing a contract with its supplier, Paxton Packaging.

- **straight purchase**, in which a new good or service of little strategic importance is desired. Because the product is less important, the time and energy needed to write RFIs, RFPs, or RFQs to purchase goods cannot be justified. When Honey-Bee-Good purchases toilet paper for its production facility restrooms, for example, it does not take the time to send out an RFI to purchase products for its two bathrooms serving twenty employees. Instead, the Purchasing Manager makes bulk purchases from a local warehouse-style wholesaler.

- **modified purchase**, in which there is an existing supplier under contract but also a change in the need, such as a larger number or different type of product. In this situation, the organization may ask the existing supplier to outline how it will meet the new or changing requirement. It may also solicit information from a few additional suppliers to compare against their existing supplier. For example, if Honey-Bee-Good, Inc. bought out three other honey producers in neighboring states, it would triple its output o 100,000 jars of honey per year to 300,000 jars. The Purchasing Manager would need to ascertain Paxton Packaging's ability to triple its production of jars and labels. If this packaging supplier could not meet the anticipated demand in the desired timeframe, Homey-Bee-Good would then have to submit an RFI to additional potential suppliers.

- **new competitive purchase**, in which a new good or service is required and the finished item is of high strategic importance and/or will be produced in very large quantities. In this situation, the Purchasing Manager will complete all or most of the activities covered throughout Step 2. For example, because of its threefold growth, Honey-Bee-Good needs to explore faster bottling machinery. The bottling machinery and corresponding conveyor mechanisms are costly items and are critical to the company's operations. Therefore, the Purchasing Manager will send an RFI to as many bottling machinery manufacturers as he can find. He will then spend many hours analyzing them before issuing a highly detailed RFP.

Step 3 - The Dirty Work: Supplier Selection, Bids, & Negotiations

Selecting the right supplier is often the most important decision a Purchasing Manager can make. When purchasing Grandma's 52" television, you are likely to study all the possible television's specifications and retailers' prices with great intensity. (You are spending your family's hard-earned money, after all!) You may even try to negotiate a lower price by playing one retailer against another. ("Well, Super Sam's is offering the same TV for $300 less. Maybe I should go there…") In the end, thanks to your diligent work at this stage of the purchasing process, you may spend $500 less than budgeted, allowing everyone to throw a big birthday bash for Grandma and her friends at a local family restaurant.

When selecting a supplier, a Purchasing Manager can use one of two techniques: *competitive bidding* or *negotiation*. After sending out an RFP or an RFQ for a specific product, an organization receives bids (i.e., proposals or quotes) from potential suppliers. The Purchasing Manager then examines all the bids to find a qualified supplier who best meets the organization's needs, such as low cost and high levels of service. This technique of competitive bidding, which pits potential suppliers against each another for the organization's business, is typically used: in competitive markets with multiple suppliers offering the same item; when a large volume of the good or service is needed; if the organization does not yet have a preferred supplier for the product; and when there is enough time for the time-consuming competitive bidding process.

If, after sending out an RFI, the Purchasing Manager finds that there are very few suppliers of the needed good or service, the timeframe does not allow for competitive bidding, immediate supplier involvement is needed, or the item requested must be manufactured and its complexity does not allow for accurate cost estimates, he/she may instead engage in the purchasing technique of negotiation with one potential supplier. ***Negotiation*** occurs when a buyer and one potential supplier engage in an open discussion in an attempt to reach a mutually beneficial purchasing agreement. The negotiation process may be as simple as a single telephone call or e-mail or as complex as a series of meetings, interviews, and site visits over the course of a year. It can also help to develop strong initial buyer-supplier relationships because both parties have openly discussed their abilities and expectations. Good negotiation takes great finesse and is more of an art than a science. If a Purchasing Manager is new to, uncomfortable with, or simply seeking support for an important upcoming negotiation, he or she may elect to seek the services of a third-party broker or negotiation service provider.

Throughout the process of both competitive bidding and negotiation, the Purchasing Manager uses set evaluation criteria when considering potential suppliers. These criteria might include factors such as:

- *Does the supplier have the ability, experience, physical resources, and adequately trained workforce to provide the goods or services of the right quantity and quality at the right time and place?*

- *Is the supplier financially sound and what do their current customers and employees think of them?*

- *How is their distribution handled? What is their track record for on-time deliveries?*

- *Is the supplier committed to this relationship? Are they ready to work with us now?*

During supplier selection, an organization must also consider whether its needs would be best met by selecting a ***single supplier*** or ***multiple sources of supply*** for the desired good or service. At first glance, it may seem most obvious to use select a single supplier: a single supplier can offer the best volume discount and higher levels of service, such as Just-in-Time service; it may be willing to offer an organization more control and information by introducing *vendor managed inventory (VMI)* into its inventory control system (more on this in later chapters…); and it provides a platform for a solid, long-lasting buyer-supplier relationship. An effective Purchasing Manager must also consider the advantages of selecting multiple sources of supply, such as: suppliers do not become complacent in the quality of their products and service because they are in constant competition with one another; costs can be lower when the market is extremely competitive; and, if one of the suppliers experiences labor problems or equipment failure, the flow of supply to the organization is still guaranteed.

Whether a single supplier or multiple sources of supply are selected, we cannot move on to purchase orders and Step 4 of the purchasing process until we mention a growing trend in the world of corporate purchasing - auctions! An ***auction*** is the sale of goods or services by a supplier in which potential buyers bid against one another for the desired items.

When an organization must purchase a large quantity of a basic item or service and it is not concerned with using a preferred supplier, it may consider holding a reverse auction to select a supplier. In a reverse auction, an organization announces the goods or services it needs to purchase. In-person, telephone, or online potential suppliers may then bid their cost for the goods or services against other potential buyers. The costs bid go lower and lower (as opposed to traditional auctions with rising bids) until one supplier is left offering the lowest bid. Overall, auctions offer a much quicker purchasing process and sometimes a more cost effective result than competitive bidding or negotiations, but can bring greater risks with unvetted suppliers.

A Quick Word about an Important Topic in the World of Purchasing

Before we move on to step 4, we must consider **ethics**. In the purchasing process, individual buyers such as Purchasing Managers often deal with vast sums of an organization's money. All members of the Purchasing Department are held to high ethical standards and must follow corporate Ethical Codes of Conduct. Most organizations have well established Codes of Conduct, which outlines the ethical values of the organization and the expectations it has for its employees' ethical conduct. The Codes usually provide employees guidance on how to behave when difficult situations or choices present themselves. Areas covered in Ethical Codes of Conduct range from policies on outright bribes and corporate fraud to the subtleties of what is acceptable and what is unacceptable in giving and accepting corporate gifts.

Step 4 - Get the Purchase Approved and Purchase Order Issued

When the supplier has been selected, the terms of the purchase arrangement are then established between the buyer and the supplier. These written arrangements are contained in a legally binding document called a ***purchase order*** or a ***purchase agreement***. This document, signed by authorized officials representing both the buyer and the supplier, contains details outlining the purchase, such as: a description and specifications of the goods or services; the quantity to be delivered; the exact place, time, and method of delivery; the price of the overall purchase; descriptions of the quality required of the goods and related services; and the purchase order number and purchase due date.

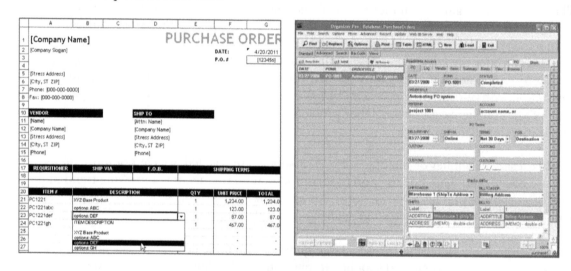

Figure 4.5 - Examples of a Purchase Order Template for Microsoft Excel Available from Vertex42 (left) and a Purchase Order Software Solution from PrimaSoft PC Software

When setting the price of the overall purchase within the purchase order or other similar contract between the buyer and supplier, both parties work toward agreeing on a fair and reasonable price. These costs set may be either *fixed* or *variable*. For situations in which the supplier is producing a new, complex item, the costs in the purchase order may be stated as ***variable costs***. For most situations, buyers and suppliers have a reasonable feel for what the cost of the desired items or services will be. In these situations, their purchase order may be a ***fixed price contract***, in which the prices for goods delivered are set at a fixed level. Also quoted may be a ***landed price***, which is the price cited by the supplier to the buyer that includes all transportation and customs duties costs.

For many years, purchase orders in large organizations had been entirely paper-based, with copies of copies of copies of purchase orders sent to multiple departments across an organization for much needed information sharing. Each department would have their file drawers full of old purchase orders at the end of each fiscal year. Today, most large organizations forward electronic copies of purchase orders to other departments or, better yet, their purchase orders are part of a larger EDI (electronic data interchange) system, with real-time information sharing. (More on what this all means in Chapter 7 ahead...)

When a good or service or range of related goods or services are to be ordered multiple times from the same supplier, an organization may issue a **blanket purchase order (BPO)**, an open order for goods or services from a specific supplier within a specific timeframe, such as a year. When goods or services covered under a BPO are needed, a **routine order release** is issued and the requested goods or services are delivered to the buyer. Blanket purchase orders are a common, efficient means of doing business for most large organizations, especially for regularly needed production and maintenance goods and services.

After an organization has sent a purchase order or a routine order release (under a BPO agreement) to a supplier, it is ready to move on to Step 5 of the purchasing process and receive the goods and check the order.

Step 5 - Receive & Check the Order

Thinking back to Grandma and her birthday surprise, you have selected the perfect 52" television at an amazingly low price and placed your order with a local retailer, Ellie's Electronics, who will be delivering it to Grandma's house while she is out of town competing at the Poker World Championship in Las Vegas. When Ellie's Electronics arrives, do you simply let them leave the delivery on the front porch and drive off because you are just too comfortable in Grandma's shiatsu massage chair to get up? If you are the responsible Purchasing Officer that your family believes you are, you instead greet the Ellie's Electronics delivery people at the door, receive the order from them, check the order (i.e., make sure the television, remote, and instruction documents are all in the box and in good condition), and sign that you have received the order.

When suppliers make a delivery to an organization, the Purchasing Department is not as directly involved in receiving the ordered goods as you were when receiving Grandma's TV. Instead, the Purchasing Manager relies on the Warehouse and Quality Control Departments to receive and inspect the order. (Remember way back in Chapter 3?)

The Purchasing Department does, however, monitor the entire order receipt process remotely. When the order is received and checked, the Purchasing Department is informed. This information is transmitted automatically in real time if the organization has a computerized inventory management system linked in to automatic identification technology. For example, the Purchasing Manager at Honey-Bee-Good immediately knows when and how many ordered jars are received into the HBG warehouse because the boxes of jars are scanned using a bar code reader and entered into the HBG inventory management software program. A short time later, after the Warehouse Manager has checked the order and entered additional information into the inventory management program, the Purchasing Manager knows the condition of the order received.

Throughout the order receipt and checking process, it is critical that the Purchasing Manager stay informed. Ensuring that the order has been received in the right quantity, of the right quality, and at the right time and place is a true measure of the success of the purchase.

Step 6 - Measure the Supplier's Performance

From the end of Step 4 through to the end of Step 5 of the purchasing process, the Purchasing Manager must vigilantly monitor the supplier's actual performance. While it is great to find a supplier who offers amazingly low prices, it is absolutely critical that the supplier deliver what it is ordered in the right quantity, of the right quality, at the right time, and to the right place. It is also important that the supplier be responsive to buyer's request, even if it just a request for additional information; be reliable, responsible, and respectful; and be flexible to changes that may arise in the buyer's needs and schedule. Another important performance measure is how good the supplier is at *expediting* orders. A buyer typically orders goods or services from a supplier according to a predetermined schedule. In some cases, the buyer may need to goods or services sooner than agreed. A supplier is viewed favorably if it can expedite the order, i.e., deliver goods or services more swiftly and efficiently than planned.

It is important for the Purchasing Manager to evaluate supplier performance to enhance future purchasing operations and supply chain efficiency. When the Purchasing Manager finds that a supplier does not meet the performance criteria stated in the purchase order or other contractual agreement, he or she can contact the supplier to allow them the opportunity to improve. Often, because the supplier wants to keep the buyer's business, being informed of poor performance can results in subsequent higher-than-expected levels of supplier service. If the supplier's level of performance does not improve, the buyer may cancel the purchase order and know to avoid that supplier in the future.

Although it is important to know when a supplier's performance is substandard, it is equally important for a Purchasing Manager to know when a supplier's performance exceeds expectations. Exceptional suppliers can become an organization's *preferred suppliers*, suppliers who have proven themselves as reliable suppliers who consistently offer higher levels of service or lower prices. Many medium- to large-size organizations keep a list or database of preferred suppliers to which they refer when sourcing for a needed product or service. Having a preferred supplier database allows for a more streamlined supplier selection process, in which a buyer may solicit competitive bids from only a few preferred suppliers (instead of the many suppliers available) or even go straight to the negotiation process with one preferred supplier.

Step 7 - Close Out the Order

After the goods or service have been received and the supplier's performance has been evaluated, the Purchasing Manager is ready to close out the order. At this stage, the Purchasing and Accounting Departments validate that what was ordered was received and that the terms and conditions of the purchase agreement or contract were met. This is also called a *three-way-match* because the purchase order, receipt documents, and supplier invoice are compared. If all three match up, the supplier's invoice is approved for payment and the purchase order is closed out, marked as completed, and filed.

IT & THE PURCHASING PROCESS

Over the past two decades, logistics management and the world of purchasing has become increasingly fast, accurate, and precise thanks to widespread computerization and rapid advances in information technology. The real-time transmission and receipt of information within purchasing and logistics management has resulted in extremely efficient organizations with streamlined supply chains.

With the variety of information technology applications now available, it is far easier for an organization's Purchasing Manager to control and improve the purchasing process. Although we will cover information technology in the supply chain in greater detail later in this book (see Chapter 7), let's take a brief look at the role IT plays in purchasing.

Thanks to the internet and the world wide web, Purchasing Managers can quickly and immediately investigate potential suppliers during the supplier selection phase of the purchasing process. On the web, suppliers' websites, corporate analysis and information sites, trade-related sites with customer blogs, and the Better Business Bureau are invaluable sources of information. The Purchasing Manager can also immediately and inexpensively send requests for information, proposals, and quotes to multiple potential suppliers via e-mail. It can also receive multiple bids via e-mail or through a template on their own corporate website. Electronic bids are far easier than their paper-based counterparts for Purchasing Managers to manage, compare, and store. For example, a company with an electronic bid submission form directly on its website immediately transfers bid information from potential suppliers to a computer spreadsheet or database as soon as it is received. When making the supplier selection decision, the Purchasing Manager can then use the spreadsheet or database to immediately and easily compare all bids by specific categories, such as cost, experience, or value-added services.

When a company is determining and transmitting information about its buying needs, creating purchase order and sending copies to other departments in the organization, receiving and checking goods at the warehouse and transmitting relevant information to the Purchasing Department, and closing out and filing the complete order, it can use an in-house intranet system for immediate information sharing across corporate departments and locations, even when they are physically thousands of miles apart.

When a company wishes to form an information-sharing relationship with its suppliers or customers, it may develop an *extranet* or use *Electronic Data Interchange (EDI)*. An extranet is a web-based system of information sharing similar to the internet, but is open only to the companies involved. An extranet can be used to transmit and receive a wide range of messages, documents, and other information. EDI is also used to share information between companies, but its focus is an immediate transmission of business information from computer to computer in a standard format. EDI transmissions contain only business data, with no accompanying files or messages.

EDI and internet-based systems are both commonly used in MRP, VMI, and e-Commerce systems. *MRP (materials requirement planning)* is a software application used to analyze production and manufacturing data to help a company determine how much of a good or service it needs to purchase and within what timeframe. MRP systems can then automatically generate purchase orders, which are sent immediately from buyers to suppliers through EDI- and internet-based systems. One mainstay of MRP systems is automatic inventory replacement, the technique of automatically ordering goods when inventory reaches a specific level. The goal of automatic inventory replacement is to maintain predetermined levels of stock within an organization.

VMI (vendor managed inventory) is the practice of a buyer allowing a supplier (or vendor) to monitor product demand in order to forecast demand patterns and set product shipment levels and schedules. Information between buyer and supplier in a VMI system may be transmitted using either EDI or the internet.

Electronic commerce (or ***e-Commerce***) systems are a typically software-driven means for a company to sell its goods to other companies (also known as ***business to business*** or ***B2B***) or directly to consumers (also known as ***business to consumer*** or ***B2C***). Information between all companies and consumers involved is transmitted most often via EDI or internet systems.

One type of e-Commerce is ***electronic procurement*** (or ***e-Procurement***), a business-to-business automated system of purchasing and payment. Because all information surrounding the purchase and receipt of the goods are captured and recorded electronically and a payment is automatically issued from the buyer, e-Procurement eliminates the need for the supplier to create and send unique transaction invoices.

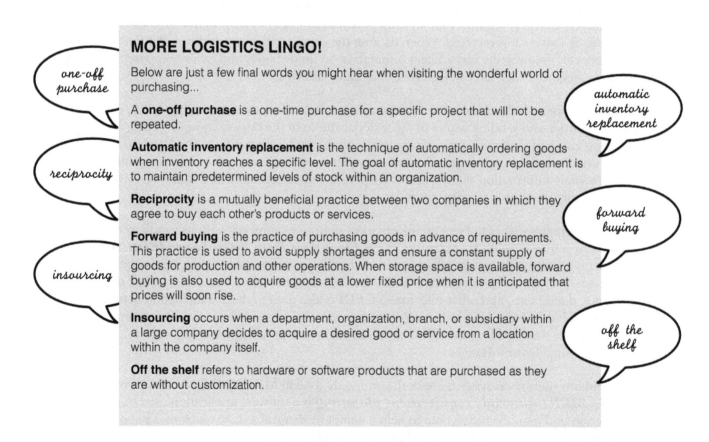

MORE LOGISTICS LINGO!

Below are just a few final words you might hear when visiting the wonderful world of purchasing...

A **one-off purchase** is a one-time purchase for a specific project that will not be repeated.

Automatic inventory replacement is the technique of automatically ordering goods when inventory reaches a specific level. The goal of automatic inventory replacement is to maintain predetermined levels of stock within an organization.

Reciprocity is a mutually beneficial practice between two companies in which they agree to buy each other's products or services.

Forward buying is the practice of purchasing goods in advance of requirements. This practice is used to avoid supply shortages and ensure a constant supply of goods for production and other operations. When storage space is available, forward buying is also used to acquire goods at a lower fixed price when it is anticipated that prices will soon rise.

Insourcing occurs when a department, organization, branch, or subsidiary within a large company decides to acquire a desired good or service from a location within the company itself.

Off the shelf refers to hardware or software products that are purchased as they are without customization.

one-off purchase *automatic inventory replacement* *reciprocity* *forward buying* *insourcing* *off the shelf*

Efficient and effective purchasing and supply management is both a science and an art. Getting the right goods and services in the right quantity, with the right quality, delivered to he right place, at the required time and at a fair market price is critical to an organization's bottom line. Unfortunately, many organizations still, to their great cost, do not appreciate or understand the importance of professional purchasing and supply management to their financial success.

CHAPTER 4 REVIEW QUESTIONS

1. What is the difference between the terms purchasing and supply management?

2. What MRO supplies might a large bakery purchase? What capital goods might it purchase?

3. For what situation is a Statement of Work typically used? What benefits would this offer over an organization's standard purchase requisition form?

4. What is the difference between an RFI and an RFP? When might each be used? Can both be used to procure the same product?

5. What role does the Purchasing Manager play when ordered goods are being received into an organization's warehouse?

6. What is a preferred supplier? Why might a company want to keep a list of preferred suppliers?

7. Describe one way in which Honey-Bee-Good could increase the efficiency of its supply chain by using information technology applications with its jar and label supplier, Paxton Purchasing.

8. Jo-Jo's Jams, a small record label, sells approximately 200,000 self-produced music CDs each year for $10 each and makes a profit of $5 from each CD sold. Jo-Jo's currently buys its blank CDs and cases from So-So-CDs for $1.00 each. Jo-Jo's Purchasing Manager has negotiated a new purchase agreement with Sili-Valley, Inc. to purchase 200,000 blank CDs and cases for $0.90 each.

    a. What was Jo-Jo's annual profit when So-So-CDs was its supplier?

    b. What will Jo-Jo's annual profit be after the switch to Sili-Valley?

    c. How much will Jo-Jo's Jams save each year by switching its suppliers? By what percentage will its annual profits increase?

    d. How many CDs would Jo-Jo's need to sell to match this increase in profit if it did not switch suppliers?

CHAPTER 4 CASE STUDY

A Look at ASCI's SmartTools

In Alaska, oil, gas, and mining are all big business. However, unlike other locations across the U.S., exploration and extraction sites in Alaska are remote. Actually, remote doesn't even begin to describe it. The North Slope, home of most of Alaska's oil and gas exploration and extraction, is located in the far northernmost reaches of the state, bordering the Arctic Sea. No railways or reliable highways reach the area and the Arctic sea is frozen over with solid ice packs for most of the year. It is also located thousands of miles away from any suppliers, making air transportation practical only for the lightest and most valuable items desired.

At the onset of the long North Slope winters, roads of ice are constructed across the frozen tundra. (Think Ice Road Truckers.) Although warm winter weather may sound like a blessing in Alaska, it is a curse for the North Slope because ice road construction can face lengthy delays. In the late spring, before the dirt roads are passable, the ice roads melt and make the tundra marshy and impassable. Compared to Texas, where most exploration, extraction, and refinery sites can be reached throughout the year by road or rail systems, Alaska's oil and gas industry faces unique supply challenges and enormous supply chain costs. One company that has devoted itself to reducing its Alaska customers' supply chain costs and risks is ASCI, Advanced Supply Chain International.

Founded in 1999 in Anchorage, Alaska to provide supply chain services to the state's oil and gas industry, ASCI is now a high tech supply chain and asset management company for some of the major players in the oil and gas, petrochemical, refining, chemical, and mining industries across the world. One of the many services ASCI offers to help customers cut costs are its web-based SmartTools. Reported to help reduce purchasing costs by up to as much as 37%, SmartTools are a type of ERP (enterprise resource planning) system that assists with supplier selection and integration, staging, order tracking, and strategic sourcing.

With ASCI's web-based and paperless SmartTools, companies can use a suite of nine IT tools that helps them manage all aspects of their inbound supply chain. One tool, the SmartCatalogue, helps purchasers quickly find the items they are looking for, from the commonplace to the obscure, all from a range of tried and tested reliable suppliers. If the purchaser then wants to find even lower prices, he can use the SmartAuction/Quote tool, which solicits, receives, and manages bids from multiple suppliers. If purchasers have large orders to place, they can use the SmartBundler tool to find the lowest costs for bulk orders. Before deciding to place an order with a particular supplier, purchasers can also use the SmartMeasures tool to peruse up-to-date performance metrics of ASCI's suppliers, such as on-time delivery statistics. Once orders has been placed, purchasers can use the SmartTracker tool, which provides real-time information for tracking orders.

Although you might imagine that finding the lowest prices are at the forefront of purchasing managers' minds, if they are working on the North Slope, they are also highly concerned with receiving goods on time. Most of the goods ordered are maintenance, repair, and operating (MRO) supplies, from highly complex widgets and thingamabobs for drilling and extraction to much needed food and toiletries for the thousands of workers on the North Slope, where the closest grocery or clothing store is hundreds of miles away. In this harsh and unforgiving environment, typical on-time arrival rates for goods can be as low as 30 to 40% for inexperienced companies and 50 to 60% for more experienced companies. This delay can lead to inventory shortages of spare parts for needed for immediate repairs, which can result in temporary shutdowns, costing oil and gas companies millions of dollars. Thanks to SmartTools and its SmartTracker and SmartMeasure, ASCI's customers typically experience an on-time arrival rate of 80% for MRO supplies, resulting in fewer costly shut downs and much happier workers who have uninterrupted supplies of peanut butter and coffee.

References

ASCI (2011) Frequently asked questions. *Advanced Supply Chain International Media Kit.*

ASCI (2011) Supply chain software. *ASCI* website. Retrieved from http://www.ascillc.com/software.php/.

Bohi, H. (2010, February) Supply chain to rural Alaska: how native villages are supplied. *Alaska Business Monthly*, 74-77.

Schwarz, M. (2010, May) Effectively managing the supply chain in remote locations. *Drilling and Exploration World*, 19 (7), 66-69.

Case Study Questions

1. What purchasing challenges do ASCI's customers face?

2. Why should these companies use services like ASCI's SmartTools?

3. Which of the seven steps of the purchasing process are handled by SmartTools?

4. How might the purchasing process have been different thirty years ago when Alaska's oil and gas companies did not have access to the information technology systems of today?

Chapter 5

Physical Distribution Management

In Chapters 1 and 2, we introduced the concepts of logistics and supply chain management. In Chapters 3 and 4, we covered the basics of inbound logistics, which includes all the logistics activities that occur at the beginning of the internal supply chain, from the moment an order for goods is placed with the supplier until the organization receives the goods from the supplier. In Chapter 3, we focused on the physical side of inbound logistics: warehousing, materials management, and inventory management. In Chapter 4, we explored the financial side of inbound logistics: purchasing and supply management.

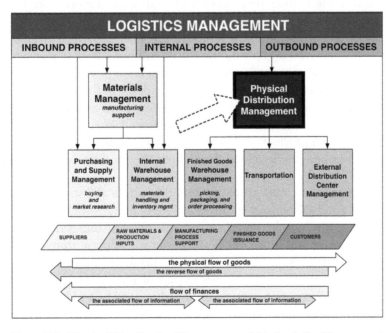

Figure 5.1 - Physical Distribution Management within Logistics Management

Now that we understand the ins and outs of getting goods to an organization, it's time to explore how an organization handles the outbound flow of its own finished product. As we saw in Chapter 3, **outbound logistics** includes all the logistics activities that occur at the tail end of internal logistics management, from the moment an organization has produced its finished product until the product is received by its immediate user. As shown in our map of logistics management above, the core of outbound logistics management processes is physical distribution management. This chapter introduces the key elements of physical distribution management, except for the topic of transportation, which needs it own chapter. (See Chapter 6.)

INTRODUCING PHYSICAL DISTRIBUTION MANAGEMENT

As we discussed in earlier chapters, the coordination of inbound logistics systems and processes is called **materials management**. The coordination of outbound logistics systems and processes is called **physical distribution**. According to both the website of the American Marketing Association and the website glossary of the Council of Supply Chain Management Professionals, **physical distribution management** (PDM) is "the management of the movement and storage functions of finished goods from manufacturing and production facilities to warehouses and customers."

Let's clarify that definition a bit, however. Physical distribution management is concerned with the movement and storage of an organization's finished products to the same organization's warehouses or customers. Therefore, extractors of raw materials, producers of component parts and semifinished goods, and manufacturers of finished goods are all engaged in physical distribution management.

Each type of organization has its own finished product, even though it may bear little resemblance to the final product seen by the end user. For example, a bauxite ore extractor is engaged in physical distribution management after it has extracted the ore from the ground and is sending it to its direct customer, an aluminum processing plant. The aluminum processing plant is likewise engaged in physical distribution management after it has produced large aluminum sheets from the bauxite ore received and is sending the aluminum sheets to its customer, a bicycle manufacturer. Finally, the bicycle manufacturer is also engaged in physical distribution management after it has produced bicycles (with frames made from the aluminum sheets provided) and is sending their finished bicycles to the regional distribution centers of their customers, national retail chains. The original finished product, bauxite ore, bears little resemblance to the final finished product, a children's bicycle, but the practice and principles of physical distribution management are involved throughout the product's entire supply chain.

Furthermore, many of the practices and principles found in physical distribution management and the outbound flow of goods also apply to physical supply management and the inbound flow of goods. For example, after our bicycle manufacturer assembles its finished product, the Raging Roadster Dirt Bike, it must store and move finished bicycles to get them to regional distribution centers for its customer, Safe-T-Toys. When it receives the finished Raging Roadsters, Safe-T-Toys must also move and store the finished bicycles as part of its inbound logistics management. The finished bicycles are stored at warehouses and moved around by forklift at both the manufacturer's and Safe-T-Toys facilities, although the first is classified as outbound physical distribution management and the second is classified as inbound physical supply management. Therefore, because the basic of movement and storage of goods were already covered previously in Chapter 4, this chapter will focus on those activities and principles that are unique to outbound logistics processes.

Since the start of the industrial age, companies have focused primarily on the manufacturing function, i.e., the cost of acquiring raw materials and producing the finished product. The activities covered within the realm of physical distribution management were given little consideration and merely regarding as necessary "delivery" functions. As we mentioned back in Chapter 2, the oil crisis of the 1970s changed all that. The entire supply chain was now under scrutiny as a possible means of reducing an organization's operating costs giving birth to three functional areas: procurement, materials management, and physical distribution.

Like its procurement and materials management counterparts, physical distribution management is still seen as an important area of study within logistics management. When practiced efficiently and effectively, physical distribution management can:

- **minimize cost**. With efficient physical distribution management, especially at the global level, logistics costs can be significantly reduced. For example, one core outbound logistics activity is physically taking items from warehouse shelves based on customers' orders, also known as order picking. When a multinational candy manufacturer Ewwey Gooey, Ltd. implemented improvements to its order picking process worldwide, it shaved 3 minutes off of each large order picked from warehouse shelves. With multiple orders picked every day at its 200 warehouses worldwide, Ewwey Gooey reduced its global order picking time by 2000 hours daily! Reductions in order picking time and similar practices in physical distribution management can result in significant decreases in an organization's overall logistics costs.

- **increase customer service**. Effective physical distribution management can have an enormous impact on the customer service an organization provides. In today's world of e-commerce and Just-in-Time deliveries, customers expect to receive goods shortly after ordering them. (Just think about the last time you ordered something online and how frustrating it felt when you had to wait five whole days for it!) The more effective its physical distribution management practices, the closer an organization can come to delivering goods at the exact time a customer desires.

- **work to fulfill Marketing's promises**. An organization's Marketing Department promises its customers that they will receive the right quantity and quality of goods at the time and place desired. Without efficient and effective physical distribution management, it would be impossible for an organization to fulfill these promises, leading to future reductions in sales.

For the remainder of this chapter, we will examine the world of physical distribution management and the role in plays in: responding to an organization's order cycle; servicing the Marketing Department's distribution channels; handling and preparing outbound goods; getting goods out the door and on the road; and engaging in reverse logistics.

RESPONDING TO THE ORDER CYCLE

One important part of outbound logistics management and effective physical distribution management is an organization's ability to respond to the order cycle. As defined by the Council of Supply Chain Management Professionals' Glossary of Terms website, the **order cycle** is the "time and process involved from the placement of an order to the receipt of the shipment." In Chapter 4, we looked at the purchasing process, which outlines the activities involved in the order of goods from the buyer's perspective. The **order cycle process** outlines the order of goods and how the order is filled from the supplier's perspective.

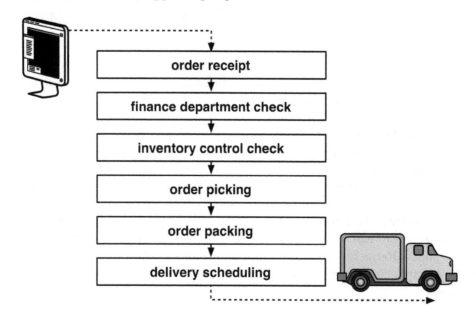

Figure 5.2 - The Order Cycle Process

For efficient and effective physical distribution management, an organization must respond to the six steps of the order cycle process efficiently and effectively. One of the goals of physical distribution management is to achieve competitive advantage for the organization. One way this can be accomplished is by reducing order cycle time, i.e., reducing the time it takes to complete the entire order cycle through its entire six steps. These six steps (and the ways in which they have an impact on overall order cycle time) are:

1. **Order Receipt.** During the purchasing process, the buyer desires specific items from a supplier and places an order for them, typically in the form of a purchase order or purchase agreement. During this first stage of the order cycle, called the order receipt step, the supplier receives this purchase order from the buyer. The degree to which an organization's order receipt procedures are automated and computerized have a substantial impact on overall order cycle time. For example, during the order receipt step for Company A, purchase orders are received from buyers by fax, manually entered into the company's computer system, and then printed and hand delivered to the company warehouse for order picking. Its competitor, Company B has streamlined its order receipt procedures by receiving buyers' purchase orders through a web-based ordering system,

which are sent directly to the warehouse computer system for pre-approved buyers. Order receipt at Company A may take up to one hour, but takes only one second at Company B!

2. **Finance Department Check.** After the buyer's order is received, it is sent to the supplier's Finance Department to verify the customer's status. This check determines if the customer: is a preexisting one, is in good credit standing with the organization, and has preexisting sales and service terms, such as whether or not an order can be sent before its payment is received. As with the order receipt example given for Companies A and B, the degree to which the Finance Department check is automated and computerized influences the speed of this stage of the order cycle process. Even for smaller organizations, where large-scale computer automation may not be cost effect, accurate and thorough computer-based record keeping can make a world of difference to a company's order cycle time and its bottom line. If a supplier does not have well kept records about its previous transactions with buyers, the Finance Department may spend ridiculously large amounts of time checking up on past buyers and extra resources in unnecessary credit checks. It may even mistakenly approve buyers who have defaulted in the past!

3. **Inventory Control Check.** After the buyer's order is approved by the Finance Department, it is sent to the Inventory Control Department or system, which then checks on the availability of the finished goods requested in the order. If the goods are available, Inventory Control then allocates the requirements or, for those of us not yet fully proficient in logistics jargon, assigns the desired goods located in inventory to the specific order. At the risk of sounding like a very broken record, this stage of the order cycle, too, can be made an instantaneous one with order processing automation and computerization.

4. **Order Picking.** Now that the customer's financial status and the availability of the items in the order have been verified, the organization can now begin to physically fill the order. The items requested are ***picked*** (or selected) from the warehouse shelves. Later in this chapter, we will explore some of the techniques used for more efficient order picking, which focus not only on automation and computerization, but also on how a company actually plans the pick in terms of which items will be picked when and by whom.

5. **Order Packing.** After the items in the order are picked, they must be prepared for shipment. An order is ***packed*** when its items are placed into packaging, ***unitized*** (placed into unit loads, such as onto pallets or into containers), and physically prepared for shipping. We will also explore order packing in greater depth later in this chapter and the importance of effective packing to a company's bottom line.

6. **Delivery Scheduling.** Finally, after the inventory is picked and packed, a delivery time and place is scheduled with the customer through the organization's transportation system. The delivery is scheduled and subsequently conducted through the *distribution channel*, the route and means by which an organization distributes its finished goods. As with all steps of the order cycle, organizations can achieve greater delivery scheduling efficiency and effectiveness when the process is automated and computerized. Imagine, for example, a Walmart regional distribution center with 40 goods-in and loading bays

and a steady stream of container trucks both bringing goods in from suppliers and taking them away to retail stores. If the scheduling of the bays alone wasn't precise down to the minute, chaos might reign, with container trucks backed up for hours waiting for available bays.

SERVICING MARKETING'S DISTRIBUTION CHANNEL

As we mentioned earlier, physical distribution management plays a significant role in servicing the Marketing Department's distribution channels. A ***distribution channel*** is the route and means by which an organization distributes its finished goods. It is the structure of the physical flow of goods and includes all members involved in this physical flow, such as the organization itself, distribution centers, third party logistics service providers, wholesalers, and retailers.

Although there is overlap between an organization's supply chain and its distribution channel, they are different concepts relevant to different disciplines. Way back in Chapter 1, we defined the *supply chain* as all the actions associated with the flow of goods, information, and finance as the goods move and transform from a raw materials or unfinished stage to a finished product received by an end user, covering both the inbound and outbound flow of goods. The distribution channel, however, is concerned solely with the physical outbound flow of goods. Also, the terms are commonly used within two different disciplines. Supply chain is a term from the world of logistics, while distribution channel is a term typically found within the world of marketing.

In an organization, the Marketing Department determines the nature and structure of its product's distribution channel and the level of service the organization will provide throughout. Selecting and following through on the most appropriate distribution channel structure will ensure that the customer receives the right quantity and quality of the right product at the right time and place. While the Marketing Department selects and designs the distribution channel, it is the mission of the Logistics Department and those involved in physical distribution management to carry out the Marketing Department's plans and strategy by physically moving goods through the distribution channel established. Therefore, it is the responsibility of physical distribution management to ensure that all of marketing's distribution channel goals and promises to customers are met.

Distribution channels are structure according to customers' needs, the nature of the product, and the location and nature of the supplier. There are a variety of types of distribution channels, with as little as two members or as many as four or more members. Below are five examples of different distribution channels of increasing complexity as more members are added to the channel based on the product, supplier, and customer's needs. As the distribution channels become more complex, so must the corresponding physical distribution management system used to meet the Marketing Department's distribution channel delivery goals and the promises to its customers.

Distribution Channel Example #1: Superior Logs

This first example of a distribution channel is the simplest one, with only two members, the manufacturer and the end user. The manufacturer, Superior Logs, produces log home kits in Alaska. The company then sells and delivers these directly to the local end user.

Distribution Channel Example #2: Dell Computers

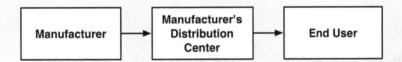

Slightly more complex is a distribution channel in which a distribution center is added, in this case, the manufacturer's regional distribution center. The manufacturer, Dell Computers, produces computers from a variety of supplier sources around the world. The company delivers many of its finished goods to the Dell Distribution Center in Ohio. From here, finished goods are sent directly to the end users. Physical distribution management is responsible for the movement and storage of goods from the completion of the computer assembly overseas to the receipt into the Dell distribution center in Ohio until the completed computers are prepared for shipment and sent to the end users.

Distribution Channel Example #3: Europa Wholesale Bakery

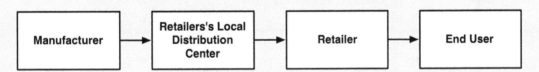

In this distribution channel structure, a fourth member is added, the retailer. The manufacturer, Europa Wholesale Bakery, is an Alaska company that produces 4000 loaves of artisan bread daily for local grocery stores and restaurants. After its finished goods are produced (i.e., the yummy loaves are baked), Europa sends many of them to the local distribution centers of retail grocery chains. From these distribution centers, the loaves are then sent directly to the retailer locations, local grocery stores across Alaska. These retailers then sell the finished goods to happy end-users.

Distribution Channel Example #4: 3M in Alaska

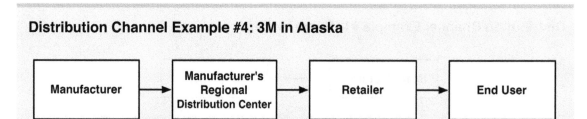

This distribution channel structure of four members is similar to the previous one of Europa Wholesale Bakery, but, instead of goods being sent form the factory to the retailer's distribution center, they are sent to the manufacturer's own regional distribution center. The manufacturer, 3M, produces a diverse range of products, but is perhaps most widely known for its office supplies, such as tape and Post-It® products. In Alaska, 3M sends its finished goods to its regional distribution center, 3M Alaska, who then distributes goods to retailers, such as Office Depot and Office Max locations. The retailers then sell the 3M finished goods to end-users.

Distribution Channel Example #5: Walmart's Faded Glory

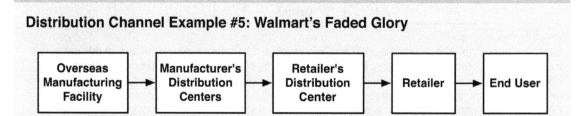

The distribution channel now becomes even more complex as we add a fifth member by including both the manufacturer's and retailer's distribution centers. The finished goods are Walmart's Faded Glory brand of clothing. The goods are produced at multiple manufacturing facilities in China. The goods are collected at the manufacturer's distribution center in China from where they are containerized and sent to various Walmart regional distribution centers around the world. Each regional distribution center then breaks down the shipment and redistributes the finished goods to a variety of local retailers, who, in turn, sell the finished goods to the end users.

As the distribution channels become more complex, the role and tasks of physical distribution management tasks become increasingly challenging requiring more computer hardware and software throughout the distribution channel to track the order. While our Superior Logs example could function with simple telephone and fax communication between manufacturer and end-user, Walmart's Faded Glory distribution channel could not. To meet the distribution channel goals and customer promises set by the Marketing Department, the physical distribution management of Faded Glory jeans would require advanced logistics information, warehouse management, and transportation management software systems, which would need to be supported by item identification hardware such as RFID readers and barcode scanners, all of which we will explore in greater depth later in Chapter 7.

HANDLING OUTBOUND GOODS

Along with servicing the Marketing Department's distribution channels, physical distribution management is also concerned with efficiently and effectively handling outbound goods. After an order from a buyer is received, for most manufacturers, the goods are not simply loaded straight onto a truck from a manufacturing facility for shipment. An organization's finished goods are typically stored and handled as they are taken from storage and prepared for shipment. When this handling of outbound goods is accomplished efficiently, an organization can decrease its physical distribution costs and increase its customer service. Within physical distribution management, three important aspects of handling outbound goods are: *finished goods materials handling, managing warehouses and distribution centers*, and *order picking and packing*.

Finished Goods Materials Handling

Remember back in Chapter 3, we defined *materials handling* as a focus on materials (physical goods in raw, semifinished, and finished states) and how they are handled (moved short distances and stored within a facility). Earlier in this chapter, we discussed how materials handling occurs during both inbound and outbound logistics processes. *Physical distribution management* is concerned with the materials handling of an organization's outbound finished goods.

Exactly the same principles and practices of materials handling found in *inbound* logistics (as we covered in Chapter 3) apply to *outbound* logistics and physical distribution management, including the importance of product flow, unitization, and equipment utilization. Often, even the same equipment is used for both inbound and outbound materials management. Imagine a small furniture retailer's warehouse with goods waiting an extra two hours on a container truck at the goods-in bay because the forklift typically used for inbound materials was still charging its batteries, even though the forklift truck designated for outbound goods was not currently being used.

Rather than cover old ground, let us charge ahead to explore more issues relevant to handling outbound goods.

Managing Warehouses and Distribution Centers

Another important aspect of handling outbound goods within physical distribution management is managing warehouses and distribution centers. The principles and practices of warehouse management for inbound logistics (that we learned earlier in Chapter 3) also apply to warehouse and distribution center management for outbound logistics and physical distribution management.

In a **warehouse**, goods are stored by an organization for subsequent picking and issuing. A **distribution center** is a facility with most of the same functions as a warehouse, except that its primary function is not storage. A distribution center instead receives finished goods from multiple vendors or locations, sorts them, and prepares them for subsequent distribution. Some items may be stored, but items are not held long-term as they often are in warehouses.

Distribution centers (or DCs) may be owned and operated by the company that manufactures the goods; its immediate customers, such as large retail chains; or third party physical distribution management service providers. While warehouses vary in size and typically serve more localized needs, such as a nearby manufacturing facility or and adjacent retail establishment, distribution centers are typically quite large and service a regional or national need within a larger physical distribution network. Therefore, warehouses are located close to the immediate organization they serve, while large-scale distribution centers are located according to access to transportation and lower labor and utilities costs. Most distribution centers are usually located close to interstate highway systems, railroads, and airport. The next time you are flying into a medium-sized city, about three to five minutes before you land, take a look down. You are likely to see multiple large structures, often the size of a football field, with container trucks lined up alongside. Then scan the area and you are also likely to find railroad tracks and maybe even a small cargo port.

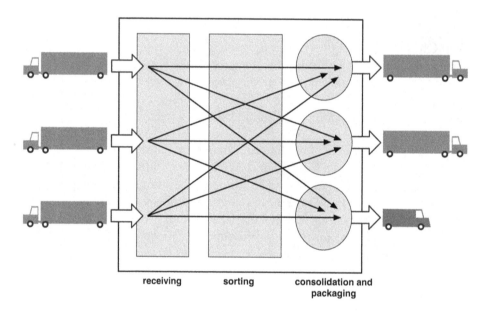

receiving   sorting   consolidation and
                                      packaging

Figure 5.3 - Cross-Docking Distribution Center

An increasingly common physical distribution management practice at distribution centers and warehouses is ***cross-docking***. In cross-docking, goods from a variety of suppliers or locations are received at one end of the facility, immediately sorted, and then immediately placed into trucks or containers at the other end of the facility for shipping. This entire process usually takes considerably less than 24 hours and can sometimes take less than a single hour! Essentially, cross-docking eliminates the need for storage and order picking because items from incoming shipments are transferred directly onto outgoing shipments. In a traditional warehouse, goods are held until a purchase order is received from a customer. At a cross-docking warehouse or distribution center, it is already known who the customers will be for each item in the incoming shipment long before they reach the cross-docking facility. For example, the home improvement retailer, Home Depot, operates an enormous cross-docking facility in Philadelphia that services more than 100 of its stores across the northeastern United States. When large truckloads of finished goods come into the cross-docking facility, employees immediately transfer items to different trucks heading for any of the retail chain's 100 plus stores in the region. Typically, cross-docking occurs throughout the day as different vendors arrive with their different wares. When a truck is full, it heads out to a retail store awaiting the products it contains, perhaps from scores of vendors!

Another increasingly common physical distribution management practice at warehouses and distribution centers is ***postponement***. Postponement is the delay of final product activities, such as assembly and packaging, until the latest possible time, typically in a regional warehouse or distribution center. Postponement allows finished goods to be assembled, packaged, or labeled in a variety of configurations. For example, a global shoe manufacturer may wait to package each individual pair of shiny new shoes into its individual box until it reaches the distribution center in its intended regional or national market. By waiting, the shoe manufacturer can now use country-specific or region-specific packaging that appeals to that local audience and is in the local language. Chances are, if you buy the same pair of designer shoes in the Mall of America in Minnesota and in a boutique on the Ginza in Tokyo, Japan, the shoes will look the same, but the shoeboxes will look very different!

Order Picking and Packing

Two final core elements of handling outbound goods within physical distribution management are order picking and order packing.

Order picking is the physical distribution management activity of selecting a required quantity of specific goods from storage, typically in response to an order received. Order picking also includes documenting that the required quantity of specific goods was moved from its storage location to the packing or shipping area. The order picking stage can have a significant impact on an organization's revenue saved or lost.

When items are picked quickly, orders can be filled quickly, users will be happy, and the organization can be paid sooner. When items are picked slowly, orders take longer to fill, users become annoyed, and the organization cannot be paid until the order is fully filled. Within the world of order picking and physical distribution, there are a variety of order picking techniques, the most common of which are: single order picking/discrete picking; wave picking; batch picking; and zone picking.

In ***single order picking*** (also known as ***discrete picking***), each order is picked by one person working from a single picking document. Orders may be picked at any time within the picker's schedule, as long as the delivery deadline is met. Compared to other styles of order picking, accountability is increased and errors are reduced, but it is slow and at the mercy of human limitations. One variation of single order picking is wave picking, in which orders are picked by one picker, one item at a time, but orders are scheduled to be picked within specific times.

In **batch picking**, one person picks multiple orders (i.e., a *batch* of orders) following multiple picking documents, at the same time. Batch picking reduces the traveling labor time of the picker by picking multiple orders at once, but can increase the risk of incorrect picking and sorting. These risks are greatly reduced, however, in computer-based automated picking systems.

In **zone picking**, a warehouse is divided into sections or zones. A different employee is assigned to and responsible for picking items within his or her section. Once picked, these items are brought to the central order consolidation and issue section where the entire order, with items picked from different zones by different pickers, can be consolidated. Zone picking does not reduce the labor used, but it can speed up the order picking process.

The materials handling equipment used during inbound logistics processes (inventory receipt and storage) are often the same equipment used for the outbound logistics process of order picking. Automated and robotic order picking equipment can be found in larger warehouse operations. Although this equipment is costly to purchase and set up, but can save an organization significant labor costs and can dramatically increase picking time.

After the items on an order have been picked from the warehouse, they must undergo **order packing** to be prepared for subsequent shipment. Order packing is the physical distribution management activity of placing goods securely into packages so that they are ready for outbound transportation. After the order has been picked, the order is **consolidated**, i.e., all of its separate items are brought together to a single location within the warehouse.

Then, after the order's items have been consolidated, they are placed securely into a box or other package for subsequent shipment. This process may include unitization of items onto pallets or into containers. One of the key components of the order packing process is packaging. **Packaging** is the term used for the physical materials into which an order's items are placed. This also includes additional materials used to secure the items within the package, such as straps or Styrofoam package filler. The packaging used during the order packing process has an enormous impact on the efficiency and effectiveness of the supply chain. Poor packaging can lead to stolen or broken products, less efficient use of transportation and subsequent storage space, and materials handling equipment malfunction. Efficient and effective packaging, however, should:

- *Keep items safe and secure.* When packaging is insufficient or inadequate, items can be damaged in transit. When packaging can be opened too easily, items can be stolen by "opportunity thieves" at any point along the supply chain.

- *Be easily labeled, transported, and stored.* Packaging must be easily labeled so that the customer's inventory receipt department can identify its contents. Packaging must also meet an organization's and its customers' requirements for transportation and storage. For example, packaging may have to be designed so that it can be placed and stacked easily onto pallets or into containers. It may also have to be placed onto storage racks of specific dimensions.

- *Be handled properly by materials handling equipment.* It is inevitable that packaged goods will be handled at both the producer's and customer's facilities. Packaging must be easily handled by both the producer's and the customer's materials handling equipment, which are not necessarily the same. For example, packaging may have to be handled by a forklift truck at one location and a conveyor at another.

For physical distribution management, packaging provides necessary safety and security for valuable goods. Without it, goods can lose all of their value in transit. Just imagine the mess, spoilage, and smell of a truckload of raw eggs being transported loosely in a 3'x3' boxes! Within the world of physical distribution management, packaging presents a bit of a conundrum. For items to be the safest and most secure, extra layers of thick packaging are required. Both the materials used and the extra space consumed for this safe and secure packaging are quite costly, however. Therefore, many organizations are now looking at cost efficient yet effective packaging. For example, organizations are looking for "greener," reusable packaging and for packaging that allows for more space utilization.

WHAT HAPPENS WHEN GOODS ARE OUT THE DOOR?

Besides servicing the Marketing Department's distribution channels and handling outbound goods, physical distribution management is also concerned with a few more activities after the ordered goods have left the warehouse and are on the way to the buyer. Three of these "out-the-door" activities found at the tail end of physical distribution management are: *controlling inventory in the distribution system, coordinating transportation,* and *reverse logistics.*

In Chapter 3, we learned that inventory control systems are used to help organizations determine the most efficient and effective inventory holding levels for individual items. **Inventory control systems** are also used within physical distribution management to keep an organization informed about its inventory, including how much of an item is available and where it is located.

For many physical distribution managers, it is important to know where inventory is, not only within the organization's manufacturing or warehouse facility, but also within the supply chain or distribution channel. Different locations and organizations within the supply chain use information technology to share accurate and real-time information about inventory location. This information makes inventory visible to the organization, even when the inventory is no longer under its control. This inventory visibility allows organizations to plan more effectively for manufacturing, warehousing, and transportation operations. It also helps reduce cost by allowing an organization to move more to Just-in-Time operations and hold less "just-in-case" inventory.

Inventory visibility also enhances customer service because it helps an organization control the process of getting the right quantity and quality of finished goods to the exact time and place a customer desires. Inventory visibility has become possible only through advances in information technology, including: computerized inventory information systems; bar code printing and scanning; RFID (radio frequency identification) technology; GPS (Global Positioning System) technology; and wireless connectivity. (Don't worry. We'll explain all of these late in Chapter 7 when we uncover the exciting world of information technology in the supply chain!)

For an organization's finished goods, **_transportation_** forms the critical bridge between those who have the goods (such as a manufacturing or warehouse facility) and those who want the goods (such as a retailer or customer). One role of the Physical Distribution Manager is to coordinate and control the outbound transportation of an organization's finished goods. This includes transportation scheduling and, when relevant, management of third-party transportation suppliers.

The primary modes of transportation used to get goods to customers include: road, rail, waterways, air, and pipeline. In the next chapter, we'll explore each of these modes of transportation in greater depth as well as current transportation industry terminology, practices, and regulations.

The Logistics Chain

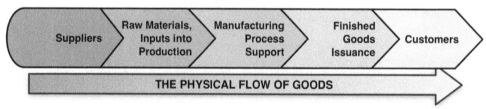

The Reverse Logistics Chain

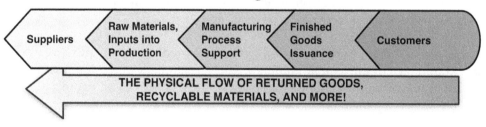

Figure 5.4 - The Direction of the Flow of Goods in the Logistics and Reverse Logistics Chains

After the goods have been delivered from the supplier to the buyer, there is often a corresponding backwards flow of related goods from the buyer to the supplier, which involves a physical distribution management function called ***reverse logistics***. According to the online *Glossary of Terms of the Council of Supply Chain Management Professionals*, reverse logistics is: "a specialized segment of logistics focusing on the movement and management of products and resources after the sale and after delivery to the customer, which includes product returns for repair and/or credit." Goods flow along the supply chain in a forward direction from the raw materials extractor through the manufacturer to the retailer and end user. Reverse logistics concentrates on how goods flow backwards along the chain from the end user.

Reverse logistics occurs if there is product and packaging returns. It is becoming increasingly common with the "greening" of logistics as the business environment attempts to become more environmentally responsible by reusing products and packaging. According to packaging-gateway.com, companies around the world spend $424 million on packaging every year, with plastic making a whopping 34% of our global packaging material. Companies are now looking for ways to get non-recyclable packaging back from customers for reuse. In Chapter 12, we'll look at some virtuous things that the "Sin City" of Las Vegas is doing in the world of reverse logistics!

CHAPTER 5 REVIEW QUESTIONS

1. How are materials management and physical distribution management similar? How do they differ?

2. What role does an organization's Marketing Department play in its physical distribution management?

3. What can an organization do to reduce its order cycle time?

4. In what discipline is the term distribution channel primarily used? What role does information technology play in managing and servicing distribution channels?

5. Under normal supply chain circumstances, is it preferable to locate a distribution center in the middle of a large, heavily populated city as close to the downtown as possible or just outside a medium-sized city where there is easy access to multiple transportation industries? Why do you think so?

6. In what types of situations and for what types of organizations would the physical distribution management practice of cross-docking be most useful?

7. If you needed a single order picked quickly, which order picking technique would you use? Why?

8. After an order is picked, what happens just before it is packed?

9. Would inventory visibility be more important for a small warehouse operation or global distribution of a product line? How might inventory visibility be achieved?

10. Do you think reverse logistics will have a more or less significant role in supply chain management in the future? Why?

CHAPTER 5 CASE STUDY

Physical Distribution & Walmart's Competitive Advantage

If you live anywhere in the United States, you have most likely been to a Walmart store. These enormous stores sell everything from clothing to electronics to furniture to groceries, all with Walmart's promise of "Everyday Low Prices." Since 1962, this Arkansas-based discount store has grown to a gargantuan worldwide retail chain with almost 2 million employees and annual sales of over $300 billion. Walmart's popularity and explosive growth has been attributed to its ability to offer a wide range of goods at prices consistently lower than its competitors. The company's undying ability to offer low prices lies in its ability to control the structure and costs of its physical distribution practices. Ah, the power of logistics management!

The roots of this retail giant lie in rural America. In its nascency, Walmart stores were located in small country towns not served by reliable distributors. To get reliable and affordable shipments of discount goods, the company decided to purchase a fleet of trucks and establish its own distribution network. Over the years, Walmart's fleet of trucks has grown to over 3000 across the U.S. Complete control of its trucking network allows the company to have complete control over its distribution schedule. Peak seasonal deliveries, nighttime deliveries, and expedited shipments when rush orders are needed are all easily accommodated, allowing the company to replenish its shelves four times faster than comparable discount chains. For example, if your local Walmart suddenly ran out of an unexpected must-have Christmas toy, you are very likely to find it restocked on Walmart shelves in a quick day or two.

In addition to owning a significantly sized fleet of trucks, Walmart also owns and operates an extensive network of more than 120 distribution centers. Each distribution center is approximately one million square feet and operated by highly advanced information technology systems, RFID and bar coding systems, and automated materials handling equipment. (You are also likely to find people and hand trucks there, too!) Every store owned by Walmart is serviced by at least one distribution center (DC) and each DC can accommodate up to 150 retail stores surrounding it. Some of the distribution centers are specialized, with approximately forty handling only grocery items, seven handing clothing, and more than ten handling specialty items. More than 80% of the goods sold on Walmart's shelves have passed through one of its distribution centers, while only 50% of goods at competing stores are likely to have passed through one.

Another important component of Walmart's physical distribution system is the practice of cross docking, which speeds goods rapidly through the supply chain and decreases the need to store goods in its distribution centers. Suppliers' trucks simply pull up to a Walmart distribution center and goods are immediately pulled from these trucks and placed onto a series of Walmart trucks bound for different retail stores. The amount placed on each Walmart truck is exactly the amount of goods that store needs. This practice allows for goods to be delivered quickly without having to be inventoried and stored. With the extensive use of cross docking and distribution centers, Walmart stores are able to receive goods and get them on the shelves in under 48 hours from the time goods are requested.

Another standard physical distribution practice of Walmart is realtime connectivity between its distribution centers and the Electronic Point of Sale (EPOS) system in each of its retail stores. When a customer buys an item, it is scanned at the cash register into the store's EPOS system. This information is then sent directly to the distribution center service the store so that it knows to send one more of the item that has just been sold. This IT connection between the store and its distribution center allows for immediate order placement and fulfillment.

Thanks to the control over its physical distribution network and its adherence to practices such as cross docking and full EPOS connectivity, Walmart is able to reap substantial cost benefits. The company's total distribution cost is only 1.3% of its sales, while most discount chains and retail stores pay 3.5 to 5% of their sales. A difference of 2 or 3% may not sound like much, but for a company with annual sales of more than $300 billion, a 2% savings in distribution costs would equal a whopping $6 billion. This enormous savings allows the company to continue to reign supreme in its promise of "Everyday Low Prices."

References

Case Study, Inc. (2008) *Walmart's Supply Chain Management Practices.* Retrieved from http://www.casestudyinc.com/case-study-walmart-supply-chain.

CFN Services (2011) *Bringing Walmart Scale Economics to Network Operators.* Retrieved from http://www.cfnservices.com.

Case Study Questions

1. How does Walmart use physical distribution management to its benefit?

2. What part does information technology play in the Walmart order cycle?

3. How does Walmart achieve competitive advantage with its use of distribution centers?

4. In terms of physical distribution management, what should Walmart do to maintain its competitive advantage?

Chapter 6

Outbound Logistics: Transportation

At the beginning of Chapter 4 when we introduced the concept of purchasing, we asked you to take a look around and notice all the items that had, at one time or another, been purchased by someone. Now take a look around again and make a note of all the items in your surroundings that have been purchased by someone at some time. Now consider each of these items on your "purchased" list. Where were all of them made? If you're not sure, pick the items up, turn them over, and look for a "Made in" label. Were they all made in your hometown? Better still, were any of them even made within 500 miles of where you are standing or sitting right now?

Chances are, very few or perhaps none of the purchased items in your surroundings were made within 500 miles of you and most were probably made in another country. But how did these items find their way to your surroundings? Did they suddenly sprout up from the ground one day or did Scottie beam them down from the Starship Enterprise overhead? Unless you have a far more exciting life than most of us (or have watched a few too many episodes of Star Trek), neither of these options is possible, so the items must have arrived at your location by way of transportation.

INTRODUCING TRANSPORTATION

The focus of logistics and supply chain management is the physical flow of goods. What provides, supports, and propels this flow? Transportation! The essential activity of transportation forms the backbone of logistics and supply chain management. Without it, these disciplines would not exist.

Transportation is the act of using a vehicle to move goods or people from one place to another. Within the realm of logistics and supply chain management, transportation is the movement of goods, not people, to a desired location. In Chapter 5, we learned that transportation of goods forms the critical bridge between areas of abundance, such as manufacturing or warehousing facilities where the goods are located, and areas of scarcity, such as the immediate customers' locations where the goods are desired.

In our map of logistics management processes, transportation is one of the three categories of outbound logistics activities within the area of physical distribution management. One of the roles of a company's Physical Distribution Manager is to coordinate and control the outbound transportation of an organization's finished goods.

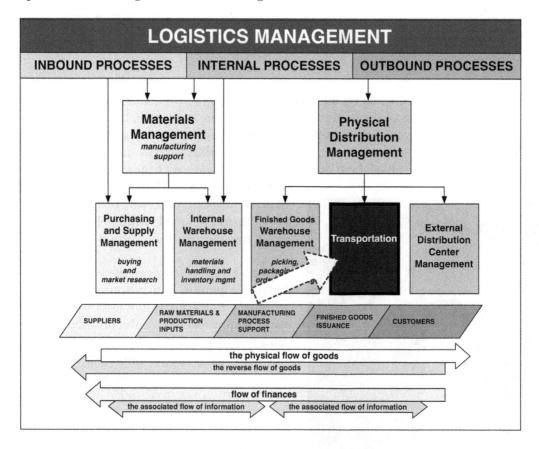

Figure 6.1 - Transportation within Logistics Management

Transportation is critical not only to physical distribution, logistics, and supply chain management, but also to the entire global economy. As most of the world has moved away from localized, hunter-gatherer and farming economies during the past few thousand years, transportation has become an increasingly essential element to human comfort and survival. It plays an essential role in providing us with the food we eat, the clothes on our backs, the books we read, the medicine we take, and the homes we live in. As a result, transportation plays a significant role in the economy of developed markets around the world. For example, according to the U.S. Department of Transportation Bureau of Transportation Statistics, contributions of the transportation industry to the U.S. gross domestic product has remained at or near 3% from 1998 to 2009 and overall transportation-related expenditures formed 10% of the U.S. gross domestic product for the year 2012.

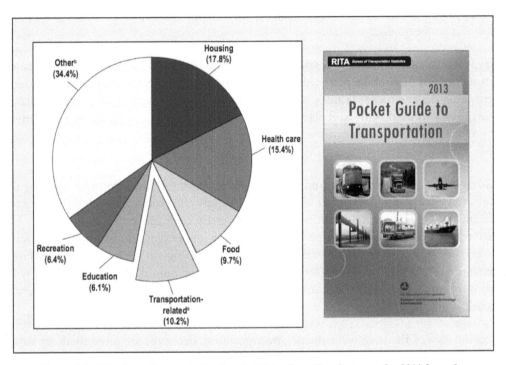

Figure 6.2 - U.S. Gross Domestic Product by Major Spending Category for 2011 from the U.S. Department of Transportation *2013 Pocket Guide to Transportation*

Transportation also allows countries to engage in global trade and build strong relationships with other countries around the world. As we will explore toward the end of this chapter, changes in transportation legislation and regulation in the 1970s and 1980s has lead to a dramatic growth in global trade over the past thirty years. For example, the *U.S. Census Commodity Flow Survey* reported that, from 1993 to 2002, the value of the goods traded with the United States increased by a whopping 45%!

Now that we have looked at the global importance of transportation, let's take a deeper look at the discipline of transportation. Back in Chapter 2, we introduced the concept of utility. Remember that, along with minimizing cost and maximizing customer service, logistics and supply chain management create value for the members of a supply chain. This value is also called ***utility***, a term from the field of economics that refers to the satisfaction customers experience when they consume an organization's goods or services. The four types of utility are: form, time, place, and possession.

Form utility, the value added to goods as their form changes, such as from raw materials to finished products, is typically added by an organization's manufacturing department. ***Possession utility***, the value added to goods when a desire for them has been created in the minds of the consumers, is typically added by an organization's Marketing Department. Place and time utility, however, fall within the realm of transportation.

Place utility is the value added to goods when they are at the right place within the supply chain, exactly where an organization's internal and external customer want them. Place utility is created by effective transportation and physical distribution management, which helps to get goods to customers' desired locations and to use geographically distant or widely dispersed suppliers, whose products may be cheaper or of a better quality.

Time utility is the value added to goods when they are available exactly when both internal and external customers want them. Like place utility, time utility is created by effective transportation and physical distribution management. Transportation decisions and optimization allow an organization's logistics department to provide time and place value to its customers. Throughout the remainder of this chapter, we will explore various transportation decisions and optimization methods that provide time and place value.

The relationship between transportation and supply chain cost extends far beyond establishing the cost of transporting goods and incorporating it into total supply chain cost. Transportation decisions play a significant strategic role in determining total supply chain costs and levels of service. In Chapter 2, we covered the tradeoff principle in which the advantages and disadvantages of logistics decisions are considered and evaluated based on the degree of change in the following three criteria: (1) cost, (2) resource use, and (3) customer service. The advantages and disadvantages offered within each of these three areas are weighed against one another to see if the decision under consideration would be an advantageous one.

Expanding on the idea of the tradeoff principle, transportation decisions are often made by striking a balance between the advantages and disadvantages offered by the following six criteria:

1. **Cost.** Obviously, transportation costs increase as delivery distances increase, making cost a central factor in determining the geographic limits within which a product can be sold cost-effectively.

2. **Speed.** For many products or situations, a speedy delivery time may be more important than delivery cost. For example, speedy delivery is essential for perishable goods (such as Maine lobster and Alaska King crab, both of which must be flown to their hungry customers) and goods immediately essential to a large manufacturing operation (such as a spare part needed to repair an ice cream producer's freezer, which will be flown in as quickly as possible before too much product melts).

3. **Safety & Security.** An organization's goods are often its most substantial financial assets. To protect the value of these assets, the organization must ensure that the transportation system handling its goods keeps them safe from damage and secure from theft at all times. Safety and

security are especially important criteria for transportation decisions involving high-cost or hazardous goods.

4. **Convenience.** For a transportation plan or system to be the successful backbone of any logistics or supply chain, it must be convenient to all members of the chain. Transportation decisions made must consider how easy it is for customers, retailers, wholesalers, distribution centers, warehouses, and manufacturers to interface with those transporting goods. Consider a furniture retail store in Hawaii that needs to ship goods from Los Angeles to Honolulu. If the proposed transportation agent, which is slightly cheaper than other transport agents, does not offer en route communication about the approximate time of shipment delivery, the furniture store would be less likely to consider selecting it because it does not offer the convenience of informing their customers of approximate delivery time.

5. **Reliability.** Even when costs are low, deliveries are fast and convenient, and goods are kept safe and secure, a transportation system or agent is no good to an organization when it is not reliable. If transportation can't consistently and reliably get goods where they need to be when they need to be, an organization loses the time and place utility that reliable transportation provides.

6. **Flexibility.** For organizations that need to transport a wide range of goods of different sizes, weights, and handling needs, a flexible transportation system is essential. For example, the transportation system of warehouse-style retailers carrying goods from regional distribution centers to individual stores would need to be flexible enough to handle a wide range of goods within one shipment, from dish detergent to televisions to king-size mattresses.

Now that we have discussed the six criteria that are weighed against each other when transportation decision are being made, let's address two important transportation decisions, typically asked and answered in conjunction with one another: *Who will handle the transportation?* and *What mode or modes of transportation will be used?*

By definition, *transportation* is the movement of goods by vehicle. A *vehicle* is a propelled means of conveyance that moves the goods from one point to another. When we use the term vehicle, we generally think of land and air travel. The term *vessel* is typically used to describe a vehicle for water transport. Vehicle move goods from one stopping point in the logistics chain to another. These starting and stopping points, called *terminals*, are locations where goods can be unloaded and reloaded onto different vehicles using different modes of transportation, such as sea to air. Terminals are also locations for vehicle maintenance, routing, and dispatch; weighing shipments; and conducting administrative work.

When an organization has goods to be moved from one location or one terminal to another, it must first decide who will physically move these goods: (1) the organization itself or (2) a *carrier*, i.e., a second company that transports goods. An organization typically uses a carrier when it must move goods a great distance and/or using specialized transport modes, such as by rail or ocean cargo ships (because most companies don't own their own rail lines or cargo ships).

A single carrier may use any combination of one or more of the five modes of transportation (road, rail, water, air, and pipeline). Carriers also may own or lease the vehicles and vessels they use. Furthermore, terminals are typically privately owned or leased by carriers. Carriers, along with government entities and other private parties, may also own the ways in transportation. ***Ways*** are the paths over which transportation carriers operate. In addition to railways tracks, roads, and seaways, ways also include any physical facilities needed to make the ways passable.

Carriers You May Just Know...

A few examples of commonly used carriers include:

❖ **CSX Transportation**, which operates the largest railroad in the eastern United States

❖ **Horizon Lines, Inc.**, a leading domestic marine container shipper for shipments within the United States and its territories

❖ **Lynden Air Cargo**, which provides regularly scheduled air cargo transportation between Anchorage and various Alaskan cities that can be reach be air only

❖ **Celadon**, a leading truckload carrier company operating within and between NAFTA countries

While most carriers specialize in providing cost-effective transportation of large shipments, some focus on the transportation of smaller shipments. This special category of carriers is known as small-package carriers, and includes widely known companies such as FedEx, UPS, and DHL.

Two other types of transportation service providers that work closely with carriers are consolidators and freight forwarders. Although it does not move goods itself, a consolidator is a type of indirect carrier that collects and combines small, separate shipments into larger ones to achieve lower transportation rates. For most carriers, the cost of delivering a container of goods is just about the same no matter how empty or full the container is. Therefore, it is less than ideal to have a situation of less-than-truckload (LTL) shipments. A consolidator works to combine small shipments to create full container-load or truckload shipments, thus achieving a significant cost savings for the organizations shipping smaller quantities of goods. A freight forwarder is a type of consolidator that specializes in combining smaller shipments for subsequent road or rail transportation.

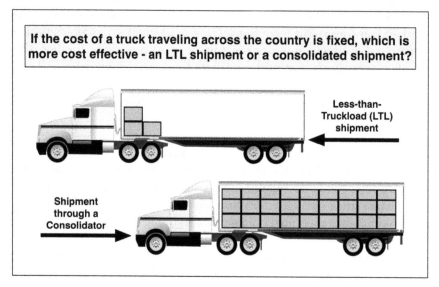

Figure 6.3 - Less-Than-Truckload Versus Consolidation

Transportation involves more than an organization or a carrier simply picking up and moving goods from one location to another. Transportation includes the complex world of **transportation management**, i.e., planning, directing, and controlling how goods are moved and handled throughout the transportation process.

Most raw materials and consumer goods today are not only moved across countries, but also across oceans. To navigate the murky and complex waters of transportation management, companies often turn to **third party logistics service providers**, also known as **3PLPs** or 3PLs, to provide some or all of the transportation and transportation management services needed. 3PLPs typically bundle a range of these services under one cost structure. Some of the transportation management activities covered by a 3PLP might include:

- *planning shipments and selecting transport carriers;*

- *keeping track of shipments in transit;*

- *determining freight costs prior to shipping;*

- *checking and paying carriers' freight bills;*

- *filing claims with carriers for damaged goods;*

- *transportation budget planning and management;*

- *transportation administration and human resource management;*

- *monitoring and maintaining service quality;*

- *conducting carrier rate negotiations;*

- *keeping up with local, state, federal, and international transport regulations;*

- *planning and handling transport information systems; and*

- *conducting transport systems analysis.*

MODES OF TRANSPORTATION

When a company is deciding who will transport its goods, it must also decide the mode by which its goods will be moved. In the world of logistics and physical distribution management, a **mode of transportation** is the physical means across or through which the goods are carried. The five modes of transportation are: (1) road, (2) rail, (3) water, (4) air, and (5) pipeline. In this section of the chapter, we will explore each of these modes of transportation in greater depth.

Road Transportation

At the risk of stating the extremely obvious, a **road** is a surfaced route used by vehicles for moving goods or people. Within most countries around the world, road is, by far, the most commonly used mode of transportation. For example, according to the 2007 *U.S. Census Commodity Flow Survey*, road is the primary mode of transportation for goods transported within the United States. A total of 71% of goods by value and 70% of goods by weight are transported by road across the U.S.

A variety of motor carriers use road as their mode of transport, including companies using vans and a variety of truck configurations. A company whose goods are transported can either privately own or rent the trucks it uses. Rented (or for-hire) trucks tend to carry more valuable goods. The 2007 U.S. Census reported that 42% of the goods (by value) were moved by for-hire trucks and 30% were moved by privately owned trucks. Conversely, privately owned trucks tend to carry more of the heavy goods. The 2007 U.S. Census reported that 38% of the total tonnage of goods was moved by privately owned trucks and 33% was moved by for-hire trucks.

The primary advantage offered by road as a mode of transportation is that, within most countries, more locations are accessible by road than any other mode of transportation. For example, in the United States, the National Highway System measures approximately 160,000 miles! On road networks, vehicles can also operate 24 hours a day, 7 days a week.

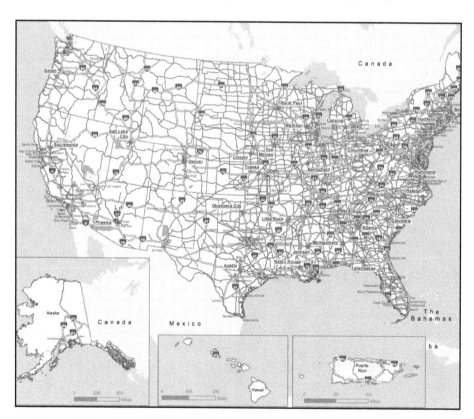

Figure 6.4 - 2012 Map of the National Highway System from the U.S. Department of Transportation Federal Highway Administration (www.fwha.dot.gov)

Compared to other modes of transportation, road offers more cost-effective movement for smaller deliveries and shorter distances, such as those up to 500 to 800 miles. It is also highly flexible and allows for last minute changes and adjustments. For example, if there are production delays at a factory, it is far easier to change a delivery schedule when a container of goods are being moved by road than when they are being moved by a prescheduled barge.

Although flexible and highly accessible, road also presents disadvantages as a mode of transportation. Traffic jams, congestion, and adverse weather can all affect road delivery times. Labor costs are also higher because the number of drivers or operators required per amount carried is much higher than for other modes of transportation. For example, one truck driver can transport one or two container loads of goods while a crew of five people can transport over 1000 forty-foot containers by way of cargo ship.

Weight also plays a factor in road transport. The per ton-mile cost of road transport is higher than those of rail or water. Also, size and weight limitations on national road networks limit carrying very heavy items and large pieces of machinery.

Rail Transportation

The transportation mode of *rail* is commonly used to transport large, heavy, and bulky items and large quantities for long distances. Although rail offers the advantage of transporting large and heavy goods that can't be transported by road, it is not used as frequently. According to the 2007 *U.S. Census Commodity Flow Survey*, which is conducted every seven years, rail is used to transport 4% of the total value of all U.S. goods and 15% of all goods by weight.

More than 90% of all U.S. freight railroads are privately owned and operated. Most of the track is also owned by the rail companies. These privately owned freight railroads can be broken down into four classification: (1) Class I railroads; (2) regional railroads; (3) local line-haul carriers; and (4) switching and terminal carriers.

Class I railroads are those that have an operating revenue of at least $319.3 million. Although small in number, Class I railroads carry most of the goods being moved by rail. The seven Class I railroads currently operating in the U.S. make up just more than 1% of the 562 freight railroads, but account for 68% of industry mileage, 89% of industry employees, and 93% of industry freight revenue. *Regional railroads* have at least 350 route-miles or an operating revenue between $40 and $319.3 million. There are currently thirty in the U.S. In addition, regional railroads typically have between 75 to 500 employees and operate 400 to 650 miles of track across two to four state.

Local line-haul carriers cover less than 350 miles and have an annual operating budget of less than $40 million. There are currently 320 local line-haul carrier in the U.S. and most operate within one state and have less than 75 miles of track. While there are no revenue or size restrictions to define them, *switching and terminal (S&T) carriers* are those that provide switching and/or terminal services instead of point-to-point services. S&T carriers complete pickup and delivery services for other railroad carriers and sometimes funnel traffic between railroads. There are currently 203 in the U.S.

The primary advantage of rail is that rail cars can accommodate very large, heavy items and it is a less expensive mode of transportation for larger volumes over longer distances than road. Rail also offers greater reliability than many other transportation modes because it is less likely to experience traffic delays or adverse weather. Furthermore, most maritime cargo ports are connected to rail networks, making rail a vital element of global supply chains.

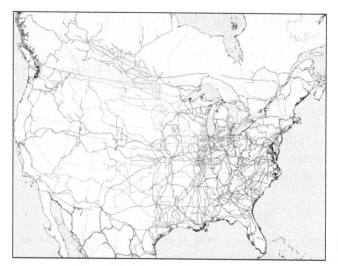

Figure 6.5 - Map of the Class I U.S. Railway System (Wikimedia Commons)

The primary disadvantages of rail are its geographic and time limitations. Rail networks are in limited, fixed locations. Also, rail carriers typically operate only at specific times, making them less flexible than motor carriers. It is also not a suitable mode of transportation for fragile goods nor is it cost effective for small quantities moving short distances. Finally, there are sometimes very long transit times due to the labor-intensive nature of boxcar consolidation.

Water Transportation

Water is a mode of transportation used to transport large quantities of nonperishable and bulk goods both domestically and internationally. In domestic trade, goods travel by water within and along the United States through *inland and intracoastal waterways*. In international trade, the majority of goods travel by ocean and enter and leave through *container ports*.

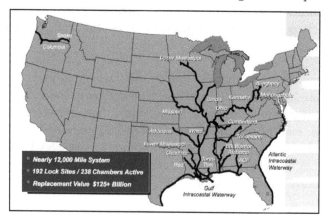

Figure 6.6 - Map of U.S. Inland and Intracoastal Waterways, from U.S. Army Corps of Engineers, *Inland Waterway Navigation Value to the Nation*, www.mvr.usace.army.mil.

In the United States, there are approximately 25,000 miles of inland, intracoastal, and coastal waterways. Twelve thousand of these miles are part of a commercially active waterway system maintained by the U.S. Army Corps of Engineers. This ***inland and intracoastal waterway system*** serves 38 states and carries one-sixth of the U.S. intercity cargo by volume. According to the 2007 *U.S. Census Commodity Flow Survey*, water is the domestic mode of transportation used for 1% of all goods by value and 3% of all goods by weight.

A ***container port*** is a facility that receives and docks cargo ships. It uses specialized equipment, including a variety of cranes, to transfer containerized goods to and from the ships. There are currently 118 coastal ports in the United States, most of which are equipped to handle containers in some form. Container ports are growing rapidly around the world as container ships become larger and faster. According to the 2005 *Containership Market Indicators* from the U.S. Maritime Administration, container imports into the U.S. increased by 58% from 1999 to 2004 and container exports increased by 22%.

Figure 6.7 - Container Port and Container Ship

To move goods by water, there are a variety of specialized vessels according to the type and amount of goods and the nature of the waterway. Some of the most common categories of vessels used to transport goods are:

- ***container ships***, which carry containerized goods;

- ***bulk carriers***, which carry bulk cargo such as grain or ore;

- ***tankers***, which carry bulk fluids, such as crude oil and chemicals;

- ***roll-on/roll-off ships***, which carry cargo on wheels, such as trucks, trailers, and railway carriages; and

- ***barges***, which are flat-bottomed and used to transport heavy goods along rivers and canals.

One of the primary advantages of using water transport is that massive quantities of goods and bulky items can be carried at one time. It is also reliable and does not suffer the traffic-related delays of road transportation. Water can also be less costly because it is far less expensive than air for international trade and there are no costs for using ocean waterways.

Water is, however, perhaps the slowest mode of transportation, making it unrealistic for shipping perishable or time-sensitive goods. These long transit times also increase the insurance costs of goods. Scheduling can also be limited with water transport. Ships sail on fixed schedules, limiting delivery scheduling flexibility, and fog or severe weather can easily cause sailing cancellations.

Air Transportation

Air is the mode of transportation more commonly used for perishable and time-sensitive goods. According to the 2007 *U.S. Census Commodity Flow Survey*, air is used to transport 2% of the total value of all goods within the U.S. and less than 0.04% of goods by weight.

In the air cargo industry, there are both all-cargo airlines (such as FedEx and UPS) and all-cargo subsidiaries of passenger airlines (such as British Airways World Cargo and Alaska Airlines Cargo). According to the World Air Transport Statistics, 57th Edition, of the International Air Transport Association (IATA), the top five international air cargo carriers (in freight ton-kilometers carried) in 2012 were: Federal Express, United Parcel Service Airlines, Emirates, Cathay Pacific Airways, and Korean Air Lines.

The primary advantage of air is that it is the fastest mode of transportation available, allowing it to dramatically reduce delivery times. Because of the shorter delivery time, it is also suitable for perishable goods, reduces the risk of damage, and requires less packaging of goods. Also, as long as airports are available, air transport can be used to move goods to anywhere in the world.

With air, all of these great advantages come at a price, however. Air transport is very costly, especially compared to other modes of transport. Like water, air also allows for less scheduling flexibility. Flights are generally at fixed times and adverse weather can delay flights and cause transportation delays. Furthermore, airplanes are strictly limited in the weights and item dimensions they can carry.

Pipeline Transportation

Pipeline is the mode of transportation used to carrying goods from point to point through a steel or plastic pipe. While oil and natural gas are the goods most commonly transported by pipeline,

Figure 6.8 - The Trans-Alaska Pipeline System, a crude-oil pipeline system that traverses Alaska from the Prudhoe Bay oil field in the north to the port of Valdez in the south

any form of liquid, such as water or sewage, can be carried by pipeline. Although expensive to construct, pipelines yield extremely low transportation cost. According to the 2007 *U.S. Census Commodity Flow Survey*, pipeline systems are used to transport 3% of the total value of all U.S. goods and 5% of all U.S. goods by weight.

When goods are transported, they are not restricted to a single mode of transportation. ***Intermodal transportation*** occurs when different modes of transportation are used to carry goods in the same through shipment. A ***through shipment*** is the entire transportation flow of goods from their point of origin to point of consumption. Intermodal transportation is especially common in global trade. For example, as container ships arrive into U.S. ports, their containers are automatically transferred to rail or motor carriers. According to the 2007 *U.S. Census Commodity Flow Survey*, multiple modes of transport are used to transport 16% of the total value of all U.S. goods.

As companies look to the supply chain as a means of cutting operating costs, competition is heating up between transportation carriers. Two primary forms of this competition are:

- ***Intramodal competition***, in which carriers of the same mode of transportation compete, such as one container ship line trying to come in at a lower cost than another container ship line following the same route; and

- ***Intermodal competition***, in which carriers of different modes of transportation compete, such as a trucking company trying to cut costs to meet those of a railway following the same route.

THE LEGAL SIDE OF TRANSPORTATION

The history of transportation in the United States is essentially one of *regulation* and *deregulation*. ***Regulation*** occurs when human or societal behavior is controlled by rules or restrictions. ***Deregulation*** occurs when government rules or regulations that constrain the market forces are simplified or removed entirely.

Toward the end of the nineteenth century, a small handful railroads became very powerful in the United States. Unchecked competition abounded, bankrupting some railroads while making monopolies of others. In 1887, the federal government enacted the Interstate Commerce Act to tackle the tough job of regulating American railroads. In the early 1900s, Congress gave a broad range of powers to the Interstate Commerce Commission (ICC), which included control of entry and exit into the industry, setting shipping rates, allocating routes, and overseeing services. While the ICC was originally established to control the railroad industry, Congress began to expand its powers in the 1930s to cover the emerging motor and air carrier industries. (The ICC was later replaced when the Surface Transportation Board (STB) was created with the Termination Act of 1995.) Regulation provided a valuable stabilizing force to transportation industries for many years, but its resulting lack of competition led to inefficiencies, higher prices, and railroad bankruptcies by the 1970s. The federal government then began to reverse it regulatory policies and deregulate the transportation industry.

Not to leave American transportation completely deregulated, on October 15, 1966, Congress established the Department of Transportation (DOT) to "serve the United States by ensuring a fast, safe, efficient, accessible and convenient transportation system that meets our vital national interests and enhances the quality of life of the American people, today and into the future." This cabinet-level department currently has eleven individual Operating Administrations: the Federal Aviation Administration, the Federal Highway Administration, the Federal Motor Carrier Safety Administration, the Federal Railroad Administration, the National Highway Traffic Safety Administration, the Federal Transit Administration, the Maritime Administration, the Saint Lawrence Seaway Development Corporation, the Research and Innovative Technologies Administration, the Pipeline and Hazardous Materials Safety Administration, and the Surface Transportation Board. More information about the Department of Transport can be found on its website at www.dot.gov.

CHAPTER 6 REVIEW QUESTIONS

1. What forms the bridge between areas of abundance and areas of scarcity for the movement of goods? What are the areas of abundance and areas of scarcity?

2. What is the difference between a vehicle and a vessel? Please provide two examples of each.

3. In which transportation situation might a consolidator be necessary?

4. What advantages does road offer as a mode of transportation over rail?

5. What advantages does air offer as a mode of transportation over water?

6. In each of the following situations, please select which of the five modes of transportation would be most the advantageous. Explain your answer.

    a. sending 350 40' containers from Shanghai, China to Los Angeles, California

    b. sending a live heart from Anchorage, Alaska to a patient waiting in Philadelphia, Pennsylvania

    c. transporting oil from a field in the Caspian Sea to a refinery in Azerbaijan

    d. sending large shipyard cranes from the manufacturer in Maine to the Port of Vancouver, Canada

    e. transporting apples from a grove in upstate Washington to a grocery store distribution center in rural Idaho

7. Please provide three examples of intermodal transportation.

8. What is the difference between intramodal and intermodal competition in transportation? Which type of competition do you think is more prevalent?

CHAPTER 6 CASE STUDY

Outbound Logistics at HarperCollins

For many years, the nation's large publishing houses have either printed their books themselves and/or outsourced printing to a variety of third party printers. The publishers would then amass the books in their warehouses across the United States and distribute them to retail booksellers using their own transportation network or that of a variety of third party service providers. This style of physical distribution has been the style of choice for decades. With the advent of electronic publishing, print publishers have begun to realize that they must reconsider the status quo of physical distribution. They must look to supply chain management to cut costs and increase customer service or risk suffering the fate of print-based newspapers. In May 2011, one of the world's large publishing houses decided to make a drastic change that may prove to be a game changer for the publishing industry.

For the past twenty years, RR Donnelley has been a printer for many of publishing giant HarperCollins' books. In 2011, HarperCollins announce that RR Donnelley would now handle all printing, fulfillment, and shipping services for their entire voluminous catalog of book titles, which marked the first agreement of its kind for a major publishing house. HarperCollins anticipates that this agreement will reduce freight costs, create a more efficient distribution system, and get books to market much quicker. While their books used to be printed and sent to multiple warehouse locations across the country before being distributed, HarperCollins is now closing its warehouses and leaving the fate of its printing and distribution entirely in the hands of RR Donnelley.

A large part of what will make this agreement both efficient and cost effective is that RR Donnelley will have a digital printing agreement for all the titles that HarperCollins sells. This means that RR Donnelley will form a global Print on Demand (POD) service in which books can be printed in a matter of minutes anywhere in the world where HarperCollins hold publishing rights to the title to be printed. This can only be possible with RR Donnelley's sophisticated digital infrastructure, complete with high speed digital printing presses and automated binding equipment in multiple locations around the world.

HarperCollins believes that co-locating its printing, fulfillment, and transportation needs all within RR Donnelley will result in substantial savings for trade bestsellers and other fast moving titles. The use of POD service will also reap significant benefits in overseas English language markets, such as Australia and the U.K. With digital printing, these overseas customers can select any title from the HarperCollins catalog and have it printed and bound immediately at a local RR Donnelley facility, thus avoiding the long lead times and expensive freight costs of overseas shipping.

References

Martinez, S. (2011, May 13) Zondervan will move headquarters when it closes warehouse in 2012. *The Grand Rapids Press*. Retrieved from http://www.mlive.com/business/west-michigan/index.ssf/2011/05/zondervan_will_move_headquarte.html.

RR Donnelley (2011, May 12) HarperCollins and RR Donnelley announce intent to enter into strategic printing and supply chain management agreement. *Globe Newswire*. Retrieved from http://www.globenewswire.com/newsroom/news.html?d=221847.

Case Study Questions

1. In which utilities has HarperCollins added value through its partnership with RR Donnelley?

2. In its transportation decision to hand over all order fulfillment and distribution to RR Donnelley, how might HarperCollins have used the trade off principle?

3. Why might HarperCollins have decided to allow RR Donnelley to handle all of its activities worldwide rather that rely on a series of local third party service providers in each country?

Chapter 7

Information Technology Systems

One of the earliest global supply chains was the Silk Road, linking the farthest western reaches of Europe to the farthest eastern reaches of Asia. The transcontinental Silk Road encompassed a more-than 5000-mile stretch of trade routes from China's Han Dynasty to Europe's Roman Empire. When an emperor in Rome wanted to place an order for specific colors of fine silks from Luoyang, his order could travel to silk merchants only as fast as human or horse could carry it. The emperor would also have little to no idea of where his silks were en route and when they might arrive.

Figure 7.1 - The Silk Road, a Global Supply Chains Predating Information Technology and IT Systems

Had our emperor lived in today's age of advanced information technology systems, he would be able to transmit his order to China in the blink of an eye, such as a Walmart in Arkansas does today when it orders flip flop sandals from Beijing manufacturers. With today's technology, the emperor would also have been able to know exactly where his order was as it traversed vast geographic distances on its way to Rome. He would also know when the order would be delivered and would be alerted to transportation delays, such as heavy rains or highway robberies by bandits in the Central Asian steppes.

Information technology and information systems have become an integral and critical part of logistics, woven deeply and entirely into and throughout every supply chain. Although it would take many tomes to cover the broad spectrum of information technology and information systems used in global and local supply chain, this chapter provides a basic introduction to information technology systems and the role they play in logistics and supply chain management.

WHAT IS INFORMATION?

Before exploring information systems and technology in the world of logistics, we'll first take a moment to discuss what we mean by *information* and the role it plays in decision-making. Let's begin where it all starts, with *data*.

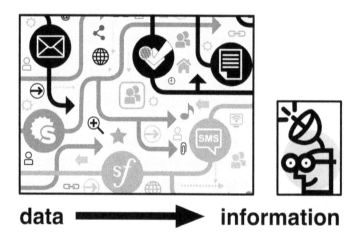

data ➡ information

Figure 7.2 - The Difference Between Data and Information

The terms data and information are often used interchangeably, but they are quite different. **Data** are facts gathered by research or observation and then represented by groupings of nonrandom symbols, such as letters, words, numbers, values, and other symbols. For example, an inventory checker in a hardware store counting the number of powered tools counts that there are eight Nervous Neil's No-Nonsense Nail Guns in stock. The data regarding the quantity of nail guns observed is eight.

The inventory checker then needs to enter this data (eight Nervous Neil's Nail Guns) into a hand-held computer or onto a piece of paper on a clipboard so that others may subsequently receive the message that there are currently eight nail guns in stock. By recording and transmitting this data that others receive, the inventory checker is transforming data into information. *Information*, therefore, is data that has been received and understood by the recipient of a message. In our example, the recipient may be the logistics manager or even the computerized inventory control system.

Information is a critical component of decision-making. Without information, there is no basis upon which to make productive decisions. Imagine selecting a new car to buy without basic information such as gas mileage, safety ratings, and purchase price! In the world of logistics management, information is used to make a wide range of decisions on an ongoing basis. At each phase of the supply chain, both within and between the chain's members and their corresponding departments, many important decisions must be made. Clear, accurate, and timely information is critical to this process. Ultimately, decisions can only be as good as the information used to make them.

To ensure that information is clear, accurate, and timely, businesses have turned to the myriad of tools and techniques offered by information technology. Before the days of computers, the speed, accuracy, and volume of information transmitted were a fraction of what they are today. The speed, accuracy, and volume of information transmissions were dependent on man's limitations, such as how quickly someone could run or ride a horse to hand deliver information, how neatly and thoroughly someone could write the information, and how much information someone could write onto a parchment or sheet of paper so that it could still be read.

In the early days of man, information was conveyed by word of mouth, from one person to the next. Then, in approximately 3000 B.C.E., one of the earliest forms of written communication, cuneiform, was developed in Mesopotamia. Written communication helped to convey information more accurately and consistently. The volume of information able to be transmitted through the written word increased over time, beginning with scrolls in ancient Egypt and Greece, manuscript and block print books hundreds of years later, and the invention of Johannes Gutenberg's moveable type in the 1450s. While books allowed large volumes of information to be transmitted accurately, it was a slow process, dependent on how quickly books could be printed and then distributed by man or horse.

The speed of information transmission took a dramatic leap in the mid-1800s, however, with Samuel Morse's development of the telegraph transmitter and receiver. With the telegraph, information was transmitted instantaneously from one person to another by cable, and later,

Figure 7.3 - Guglielmo Marconi and Signal Hill in Saint Johns, Newfoundland, where his first transatlantic wireless transmission was received in 1901

wirelessly. Instantaneous communication took a further leap forward with Alexander Graham Bell's telephone in 1877, which allowed instantaneous verbal communication between two people separated by great distances.

Although the telephone and telegraph increased the speed of information transmission, they did not provide the accuracy and higher volumes of information transmission provided by books and other written communication forms. Telephones and telegraphs were limited by how quickly someone could speak or produce taps, how well the recipient could hear and interpret the information, and how much information could be conveyed within a limited timeframe.

The development of the computer and information technology throughout the second half of the twentieth century provided the perfect marriage of speed, accuracy, and capacity for information transmissions. With today's computer technology and communication systems such as the Internet, thousands of pages of information can be transmitted immediately and accurately from one end of the world to another. The information recipient can then use computer software to instantaneously sift through the thousands of pages received, resulting in a single page of needed information. Wow!

As we mentioned earlier, information is the essential component of decision-making. Information systems and technology have made this process easier, faster, and more reliable, from the collection of data to the final decision being enacted. ***Raw data***, which are the facts and figures surrounding an actual thing or event, are now instantly collected, compiled, and transmitted using technology tools such as computer-linked RFID readers and bar code scanners. This raw *data* is then received by a recipient through Internet or intranet. The recipient may then use software programs to help sort, count, and categorize the data so that it can the be interpreted, transforming it into *information*. This new information may then be compared to additional information, perhaps stored within computer systems, to transform it into decision-making *knowledge* within the mind of the recipient.

DATA   INFORMATION   KNOWLEDGE   DECISIONS

Figure 7.4 - From Data to Decisions

INFORMATION IN LOGISTICS

Information is used for decision-making throughout all logistics management processes. Physical goods flow downstream along a logistics supply chain, but information must pervade every aspect of the chain and flow between members in both downstream and upstream directions. This permeation of information sharing throughout all logistics management processes makes for highly effective and efficient supply chains.

A few examples of information flowing to and from members of the supply chain include:

- the **customer**, who provides information about product needs and requires information about product availability, quality, price, and delivery times;

- the **Marketing Department**, which provides information to the customer and requires information from Production and finished goods Warehousing about product availability;

- the **Production Department**, which provides information about production lead-times and production capabilities and requires information about supply deliveries;

- the **Purchasing Department**, which provides information to suppliers about goods needed and requires information from other departments about needs and timeframes;

- the **supplier**, who provides information about the availability of goods and transportation and requires information about quantities and timeframes of goods to be purchased and delivered; and

- the **warehouse**, which provides information about orders for dispatch and loading schedules for transport and requires information from purchase orders.

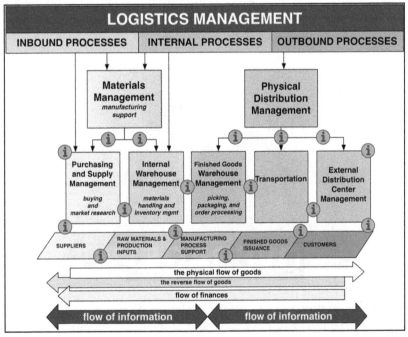

Figure 7.5 - Information and Logistics Management. Information is regularly and continuously conveyed between and within *all* sections of our map of logistics management.

As we've already mentioned, information is used for decision-making. In the world of logistics and supply chain management, information is used to make a wide range of decisions about: (1) inventory management and control; (2) transportation; and (3) physical distribution facilities placement and management. When determining the optimal levels of inventory to hold, companies need information on inventory holding and issuing costs, customer demand patterns, and ordering costs. When selecting transportation routes, modes, and vendors, companies need information concerning transportation costs for various options, shipment frequency and size, and customer delivery receipt locations. Finally, when determining the optimal location, layout, scheduling, and management of a warehouse or distribution center, companies need information regarding customer demand and locations, local regulations and taxes, and inventory type and quantity. Throughout the range of a company's inbound, internal, and outbound processes, information is truly the lifeblood of efficient and effective logistics management.

Within logistics and supply chain management, one possible result of insufficient information for decision-making is the bullwhip effect. In a supply chain, each member places an order for goods from its preceding member based on the predicted demand for a product. Each member of the chain, however, often act and think in isolation, creating their own sometime incomplete picture of the actual demand for the product. For example, a retailer predicts customer demand for an item and places an order for a specific quantity with a wholesaler. Wanting to meet customer (retailer) demand and be ready for additional customer orders, the wholesaler might then order the quantity desired by the retailer plus an additional 20% from the distributor. The distributor, unknowingly using the same thinking as the wholesaler, then orders an additional 20% of the quantity in addition to the retailer's desired quantity and the wholesaler's added 20%. As orders are filled by the manufacturer and the product begins flowing back downstream to members of the supply chain, all members of the supply chain are stuck with an *overage* or overstock situation, i.e., when the supply of an item exceeds its demand. Whenever you see a store trying to sell off excess Halloween candy during the first few days of November at drastically reduced prices, it's likely that the retailer was stuck with an overage.

Members of the supply chain then want to rid themselves of their excess stock and begin ordering less than the desired quantity, not knowing that the other members of the supply chain are doing the same thing. This then results in a *shortfall* or backlog of products, i.e., when the demand for an item exceeds its supply or the supply is less than expected. This yo-yoing of overstock and backlog, continues due to a lack of coordination and communication across the supply chain, is called the *bullwhip effect*.

The Bullwhip Effect is well illustrated in the Beer Game, a game developed by professors at the Massachusetts Institute of Technology Sloan School of Management. The game is a simulation in which players adopt the roles of members of a beer supply chain, including retailers, wholesalers, distributors, and brewers. Each member of the chain receives order information only from its preceding member, which inevitably creates backlogs, overstocks, and temper flare-ups.

To help reduce the bullwhip effect, logistics and supply chain managers today rely on information technology and systems, such as EPOS, EDI, and VMI. (Don't worry. We'll cover these plus a few more in the second half of this chapter.) Furthermore, to make suitable and productive logistics decisions and avoid negative results such as the Bullwhip Effect, information must be:

- *Clear, complete, and accurate.* If information is incorrect or incomplete, decisions made will suffer a similar fate. Imagine placing a delivery order for eighteen pizzas for an office party and being misheard over the telephone, resulting in eighty pizzas landing on your doorstep!

- *Accessible in the right place.* Great information is as good as no information if it can't be found. A scene from the film *Zoolander*, a comedy about the world of male modeling, provides a great illustration of this point. While trying to stop an evil fashion designer from taking over the world, two heroic (but less than computer-savvy) male models are told that the files they need to find are "in the computer." As a result, the protagonists demolish the computer as they try to get the files they believe are literally "inside" the machine.

- *Accessible at the right time.* Needed information is of little use after a decision has been made. For example, a traffic light would be of little use if it were only visible from the middle of an intersection.

- *The kind of information needed.* If the information available is not relevant to the decision to be made or cannot be interpreted, it can be even more harmful that having no information at all. Imagine again that you are buying a car and the only information you have about it are its color and model name (i.e., no information about miles per gallon, safety features, and cost). Many of us might be tempted to select a car based solely on its color and model name, but, with this insufficient information, we might end up with a lemon that we can't even afford!

To ensure that logistics information is clear, accurate, and of the right type accessible at the right time and in the right place, logistics and supply chain management professionals have turned to information systems and information technology. Today, both *information systems* and *information technology* smooth logistics flow by efficiently and accurately recording, analyzing, and transmitting logistics information. **Information systems** are the systems and software programs that manage the flow of logistics data in an organization in a systematic, structured way to assist in planning, implementing, and controlling. **Information technology** is the hardware used to implement information systems to help achieve supply chain efficiencies.

LOGISTICS INFORMATION SYSTEMS

As we've already mentioned, an information system is a set of systems, software programs, and hardware that manages the flow of data into and within an organization. Within a logistics and supply chain setting, a **logistics information system (LIS)** is an interacting structure of people, computer hardware, software, equipment, and procedures which together make relevant and needed information available to a logistics manager for planning, implementing, and controlling activities related to the supply chain.

Thus, a logistics manager does not simply go to the nearest big-box electronics store and pick up a "logistics information system." Instead, an organization's logistics department works together with customers, suppliers, and members of other departments within the same company to construct an LIS. The resulting LIS is likely to be quite complex, using multiple software programs and pieces of hardware, in addition to an exhaustive set of procedures for how to really maintain and run the system, input data, and extract needed information.

Logistics information systems usually follow one of the following three patterns:

- ***Intra-Organizational System***, an LIS used within a single organization, such as an in-house system used to collect and disseminate logistics-related information from multiple global locations of the same company

- ***Inter-Organizational System***, an LIS used between one organization and another, such as its supplier or customer, such as an ordering system used between a prefabricated home builder and its lumber supplier

- ***Total Supply Chain System***, an LIS between members across larger segments of a supply chain, such as an ordering and distribution system to collect and provide information between an automobile manufacturer, its many suppliers, and its many franchises worldwide

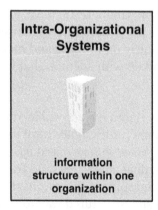 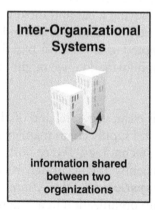 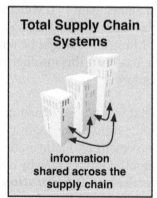

Figure 7.6 - Intra-Organizational, Inter-Organizational, and Total Supply Chain Systems

In addition to varying by how they are organized, logistics information systems also vary according to their application and how they are used. Some more commonly used types of logistics information systems include DSS, WMS, TMS, ERP, intranet/extranet, MRP, DRP, EDI, EPOS, JIT, e-Commerce, VMI, QR, and ECR. But what on earth do all of these letter and words mean?

A decision support system (DSS) is an intra-organizational, interactive, computer-based system used to provide information to help a company make more effective decisions. A DSS uses analytic models to solve complex problems and is typically designed to suit a particular need or function. Within the world of logistics management, examples of a DSS include both warehouse management systems and transportation management systems.

A *warehouse management system (WMS)* manages warehouse business processes and directs warehouse activities. These activities and processes include: order receipt and shelving; order picking and shipping; inventory cycle counting; integration with RFID or voice recognition technology; and layout planning. Warehouse management systems are typically intra-organizational and software-based.

A *transportation management system (TMS)* is a software-based system used to manage and optimize transportation in areas including: transportation and labor planning; auditing freight payments and managing carriers and third party transport providers; shipment loading and scheduling; and managing documentation and mileage. Although commonly intra-organizational, a TMS may also involve information-sharing between multiple companies in the supply chain.

An *enterprise resource planning (ERP) system* is a type of software system used across an entire company for planning and managing its resources. It replaces a company's many, often incompatible information systems with a single, integrated database system with seamless, real-time information sharing, storage, and retrieval. ERP systems play a large role in order receipt, shipments, and inventory management. ERP systems are typically intra-organizational, although aspects of a system may interface with customers and suppliers. The most commonly used ERP systems are those developed by SAP, Oracle, PeopleSoft, and BAAN.

An *intranet* is an intra-organizational information system used to facilitate communication across the many departments and locations of an organization. Although it uses Internet technology, an organization's intranet can only be accessed by members of that organization. An extranet is a total supply chain information system used to facilitate communication across the many organizations involved in a product's or company's supply chain. Like an intranet, an *extranet* uses Internet technology and can only be accessed by designated members of that supply chain.

Materials requirements planning (MRP) is a software application used for inventory control and production planning in the manufacturing process. It helps determine when and how much inventory an organization should purchase. *Distribution resource planning (DRP)* is a method of determining inventory demand at distribution centers and then consolidating demand information into an organization's production and materials systems. Both MRP and DRP are typically intra-organizational applications but both may also interface with suppliers and customers.

Electronic Data Interchange (EDI) is a system of standards for structuring information for instantaneous, inter-organizational transmission and receipt. EDI allows many processes and documentation to become automated, such as creating and completing purchase orders. Unlike intranet and extranet communications, EDI transmissions include only the data allowed by the preset structure, not accompanying words or messages. EDI is, however, the primary data transmission system used for e-commerce transactions around the world.

Electronic point of sale (EPOS) is a method and computerized system of recording retail sales by scanning products' bar codes at the cash register. EPOS systems used by many retailers are quite powerful and perform more complex tasks than recording sale information alone. They also link with or perform other functions, including inventory management, forecasting, customer relations and service management, and accounting. Depending on its application, a company's EPOS may be an intra-organizational, inter-organizational, or total supply chain system.

Just-in-time (JIT) is an inventory strategy in which inventory is moved along to the next segment of the supply chain (such as a manufacturing facility or a retailer's distribution center) so that it arrives at the exact time and in the exact quantity needed. JIT and its corresponding software and communications applications can dramatically reduce in-process inventory and its associated costs. JIT is typically an inter-organizational or total supply chain application.

Electronic commerce, or *e-commerce*, systems are total supply chain information systems used to conduct business electronically using Internet or EDI technologies. E-commerce systems are a typically software-driven means for a company to sell its goods to other companies (also known as business to business or B2B) or directly to consumers (also known as business to consumer or B2C). E-commerce systems are total supply chain to inter-organizational systems.

Vendor managed inventory (VMI) is the practice of a buyer allowing a seller (or vendor) to monitor product demand in order to forecast demand patterns and set product shipment levels and schedules. VMI applications may be EDI, EPOS, Internet, or software-based. Their ultimate goal is to ensure that the buyer has enough inventory needed while keeping inventory holding costs at a minimum. VMI applications are typically total supply chain or inter-organizational in nature.

Quick response (QR) is a strategy in which multiple members of a supply chain work together to provide immediate response to consumer demands. QR is a total supply chain strategy and its applications focus on sharing sales, forecasting, and manufacturing data.

Efficient consumer response (ECR) is a total supply chain strategy in which multiple members of the supply chain work together to optimize the supply chain and enhance product availability. ECR systems are typically demand-driven replenishment systems that link members of a logistics chain to create a large, seamless flow-through distribution network. With an ECR system, product replenishment is based on consumer demand and point of sale (or electronic point of sale) information.

LOGISTICS AND INFORMATION TECHNOLOGY

A critical component of all logistics information systems is the actual technology used to collect, house, sort, analyze, and distribute the information needed by logistics managers. Earlier in the chapter, we defined information technology in logistics management as the hardware used to implement information systems to help achieve supply chain efficiencies. When we think of hardware, we typically think of computer equipment, such as CPUs, keyboards, and monitors. Three additional forms of information technology that are playing an increasingly important role in logistics and supply chain management are bar code, RFID, and voice-based technologies.

Bar codes, the most widely used form of technology-based item identification, consist of a series of bars and spaces printed onto a label, which is adhered to an item or unit load. Information is associated with these bars and spaces. A ***bar code scanner*** reads the label and communicates the information to a central inventory control system. Bar code technology is used within many logistics information systems, such as electronic point of sale and warehouse management systems. When we step into the self-scanning express aisle of a large grocery store, we ourselves become frontline users of bar code technology. As we scan the bar code of our Wheatie-Bites cereal, our purchase is entered into the grocery store's electronic point of sale system, which helps the store record its inventory levels and plan for future orders.

 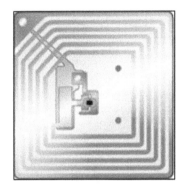

Figure 7.7 - Example of a Barcode Being Scanned with an Optical Scanner and an RFID Tag

RFID, an acronym for radio frequency identification, is a technology that uses programmed transponder tags, which are attached to items or unit loads. The transponder tags send out information about the items through radio waves. An ***RFID reader*** with an antenna reads this information and transmits it to a central inventory control system. Like bar coding, RFID technology is used within logistics information systems, such as transportation management systems. Unlike bar codes, RFID tags can be programmed with additional information and can be read when not in the line of sight, at distances of 90 feet or more, and when the tagged item or load is in motion.

Voice-activated or ***voice-directed technology*** can be used in systems that guide users to complete specific actions using voice commands. For example, voice technology is gaining popularity in warehouse order picking systems, in which an order picker wearing a handsfree headset listens to each item to be picked along with its location. The order picker then uses voice commands to confirm that the correct items and quantities have been selected.

Thanks to a longer history, less expensive equipment, and its prevalence in retail, bar code technology is one of the more commonly used forms of information technology in logistics management. Bar code technology is currently used in a variety of settings, from extensive global supply chain networks to smaller local warehouses. Some of the newer and more expensive information technologies, such as RFID and voice-based technologies, are used primarily in the warehouses, distribution centers, and transportation networks of large, multinational companies and 3PLPs. To stay competitive in the rapidly changing global marketplace, all logistics and supply chain managers, including those of smaller supply chains, must become familiar with these newer technologies.

How Does Voice-Activated Technology Work?

As you enter the wonderful world of logistics, you are likely to hear more and more about voice-activated technology. We have already mentioned that it can be used in order picking systems, but exactly how would the work and what would it look like? Here's a step by step example of what happen when voice-activated technology is used for order picking:

Step 1: Armed with a handsfree, wireless headset, the picker enters the warehouse and listens to the system's command.

Step 2: The system, usually in the form of a computer generated voice, tells the picker to go to location 1.1.2.4 in the warehouse.

Step 3: The picker goes to the location as instructed and reads a validation code found on the location racking through the microphone on the wireless headset. This will allow the system to either confirm that the picker is in the right location or direct him to the correct location.

Step 4: Because the picker is indeed at the correct location, the system then tells him through his headset the exact quantity of the item (at location 1.1.2.4) that he must pick.

Step 5: The picker then confirms the quantity picked by restating this quantity into the headset's microphone, such as "Five picked."

Step 6: After the picker has confirmed that he has picked the correct quantity, the process will start over and the system will direct him to his next location.

CHAPTER 7 REVIEW QUESTIONS

1. What is the difference between data and information?

2. What were the limitations of pre-computer forms of information transmission? What advantages has computerization brought to decision-making?

3. Which members of the supply chain provide and require information? What types of information do they provide and require? Please provide three examples.

4. Explain a situation in which the bullwhip effect might occur. How would the bullwhip effect influence this situation?

5. What is the difference between information systems and information technology? Please provide two examples of each.

6. Which type of LIS is used between one organization and another? Please provide one example of this type of LIS.

7. What is a WMS? With which information technologies is it often associated?

8. If a logistics manager wanted to optimize shipment loading and manage shipment documentation, which type of logistics information system would she use?

9. Which type of logistics information system utilizes bar code technology at retail cash registers?

10. Which type of information technology would be useful for increasing order-picking speed in a warehouse? Why?

CHAPTER 7 CASE STUDY

CASE
STUDY

RFID at Walgreens

For the past five years, many large retail companies around the world have begun to use RFID for physical distribution. In the United States, most of the retail giants have run test pilots using RFID, but few have made it a bona fide part of their logistics operations. Leading the charge, however, is Walgreens, a drugstore retail chain with 6,658 stores across the U.S. Not only has the pharmacy giant made RFID an integral part of its logistics management, but it is also now using it for marketing and promotional campaigns.

In 2008, Walgreens began using RFID throughout its distribution operations to achieve its goal of 100% shipping accuracy between the distribution center and each retail store. The company began using the Blue Vector RFID system in its 600,000 square foot South Carolina distribution center, which services over 700 retail locations in the southeastern United States. The system is now used in all of its distribution centers and has dramatically reduced shipping errors and the time-consuming paperwork associated with errors. In the pharmacy business, accurate drug shipments can be a matter of life and death because some consumers are just not able to wait for critical lifesaving medications.

In the Walgreens distribution centers, it's all about accuracy. Orders for retail locations are placed in 24"x18"x12" plastic totes that have RFID tags attached to them. Every day, a whopping 80,000 RFID-tagged totes are shipped from the South Carolina distribution center alone. When read with RFID scanners, these tags let distribution center workers know which retail location has ordered the tote, which truck is the correct one for the tote, and what order the tote should be in when loaded onto the truck. Because trucks may deliver to multiple retail stores on one trip, it is important to place the totes destined for the first location close to the loading door so they can be unloaded first.

Before implementing the RFID system, distribution center workers would read printouts of items to be shipped and manually scan the barcodes on each tote using a handheld scanner. They would then read the information on the scanner and input it into the computerized warehouse management system. Because there were so many opportunities for human error, many errors did indeed occur, with retail locations sometimes receiving incorrect or incomplete orders and distribution centers having to spend valuable time accounting for and correcting these errors.

With the RFID system, the tags attached to each of the distribution center's totes is connected to the warehouse information system software. Filled totes are placed on dollies bound for specific locations in specific trucks. To reduce the risk of errors even further, each dolly (hand truck) has a unique RFID tag attached to it, which contains information about the truck and load order for its corresponding totes. As each dolly filled with totes is rolled toward the truck bay, it passes through an RFID scanning portal with an LED screen. As dollies are rolled through, the screen displays information about exactly where the dolly needs to go. The dolly is then rolled to the correct dock for the truck onto which its contents will be loaded. At each of the dock doors for the 45 loading bays is an additional RFID portal. If a dolly is rolled passed a portal and onto an incorrect truck or if it is loaded in the incorrect order, a loud alarm sounds so that the person rolling the dolly knows that a mistake is about to be made. With this system, mistakes can immediately be corrected, even before they happen!

When dollies are rolled onto the correct trucks and in the correct order, the corresponding RFID portal sends the information via a cable connection to the warehouse management system. This information is then automatically forwarded to the store receiving the items so that they know when to expect them. The connection between the RFID and warehouse management systems also alert the distribution center as soon as it recognizes that ordered items are missing from a shipment. Distribution center employees can immediately rectify this and ensure that the order is complete long before the truck drives away.

Walgreens has not limited its use of RFID to shipping alone. The company now uses a Goliath RFID system to determine and record the location and execution of promotional displays in 5000 of its retail stores nationwide. Promotional displays are the special displays on counters or on the ends of aisles that are created by a product's supplier to provide advertising, information, and the product itself. Walk into the cosmetics section of any drugstore and you are bound to see loads of promotional displays containing not only specific product lines, but also color charts, attractive celebrities, or tag-lines extolling the product's elegance, simplicity, or earth-friendliness. With an RFID scanner in the ceiling of each retail location connected to a central software system, the RFID tags attached to each display provide store-level information on what displays are up and where they are located. The system also provides Walgreens the means to assess the effectiveness of each display by comparing a store's point of sale information with the display's location, timing, and other execution data. Essentially, it can help show Walgreens and its suppliers what works and what doesn't work with the store's consumers. Since implementing the RFID program, Walgreens has found that sales on promotional display items have increases 200 to 400%.

References

Martinez, S. (2011, May 13) Zondervan will move headquarters when it closes warehouse in 2012. *The Grand Rapids Press*. Retrieved from http://www.mlive.com/business/west-michigan/index.ssf/2011/05/zondervan_will_move_headquarte.html.

RR Donnelley (2011, May 12) HarperCollins and RR Donnelley announce intent to enter into strategic printing and supply chain management agreement. *Globe Newswire*. Retrieved from http://www.globenewswire.com/newsroom/news.html?d=221847.

Case Study Questions

1. Why would bar code technology be more time consuming than RFID technology in the case of the Walgreens distribution center?

2. Why is it a good idea to also place RFID tags on the distribution center dollies?

3. How many RFID portals do the totes pass through? Why is this duplication necessary?

4. In the future, how might even further use be made of RFID technology for a company like Walgreens?

Chapter 8

Finance in Logistics
and Supply Chain Management

Throughout many of the previous chapters, we have repeatedly stated that it is the job of logistics management to increase supply chain efficiency and effectiveness. Logistics managers must examine the company's current supply chain processes, procedures, and technologies in search of ways to change and improve them while saving the company money and increasing levels of service provided to customers.

When changes need to be made in logistics and supply chain management, logistics managers must often face their stalwart peers and CEOs, who, although working hard to improve the company themselves, often don't want to hear about changing distribution center locations, using 3PLPs, or purchasing and implementing RFID technology. To an ear untrained in logistics management, much of this may sound like expensive, unnecessary, complex logistics gobbledygook. How then can a logistics manager speak the language of the CEO and the manufacturing, marketing, and financial decision-makers at the organization to get their attention? The answer to this question can be summed up in one word: *money*.

In the business world, money talks. At the core of most decisions within an organization is the effect of a change on the organization's bottom line. To be well equipped for discussing new ideas and potential changes with the top echelons of an organization's management, logistics managers must know the basics of finance, especially how to outline the impact of changes in logistics management on the organization's profits.

Throughout this chapter, you will be the logistics manager of a local toy manufacturer, Kearney's Crazy Kazoos. We will introduce a few core concepts of finance that will help you speak the language of the company's CEO, Crazy Jim Kearney, so that you can illustrate the positive impact of logistics management changes on Kearney's Crazy Kazoos' bottom line.

LOGISTICS LINGO: WHO'S WHO IN FINANCE

shareholder

A **shareholder**, also known as a stockholder, is a person or an organization that owns shares of stock within a company.

shares

The **shares** owned are actual portions of ownership of the company, which receive income from the company's profits called dividends.

stakeholder

A **stakeholder** is another person or entity that can be affected by a company's actions. Examples of stakeholders include: shareholders, company employees, suppliers, the local community, professional associations, labor unions, the government, and even competitors!

INCOME STATEMENTS

The primary goal of a typical company is to make money while satisfying customers so that it can continue to make money from sales to new and existing customers. Most large companies are publicly traded and have shareholders, to whom a company is responsible for turning a profit. A company also has other stakeholders who are concerned with its financial health, including its employees, the local communities in which it operates, and its suppliers, all of whom rely on the company's success for their own success.

A company, its shareholders, and its stakeholders are all concerned with the company's financial status. Therefore, the company generates a variety of ***financial statements***, which are formal records of its financial activities and its overall long- and short-term financial condition. Most financial statements are issued periodically at regular intervals, such as annually or quarterly. Two commonly used financial statements are the *income statement* and the *balance sheet*. The remainder of this section explores an income statement and the next section covers the balance sheet.

An ***income statement***, also known as a ***profit and loss statement (P&L)***, shows how much money an organization made or lost over a set period, typically over a financial year. It compares the actual sales value of goods to how much it cost to produce or purchase the goods and operate the company.

Let's take a closer look at the annual income statement for our company, Kearney's Crazy Kazoos, and the role logistics-related expenses play in calculating the company's net profits, as shown in Figure 8.1.

At first glance, the Kearney's income statement might seem a bit intimidating to the average logistics manager. It might be even downright horrifying to those with the slightest touch of numerophobia (i.e., fear of numbers), but, when broken down line by line, an income statement is quite simple to understand.

	KEARNEY'S CRAZY KAZOOS, INC. Income Statement for Year Ending December 31, 2014 (in millions of dollars)	
1.	Net Sales	$2000
2.	Opening Inventory	($200)
3.	Purchases	($890)
4.	Closing Inventory	$210
5.	Cost of Goods Sold	($880)
6.	Gross Profit Margin	$1120
	LOGISTICS OPERATING EXPENSES	
7.	Transportation Expenses	($50)
8.	Inventory Holding Expenses	($30)
9.	Warehousing Expenses	($20)
10.	Total Logistics Expenses	($100)
11.	Other Operating Expenses	($220)
12.	Total Operating Expenses	($320)
13.	Net Profit Before Interest and Taxes	$800
14.	Interest on Long Term Loan	($63)
15.	Net Profit After Interest, Before Taxes	$737
16.	Corporate Taxes Due, 40%	($294.80)
17.	Net Profit After Interest and Taxes	$442.20

Figure 8.1 - Income Statement for Kearney's Crazy Kazoos

Let's now break Kearney's income statement into three sections and examine each line to see what the item represents and how its value was calculated. As we look at each of the numbers, you might notice that some are written in parentheses. Accountants often use either red ink or parentheses on financial statements to indicate those values that represent *outgoings* or the money the company spends. In the three sections below, we start with Kearney's net sales and, after factoring in all the company's outgoings, arrive at the final net profit.

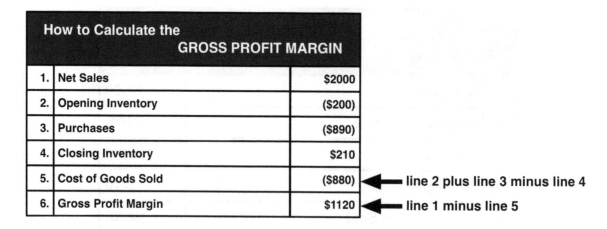

Figure 8.2 - Calculating the Gross Profit Margin on Kearney's Crazy Kazoos' Income Statement

Line 1 shows the company's **net sales**, which is the total dollar amount Kearney's made from the sales of its products throughout its 2014 financial year. Net sales typically represent sales figures after returns and discounts have been figured in. It also represents dollar amounts from sales that have been finalized but may not have yet been paid by the customer.

Line 2, **opening inventory**, represents the dollar amount of inventory Kearney's was holding in its warehouses at the start of the 2014 financial year. This inventory, left over from 2013, was available for sale in 2014. The value of opening inventory is calculated from a physical inventory check of goods held in Kearney's warehouses at the end of the 2013 financial year.

Line 3, **purchases**, includes the dollar amount of inventory purchased by Kearney's from its suppliers. This inventory purchased may be actual kazoos and toys made by other manufacturers, which Kearney's will resell, or it may be the raw materials and other inventory needed to manufacture goods.

Line 4, **closing inventory**, is the dollar amount of inventory remaining in the Kearney's warehouse at the end of the 2014 financial year. Like opening inventory, the closing inventory value is calculated from a physical inventory check of goods at the end of the financial year. This 2014 closing inventory value will then be used as the opening inventory value for Kearney's 2015 income statement.

Line 5 represents the total **cost of goods sold**, i.e., how much it costs Kearney's to produce or buy the goods it sold. It is calculated by adding the opening inventory (line 2) and the purchases (line 3) and then subtracting the closing inventory (line 4).

Finally, line 6, the **gross profit margin**, also known as the **gross income**, is the difference between Kearney's sales and the cost of its sales. It is calculated by subtracting the cost of sales (line 5) from the net sales (line 1). A company's gross profit margin is an important figure because it indicates what resources it has available for other expenses, such as operating expenses, shareholder dividends, corporate expansion, and research and development.

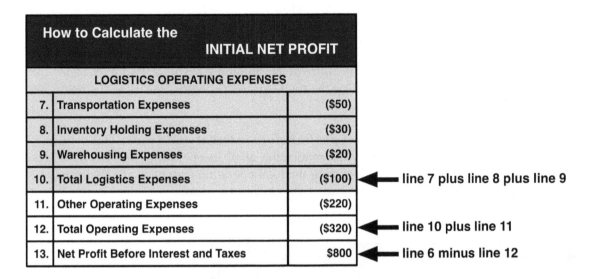

Figure 8.3 - Calculating the Initial Net Profit on Kearney's Crazy Kazoos' Income Statement

As we will see, this section calculates the net profit Kearney's makes from the sales of its goods after company operating expenses have been figured in. Some of these operating expenses include those related to logistics management, such as transportation (line 7), inventory holding (line 8), and warehousing (line 9) expenses.

Not all companies highlight separate logistics expenses in their income statements, however. Some companies even have only a single line for operating expenses, which accounts for all expenses combined, including logistics-related ones. When included in an income statement, separate logistics-related figures can provide companies with an instant snapshot of the impact logistics has on the company's bottom line, especially when figures are compared from year to year as expenses increase or decrease.

Line 7, **_transportation expenses_**, includes how much Kearney's spent in 2014 for the transport of goods into and out from its facilities. This might included shipping expenses for raw materials delivery, the use of 3PLP to deliver finished products to the customers' door, maintaining a fleet of delivery trucks, and customs brokerage charges for goods it imports from China.

Line 8, **_inventory holding expenses_**, also known as **_inventory carrying costs_**, represents the dollar amount it costs for Kearney's to hold its goods in storage. These expenses typically include obsolescence, deterioration, spoilage, depreciation, insurance, tax, and extra storage and handling expenses.

Line 9, **_warehousing expenses_**, represents Kearney's typical warehouse operating expenses, including those associated with inbound and outbound physical distribution activities.

Line 10, **_total logistics expenses_**, are all the logistics costs combined, i.e., transportation (line7) plus inventory holding (line8) plus warehousing (line 9) expenses.

Line 11 includes all of Kearney's **other operating expenses**, such as administrative costs, facilities expenses, and employee salaries.

Line 12, **total operating expenses**, is the entire dollar amount Kearney's used in 2014 to operate its business. It is calculated by adding the total logistics expenses (line10) to the operating expenses (line 11).

Finally, line 13 shows Kearney's **initial net profit before interest and taxes**. This lines represents how much money the company has made after all of its operating expenses have been taken into account. It is calculated by subtracting the total operating expenses (line12) from the gross profit margin (line 6 calculated at the end of the previous section.

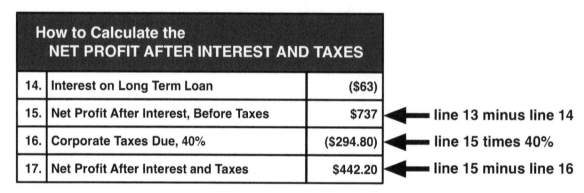

Figure 8.4 - Calculating the Net Profit After Interest and Taxes on Kearney's Crazy Kazoos' Income Statement

Line 14 represents the amount Kearney's must pay the bank in **interest on a long term loan**. It is not located in the previous section of the income statement because, although it is an expense Kearney's incurs annually, it is not a company operating expense, i.e., a regular cost for operating a business to produce a product. This value is calculated by the bank, based on the amount borrowed, the bank's interest rate, and the way in which the interest is compounded.

Line 15, Kearney's **net profit after interest, before taxes**, is calculated by subtracting the interest on the long-term loan (line 14) from Kearney's initial net profit (line 13). This is an important figure for most companies because it is the profit value from which a company's taxes are calculated.

Line 16 indicates Kearney's **corporate taxes due**. This value is calculated by multiplying the net profit after interest (line 15) by the tax rate, which happens to be 40% for Kearney's Crazy Kazoos.

Finally, the moment we have been waiting for, is line 17, the **net profit after interest and taxes**, which is calculated by subtracting the corporate taxes due (line 16) from the net profit after interest (line 15). This final amount represents the total profit or loss for Kearney's for 2014, i.e., how much the company made or lost overall. At the end of the financial year, the amount of net profit after interest and taxes can be placed into the shareholders' retained earnings account or can be shared among shareholders or owners as returns on their capital investment.

Income Statements in a World of Information Technology

Most financial statements today are created with the assistance of computers. The software used to generate income statements ranges from simple Microsoft Excel templates to complex, companywide ERP and accounting software systems that process and record all corporate transactions.

Let's look now at how an income statement can be used to show the impact of logistics cost increases or reductions. As the Logistics Manager of Kearney's Crazy Kazoos, you want to spend $5 million on RFID equipment company wide, which, according to the most conservative estimates, will reduce the company's overall transportation, inventory holding, and warehousing costs by 10%. When you propose the $5 million logistics expenditure at an upper-management meeting, everyone gasps in horror at the idea. One manager even snickers, "Hey, we'd all like to play with $5 million toys, but we just don't have that kind of money to 'play' with."

As a financially savvy logistics manager, however, you can use an income statement to get everyone's attention, as shown in Figure 8.5. When the figures from our existing 2014 income state are adjusted to reflect the 10% reduction in logistics costs the proposed RFID technology will bring, it becomes clear to all (even the RFID naysayers) that the 10% reduction would increase the final net profit (line 17) by a whopping $6 million, both covering the initial RFID expenditure and increasing profits by $1 million, even after paying the 40% tax due on the initial profits!

THE BALANCE SHEET

Earlier in the chapter, we mentioned that companies generate a variety of *financial statements*, i.e., formal records of financial activities and their overall long- and short-term financial condition. Along with the income statement, another important financial statement for companies engaged in any form of commerce is the **balance sheet**. At its core, a balance sheet is a like a snapshot of a company's financial picture taken at a given time. It is a statement showing the company's **assets**, i.e., everything the company owns, and the company's **liabilities**, also called **claims on assets**, which are all claims against the company such as the money it owes. Unlike an income statement, which is calculated at specific annual intervals, a balance sheet can be calculated on any given day to get the financial "picture" of the company on that day. For example, it may be calculated quarterly for corporate investors or an any given time when the company is applying for a loan.

As we continue our exploration of Kearney's financial statements, we will see that the company's balance sheet, like that of most companies, is divided vertically into two haves. The left side of the balance sheet lists all the company's assets and the right side lists all of its liabilities. Both of these sides must balance, which means that the total assets of a company must equal its total liabilities. In this way, a company responsible to both shareholders and stakeholders can account for every penny, making sure that no loose change here and there is being siphoned off surreptitiously from somewhere in the company.

KEARNEY'S CRAZY KAZOOS, INC.
Income Statement for Year Ending December 31, 2014 Compared to
2015 Income Statement if Logistics Expenses Reduced by 10%
(in millions of dollars)

		2014 Calculations		2015 Calculations
1.	Net Sales	$2000		$2000
2.	Opening Inventory	($200)		($200)
3.	Purchases	($890)		($890)
4.	Closing Inventory	$210		$210
5.	Cost of Goods Sold	($880)		($880)
6.	Gross Profit Margin	$1120		$1120
	LOGISTICS OPERATING EXPENSES	**10% Logistics Expense Reduction**		
7.	Transportation Expenses	($50)	$5 difference	($45)
8.	Inventory Holding Expenses	($30)	$3 difference	($27)
9.	Warehousing Expenses	($20)	$2 difference	($18)
10.	Total Logistics Expenses	($100)	$10 difference	($90)
11.	Other Operating Expenses	($220)		($220)
12.	Total Operating Expenses	($320)		($310)
13.	Net Profit Before Interest and Taxes	$800		$810
14.	Interest on Long Term Loan	($63)		($63)
15.	Net Profit After Interest, Before Taxes	$737		$747
16.	Corporate Taxes Due, 40%	($294.80)		($298.80)
17.	Net Profit After Interest and Taxes	$442.20		$448.20

Profits would INCREASE by $6 MILLION
from 2014 to 2015 if logistics expenses
reduced by 10%

Figure 8.5 - Calculating the Dramatic Increase in Net Profit with a 10% Reduction in Logistics Expenses

At first mention, this idea of a perfect balance between what a company owns and what it owes may seem preposterous. How on earth can a company ensure that its expenditures will equal the same amount as its net profits and assets? As we will see, this perfect balance is achieved when the owners or shareholders' investment in the company is brought into the equation. The dollar value difference between a company's assets and its current and *fixed liabilities* (more on these later) is the amount owned by the company's owners or shareholders as a return on their investment in the company in addition to the amount of money a company will reinvest in itself. This difference is often called the ***shareholders' equity***. Therefore, if a company's assets are greater than its liabilities, shareholders own the difference. If the company's liabilities are greater than its assets, however, shareholders do not actually owe the difference, but the company must suffer the consequences of negative equity, typically resulting in decreased share or stock values.

Let's now take a look at the balance sheet of Kearney's Crazy Kazoos item by item, focusing on where logistics-related expenses come into the picture.

KEARNEY'S CRAZY KAZOOS, INC. Balance Sheet December 31, 2014 (in millions of dollars)						
ASSETS			**LIABILITIES/CLAIMS ON ASSETS**			
1.	CURRENT ASSETS			13.	CURRENT LIABILITIES		
2.	Cash	$80		14.	Accounts Payable	$220	
3.	Accounts Receivable	$160		15.	TOTAL CURRENT LIABILITIES		$220
4.	Inventory	$210		16.	FIXED LIABILITIES		
5.	TOTAL CURRENT ASSETS		$450	17.	Long Term Loan	$315	
6.	FIXED ASSETS			18.	TOTAL FIXED LIABILITIES		$315
7.	Land	$45		19.	TOTAL CURRENT & FIXED LIABILITIES		$535
8.	Plant & Equipment	$360		20.	SHAREHOLDER EQUITY		
9.	Buildings	$220		21.	Shareholder's Invested Capital	$53	
10.	TOTAL FIXED ASSETS		$625	22.	Retained Earnings	$487	
11.				23.	TOTAL SHAREHOLDER EQUITY		$540
12.	**TOTAL ASSETS**		$1075	24.	**TOTAL LIABILITIES**		$1075

Figure 8.6 - Balance Sheet for Kearney's Crazy Kazoos (in millions of dollars)

Left Side of the Balance Sheet: The Assets of the Company

On the left side of its Balance Sheet, Kearney's lists its assets, i.e., all the company's money and everything else it owns, such as inventory, property, and equipment. The assets of the company are divided into two categories: *current assets* and *fixed assets*. **Current assets** (line 1 above left) are those assets that are typically used up within a financial period. These include all cash held and resources that will probably be converted into cash within the financial year, such as finished goods inventory. The value of a company's current assets fluctuates from day to day as cash is spent and received.

Unlike the fluctuating current assets, **fixed assets** (line 6 above left) do not fluctuate. These are the assets held by a company over a number of years to use in its efforts to generate profit. Fixed assets include the land, buildings, factories, and machinery the company owns.

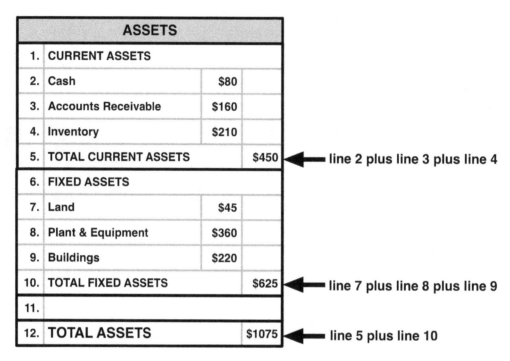

Figure 8.7 - The Assets Side on the Balance Sheet for Kearney's Crazy Kazoos (in millions of dollars)

Let's now look at the asset side of Kearney's balance sheet line by line on Figure 8.7 to see what each of the figures mean and how they are generated.

Line 2, **cash**, is the cash Kearney's have available for immediate spending. This cash may be kept in different locations, such as in a petty cash box in-house or in different bank accounts. To ensure that their balance sheets stay balanced, companies keep a tight control on their cash and record even the smallest expenditures made from cash in the petty cash box.

Line 3, **accounts receivable**, is money owed to Kearney's by customers who have received goods but not yet paid for them. Even though the accounts receivable money is not yet in hand, a company must include these impending payments on the balance sheet to make it balance. The goods received by the customers are no longer in the company's inventory, leaving a gap in the current assets that must be filled with the amount to be received.

Line 4, **inventory**, represents the value of the goods Kearney's owns that has not yet been sold to customers. This value is the estimated dollar amount of inventory remaining in the Kearney's warehouse at the time the balance sheet is calculated.

Line 5, **total current assets**, is the total amount of current assets Kearney's has at the time of the Balance Sheet. This value is calculated by adding the cash value (line 2) to the accounts receivable (line 3) and inventory (line 4) values.

Line 7, **land**, the first of our types of fixed assets, is the value of the actual land that Kearney's owns. This is typically the land on which a company's factories, warehouses, and administrative buildings are located.

Line 8, **plant and equipment**, is the value of all the machinery and equipment Kearney's owns and uses to produce and distribute its products. This might include manufacturing machinery, forklift trucks, and computer equipment.

Line 9, **buildings**, represent the estimated value of all the buildings and facilities owned by Kearney's, such as its manufacturing facility, its warehouses, and its headquarters building.

Line 10, **total fixed assets**, is the total amount of fixed assets Kearney's has at the time of the Balance Sheet. This value is calculated by adding the land value (line 7) to the plant and equipment (line 8) and buildings (line 9) values.

Finally, line 12, **total assets**, is the dollar value of Kearney's current and fixed assets combined. This value is calculated by adding the total current assets (line 5) and the total fixed assets (line 10). This final amount must equal (or "balance" with) the total liabilities, which is calculated in the second half of the balance sheet.

Right Side of the Balance Sheet: Liabilities/Claims on Assets of the Company

On the right side of its Balance Sheet, Kearney's lists its **liabilities**, also called **claims on assets**, which are all claims against the company, such as the money it owes and will pay to banks and shareholders. The liabilities of the company are divided into three categories: *current liabilities*, *fixed liabilities*, and *shareholders equity*. **Current liabilities** (line 13 of the balance sheet) are liabilities and money owed that must be paid within a short period of time. This includes outstanding accounts payable owed to creditors that fall due and will be settled within the course of a normal business year, such as short-term loans, utility bills, rent, and corporate credit card debt.

Fixed liabilities (line 16 of the balance sheet) are liabilities and money owed over a term longer than the current financial year. This includes long-term loans and mortgages. **Shareholder equity** (line 20 of the balance sheet) is the net worth of the company after all the money and inventory have been counted and all the bills have been paid. It is essentially the claim the shareholders have on the business in the shares of stock they already own plus **retained earnings**, i.e., the company's earnings that are not redistributed to shareholders but are instead retained for reinvestment in the company. The value of the shareholder equity is also called the **net worth** of the company.

Let's now look at the liabilities side of Kearney's balance sheet line by line on Figure 8.8 to see what each of the figures mean and how they are generated.

Line 14, **accounts payable**, is the money Kearney's owes immediately or in the short term to its creditors. For example, when Kearney's orders raw materials or office supplies from its suppliers, if it receives the items and has them in stock but has not yet paid for them, the amount owed would be counted as accounts payable.

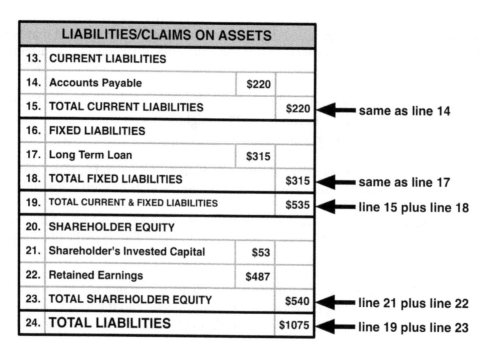

Figure 8.8 - The Liabilities Side on the Balance Sheet for Kearney's Crazy Kazoos (in millions of dollars)

Line 15, ***total current liabilities***, is the value of all current liabilities added together. For example, a company may list a variety of accounts payable and short-term loans on their balance sheet, which would be added together to calculate the total current liabilities. In our example, however, Kearney's listed accounts payable (line 14) as its only category of current liabilities, making the total current liabilities (line 15) equal to accounts payable (line 14).

Line 17, ***long term loan***, is the amount that Kearney's owes for loans taken out for longer than a one-year period. The interest on this long-term loan is also included on the company's income statement (see line 14 of Kearney's Income Statement).

Line 18, ***total fixed liabilities***, is the value of all fixed liabilities added together. For example, a company may include multiple long-term loans on their balance sheet, which would be added together to calculate the total fixed liabilities. In our example, however, Kearney's listed one long-term loan (line 17) as its only category of fixed liabilities, making the total fixed liabilities (line 18) equal to the long-term loan (line 17).

Line 19, ***total current and fixed liabilities***, is the total of all that Kearney's owes to everyone except its shareholders. It is calculated by adding the total current liabilities (line 15) to the total fixed liabilities (line 18).

We now move into the realm of shareholders! Let's jump out of order a bit and first look at line 23, ***total shareholder equity***. This is the dollar value difference between a company's total assets (line 12) and its total current and fixed liabilities (line 19), i.e., the shareholders' claim on the company after all of the bills have been paid. It is also known as the ***net worth*** of the company.

Line 21, **shareholders' invested capital**, also known as **capital stock**, is the current value of the shareholders' initial investment in the company.

As previously discussed, line 22, **retained earnings**, represents the company's earnings that are not redistributed to shareholders, but are instead retained for reinvestment in the company. These retained and subsequently reinvested earnings are still technically owned by the shareholders because they are the owners of the company and its assets.

Finally, line 24, **total liabilities**, is the dollar value of Kearney's current liabilities, fixed liabilities, and shareholder equity combined. This value is calculated by adding the total current liabilities (line 15) to the total fixed liabilities (line 18) and the shareholder equity (line 23). This final amount must equal (or "balance" with) the total assets, which was calculated in the first half of the balance sheet.

RATIOS & THE DUPONT STRATEGIC MODEL

To better understand the business implications of the figures found in financial statements such as the income statement and the balance sheet, corporate manager turn to *financial ratios*, many of which are extremely useful to logistics managers. As you may remember from way back when you learned pre-algebra, a **ratio** is a fraction or two numbers separated by a colon that represents the amount or magnitude of one thing in comparison to the amount or magnitude of another thing. For example, if there are two cats and three ferrets in the room, the ratio of cats to ferrets is two to three, also written as 2/3 or 2:3.

In the business world, a **financial ratio** is also a comparison of two numbers, but the values of these numbers are taken from financial statements, such as the balance sheet and the income statement. Business managers use financial ratios to interpret much of the information found on these financial statements by making comparisons that reveal if a company's operating expenses are too high, if it has incurred too much debt, or if it is holding too much inventory. A company uses financial ratios to gain insight into its financial health by comparing its financial ratios to those of other companies and to its own financial ratios from previous fiscal years. Like traditional mathematical ratios, financial ratios are expressed as fractions or as two numbers separated by a colon, but they can also be expressed as percentages and decimals.

Five commonly used financial ratios for strategic decision-making are: *net profit margin*, *asset turnover*, *return on assets*, *financial leverage*, and *return on net worth*. Let's now take a closer look at each of these ratios, what they mean, and how they can be calculated using data from our Kearney's Income Statement and Balance Sheet.

The **net profit margin** is the first of our five financial ratios that tells a manager or stakeholder how much profit a company makes for every $1 it generates in sales. Therefore, the higher the net profit margin, the more profitable the company. Companies and their existing and potential investors will often compare a company's net profit margins to those of other companies in the same industry to see which company is more profitable. Companies can also compare their most recent net profit margin with those calculated in previous financial years to see how the profitability of the company is changing.

The net profit margin is calculated by dividing a company's net profit (after interest and taxes) by its net sales, both of which are found on the company's income statement. In our Kearney's Income Statement, the net profit after interest and taxes value (found in line 17) was $442.2 million. The net sales value (found in line 1) was $2000 million. We then calculate the net profit margin by dividing $442.2 million (net profit) by $2000 million (net sales), equaling a net profit margin of 0.2211 or 22.11%. Net profit margins are usually expressed with percentages.

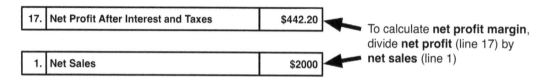

Figure 8.9 - Calculating the Net Profit Margin for Kearney's Crazy Kazoos (in millions of dollars)

The second of our five financial ratios is the ***asset turnover***, or the amount of sales a company generates for every dollar of its assets. The asset turnover ratio reveals how good a company is at using its assets to make sales. It is calculated by dividing the value of a company's net sales, found on its Income Statement, by its total assets, found on its Balance Sheet. In our Kearney's Income Statement, the net sales value (found in line 1) was $2000 million. In our Kearney's Balance Sheet, the value of the total assets (found in line 12) was $1075 million.

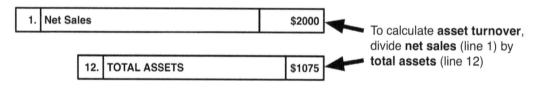

Figure 8.10 - Calculating the Asset Turnover for Kearney's Crazy Kazoos (in millions of dollars)

We can then calculate the asset turnover by dividing $2000 million (net sales) by $1075 (total assets), equaling an asset turnover of 1.86. (The asset turnover ratio is typically expressed as a decimal number.) This calculation means that for every $1 of assets Kearney's has, it generates $1.86 in sales.

Return on assets (ROA), the third of our five financial ratios, is a comparison that reveals how profitable a company is relative to its assets. This ratio is an important one for shareholders because it lets them know to what degree a company has taken their investment, which are now the assets of the company, and turned them into profits. Return on assets also serves an indicator for potential investors of how well a company can do with what it's given. It is calculated by dividing the value of a company's net profit, found on its Income Statement, by its total assets, found on its Balance Sheet.

In our Kearney's Income Statement, the net profit after interest and taxes value (found in line 17) was $442.2 million. In our Kearney's Balance Sheet, the value of the total assets (found in line 12) was $1075 million. The return on assets can then be calculated by dividing $442.2 million (net profit) by $1075 million (total assets), equaling 0.4113 or 41.13%. (Return on assets is usually expressed as a percentage.)

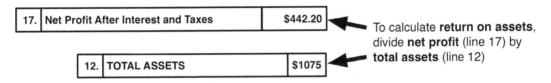

Figure 8.11 - Calculating the Return on Assets for Kearney's Crazy Kazoos (in millions of dollars)

The fourth of our five financial ratios, *financial leverage*, indicates the degree to which a company is using borrowed finances. Companies must perform a delicate balancing act when trying to achieve a good financial leverage ratio. Some financial leverage is desirable because of the tax breaks it can bring, but too much leverage can place a company in risk of bankruptcy. Financial leverage is calculated by dividing a company's total assets by its net worth, also know as shareholder's equity, with values both found on the company's Balance Sheet.

In our Kearney's Balance, the total assets value (found in line 12) was $1075 million and the net worth (found in line 23), also called the total shareholder equity, was $540 million. The financial leverage can then be calculated by dividing $1075 million (total assets) by $540 million (net worth), equaling 1.99. (The financial leverage ratio is typically expressed as a decimal number.)

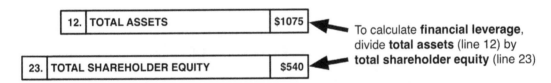

Figure 8.12 - Calculating the Financial Leverage for Kearney's Crazy Kazoos (in millions of dollars)

Our fifth and final financial ratio, *return on net worth*, also called *return on equity (ROE)*, reflects the ability of a company to obtain a return on the capital invested by its shareholders. Shareholders typically compare a company's return on net worth ratio to those of the other companies in the same industry. The return on net worth is calculated by dividing a company's net profit, found on its Income Statement, by its net worth, also know as shareholder's equity, found on the company's Balance Sheet

In our Kearney's Income Statement, the net profit after interest and taxes value (found in line 17) was $442.2 million. In our Kearney's Balance Sheet, the net worth (found in line 23), also called the total shareholder equity, was $540 million. The return on net worth can then be calculated by dividing $442.2 (net profit) million by $540 million (net worth), equaling 0.8189 or 81.89%. (The return on net worth ratio is typically expressed as a percentage.)

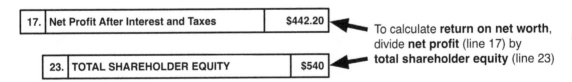

Figure 8.13 - Calculating the Return on Net Worth for Kearney's Crazy Kazoos (in millions of dollars)

A visual tool used to see a clear map of all of these ratios and the impact various items on financials statements have on a company's bottom line is the ***DuPont model***, also known as the ***strategic profit model***. The model was created in 1914 by F. Donaldson Brown, a former electrical engineer who was working for the DuPont chemical company's Treasury department. Brown developed the model after DuPont purchased 23% of General Motors Corporation and he was given the task of cleaning up GM's messy finances. The DuPont model continues to be used by companies today to get an instant overview of critical financial figures and ratios and to analyze their profitability. Logistics and supply chain managers find the model extremely useful in illustrating the impact of logistics expenses on a company's bottom line and revealing the financial implications of changes to logistics expenditures and inventory holding.

Shown in Figure 8.14 is an example of the DuPont model, modified to highlight logistics expenses, using figures taken from the Kearney's Income Statement and Balance Sheet discussed in the previous sections of this chapter.

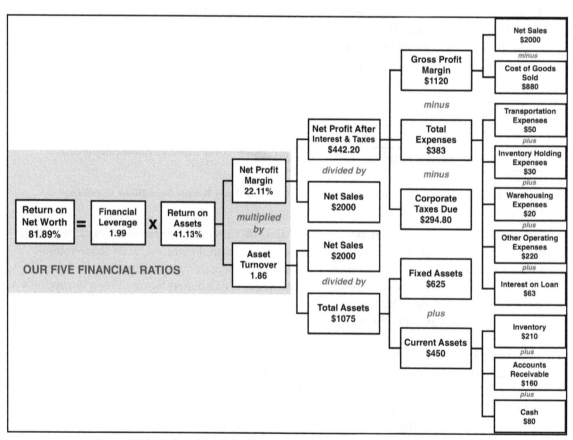

Figure 8.14 - DuPont Model for Kearney's Crazy Kazoos (in millions of dollars)

The DuPont Model illustrates the mathematical relationships between various figures on an income statement and a balance sheet and how they create a company's financial indicators, i.e., our five financial ratios. As shown in the model on the previous page, the DuPont Model is arranged so that values taken from the income statement are typically found in the top half of the model and are used to calculate the net profit. The values taken from the balance sheet are typically found in the bottom half of the model and are used to calculate the total assets.

Where Did All the Numbers in Our DuPont Model Come From?

The values used to calculate the ratios on the DuPont Model are taken from a company's Income Statement and its Balance Sheet. The values on the top half of the DuPont Model come from the Income Statement. The values on the bottom half of the DuPont Model come from the Balance Sheet.

Can **you** find all the DuPont Model's values on Kearney's Income Statement and Balance Sheet in Figures 8.1 and 8.6?

Logistics and supply chain managers can use the DuPont Model when speaking with CEOs and upper level company executive about logistics-related expenses. For example, they can use the model to show how changes they have made in logistics management have not only decreased logistics-related operating costs, such as warehousing and transportation, but have also had a positive impact on the company's financial bottom line, such an increased return on assets.

Logistics and supply chain managers can also use the DuPont Model to convince CEOs and upper level executives to make desired logistics management changes by comparing the current situation to the proposed one, thus illustrating the impact these changes could have on the company's financial ratios. For example, let's again consider the case of Kearney's Crazy Kazoos. You are again the Logistics Manager and you would like to make a case for proposed changes to the CEO. Although the company is doing very well financially, you see significant room for improvement in the area of inventory holding.

A year ago, you purchased a streamlined, top-of-the-art automatic storage/ retrieval system which, when installed, could cut your inventory holding expenses in half. Your problem is that the Warehouse Manager, who happens to be the CEO's brother, refuses to install and use the system because he argues, "Things are just fine the way they are." You mentioned this to the CEO last year and told him about all the positive benefits the new systems would bring, such as faster order picking times and decreased costs. The CEO, normally an innovative thinker and receptive to change, simply replied, "Let's just wait and see what happens."

Now that a year has passed and the new inventory equipment is still uninstalled and unused, you decide to again approach the CEO about the automatic storage/retrieval system and the positive effect its use would have on Kearney's bottom line. This time, however, you crunch the numbers and draft a DuPont Model to show the CEO the exact impact the Warehouse Manager's refusal to use the new system is having on the company's financial ratios.

Shown in Figure 8.15 is the DuPont Model with Kearney's current income statement, balance sheet, and financial ratio ratios alongside the updated values that would result if the new inventory equipment was used and the inventory holding costs were cut in half.

As seen in the reconfigured DuPont model on the previous page, if the new automatic storage/ retrieval system was put to use, the 50% reduction in inventory holding costs it would bring welcome ripples of change to the company's entire financial picture. Kearney's net profit would increase by a whopping $9 million, from $442.2 to $451 .2 million! Three of its financial ratios (the net profit margin, the return on assets, and the return on net worth) would also increase, with the ever-important return on net worth increasing by over 1.5%, from 81.89% to 83.50%!

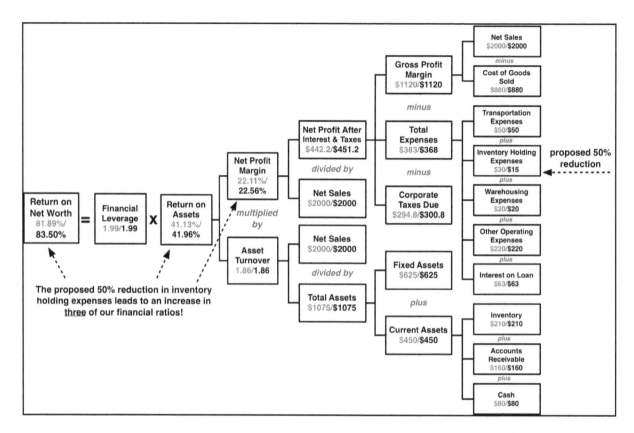

Figure 8.15 - DuPont Model for Kearney's Crazy Kazoos Comparing Original Values & Ratios (on left) to New Values & Ratios (on right) After a Proposed 50% Reduction in Inventory Holding Expenses (in millions of dollars)

After showing the Kearney's CEO your well-outlined DuPont Model, he will immediately march straight down to the warehouse, have a heart-to-heart talk with his brother (with your DuPont Model in hand), and authorize immediate use of the new automatic storage/retrieval system. As a current or future leader in the world of logistics, understanding income statements, balances sheets, financial ratios, and the DuPont Model will help you understand and communicate effectively with an organization's decision-makers, whose ultimate language is the language of money.

A Look at the Inventory Turnover Ratio

Another financial ratio of great interest to logistics and supply chain managers is the inventory turnover ratio. Below is a description of the inventory turnover ratio from the *U.S. Securities and Exchange Commission's Beginners' Guide to Financial Statements*.

The **inventory turnover ratio** compares a company's cost of sales on its income statement with its average inventory balance for the period. To calculate the average inventory balance for the period, look at the inventory numbers listed on the balance sheet. Take the balance listed for the period of the report and add it to the balance listed for the previous comparable period, and then divide by two. (Remember that balance sheets are snapshots in time. So the inventory balance for the previous period is the beginning balance for the current period, and the inventory balance for the current period is the ending balance.)

To calculate the inventory turnover ratio, you divide a company's cost of goods sold (just below the net revenues on the income statement) by the average inventory for the period, or

INVENTORY TURNOVER RATIO = COST OF GOODS SOLD / AVERAGE INVENTORY (BY PERIOD)

If a company has an inventory turnover ratio of 2 to 1, it means that the company's inventory turned over twice in the reporting period.

Time to get to work! Let's now calculate the 2014 inventory turnover ratio for Kearney's Krazy Kazoos using the data already provided throughout this chapter. We can find the **cost of goods sold** on line 5 of the Kearney's Krazy Kazoos 2014 Income Statement in Figure 8.1. Therefore, the cost of goods sold in 2014 was **$880 (in millions)**.

Let's now find the **average inventory** for 2014 for Kearney's Krazy Kazoos. To calculate the annual average inventory, we must find the average of the company's opening inventory and closing inventory. Both values can be found in the Kearney's Krazy Kazoos Income Statement for 2014 in Figure 8.1. The **opening inventory**, found in line 2, was $200 (in millions) and the **closing inventory**, found in line 4, was $210 (in millions). Therefore, the average inventory for 2014 is:

average inventory = (opening inventory + closing inventory) / 2

average inventory = ($200 million + $210 million) / 2

average inventory = $205 million

We now have all the data we need and are ready to calculate the inventory turnover ratio for Kearney's Krazy Kazoos for 2014.

inventory turnover ratio = cost of goods sold/average inventory

inventory turnover ratio = $880 million / $205 million

inventory turnover ratio = 4.2926, rounded to 4.3

Therefore, the inventory turnover ratio for Kearney's Krazy Kazoos for 2014 was 4.3, which means that the company's inventory turned over more than four times in the 2014 reporting period.

CHAPTER 8 REVIEW QUESTIONS

1. What is the difference between a shareholder and a stakeholder? Can someone be both a shareholder and a stakeholder in the same company?

2. What is the purpose of an income statement? How frequently is one calculated and issued by a company?

3. When numbers are written in parentheses in financial statements, what does this mean? What mistakes do you think might occur if these numbers were not written in parentheses? What is another alternative to writing these numbers in parentheses?

4. What is a gross profit margin? How is it calculated?

5. What are some of the logistics-related expenses that might be found on an income statement? Do all companies separate and highlight logistics operating expenses on their income statements? Why or why not might logistics-related expenses be a useful part of an income statement?

6. What is the purpose of a balance sheet? How frequently is one calculated and issued by a company?

7. How is a balance sheet structured? What does each half represent?

8. What is the difference between current assets and fixed assets? What are some examples of each?

9. What is the shareholders' equity? What are its two primary components? How is it calculated?

10. What are financial ratios? What is their relationship to the DuPont Model?

CHAPTER 8 CASE STUDY

Toby's Troublesome Toys: Part 1

Toby's Troublesome Toys is Kearney's Crazy Kazoos' oldest competitor. You have just been hired by Toby's Troublesome Toys as the company's Logistics Manager. You have just learned the following facts about your new employer:

- Toby's Troublesome Toys made $1000 million in sales in 2014.

- The company's opening inventory at the beginning of 2014 was $100 million and its closing inventory at the end of 2014 was $200 million.

- Throughout 2014, Toby's made $500 million in purchases.

- The company spent $30 million on transportation, $30 million on inventory holding expenses, and $40 million on warehousing expenses.

- Toby's also spent $300 million on other operating expenses.

- Toby's does not have any long-term loans and its corporate tax rate is 30%.

Case Study Assignment: Part 1

1. Using the information provided and the format shown in Figure 8.1 earlier in this chapter, prepare a 2014 Income Statement for Toby's Troublesome Toys.

Toby's Troublesome Toys: Part 2

As the Logistics Manager of Toby's Troublesome Toys, you have learned a few additional facts about your new employer:

- Toby's Troublesome Toys currently has $50 million in cash, $50 million in accounts receivable, and $200 million in inventory.

- The company's buildings are worth $400 million, its land is worth $100 million, and its facilities and equipment are worth $200 million.

- Toby's currently has a whopping $800 million due in accounts payable.

- The company has no long-tern loans.

- Toby's has $50 Million in shareholder's retained earnings and $150 million shareholders' invested capital.

Case Study Assignment: Part 2

2. Using this new information you have acquired, prepare a Balance Sheet for Toby's Troublesome Toys following the format shown in Figure 8.6 earlier in this chapter.

3. Using the values you have already calculated on the income statement and balance sheet for Toby's Troublesome Toys, now complete a DuPont model for the company following the format shown in Figure 8.14.

Toby's Troublesome Toys: Part 3

As the new Logistics Manager for Toby's Troublesome Toys, you are responsible for all the Logistics functions of Purchasing, Warehouse, Inventory Management, and Transportation. You have proposed to implement new systems that will reduce inventory holding costs by 20%, warehousing costs by 15%, and transportation costs by 10%. The CEO of Toby's Troublesome Toys, Samuel Stuckinthemud, is reluctant to make any changes and believes that the proposed reductions would have little impact on the corporate bottom line.

Case Study Assignment: Part 3

4. To convince the CEO of Toby's Troublesome Toys to make your proposed changes that would reduce inventory holding costs by 20%, warehousing costs by 15%, and transportation costs by 10%, create a new income statement like the one shown earlier in Figure 8.5 to highlight how these reductions would impact the company's 2014 income statement you already created in question 1 above.

Chapter 9

Logistics & the Supply Chain in the
Global Environment

Made in...?

Right now, take off one of your shoes. Take a deep breath, hold your nose, and venture to take a look at the "Made In" label inside it. I'd be willing to bet a good spaghetti dinner that they were not made in your city or even your country! Now, for the rest of the day, ask everyone you meet to take a shoe off to see where it was made. Although some countries may be more heavily represented than others, you are likely to find an entire United Nations of footwear. Why then, aren't our shoes made by a local neighborhood cobbler anymore? Why aren't 99% of the durable goods around us made in our hometowns?

Our world has become a global marketplace. Most of the goods we buy and use every day are from different parts of the world. Most large U.S. manufacturers generate significant portions of their sales and purchases overseas. Even those companies that we have traditionally been associated with the culture and history of one country have "gone global" in both their manufacturing and sales efforts. For example, Deere & Company, the manufacturers of John Deere agricultural equipment so many of us associate with farmers in America's heartland, employs 47,000 people in 27 countries worldwide and has factories overseas in Canada, India, and Germany.

As companies "Go Global," the role of logistics moves from very important to absolutely critical. Greater geographic, political, legal, and cultural distances and differences must now be traversed to move goods from raw materials to consumers, making logistics costs a significant portion of overall product costs. Therefore, it is essential for a logistics manager to understand the global market environment and how to manage logistics and supply chains effectively to minimize cost, minimize delivery time, maximize handling conditions, and increase customer service.

INTERNATIONAL MARKET ENTRY

International trade has become a fact of life for large businesses. According to the World Trade Organization's *International Trade Statistics 2011*, over $10 trillion of merchandise was exported from countries around the world in 2005, representing a staggering 13% increase from the previous year! But why are companies choosing to leave the safety and security of their home markets and venture into the vast, unknown waters of the global arena?

Companies choose to expand their operations from domestic to global for a variety of reasons, including:

Access to more consumers. Expanding from a local or domestic customer base to a global one can dramatically increase the number of customers who buy a company's products. For an America soft drink manufacturer, for example, its domestic market is the U.S. population of over 300 million people. Although this may sound like a large enough market, why stop there when the soft drink company could expand its market to the entire world's population, which, as of 2013, the United States Census Bureau estimates to be 7.082 billion. That's over seven billion people!

Less expensive production costs. Many countries around the world have lower production costs because of lower cost-of-living and standard-of-living, making labor costs much lower. Countries may also have lower production costs because of their proximity to raw materials or national financial incentives to set up manufacturing facilities there. Companies often choose to relocate their production facilities to countries with lower production costs so that they can get a greater return for their shareholders and pass savings on to their customers.

Product interest waning in domestic market. Companies may sometimes have to expand their market globally because their domestic customers are no longer interested in their product. For example, because the numbers of smokers in the United States has plummeted over the past twenty years, cigarette manufacturers moved aggressively to Asian markets to stay afloat and sustain profitability.

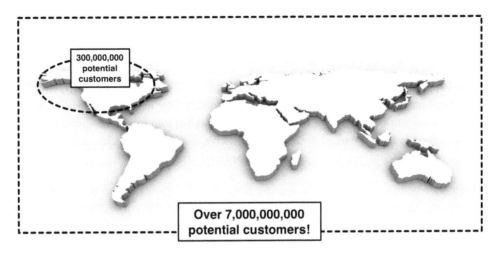

Figure 9.1 - Global Market Entry Allows Access to Many More Potential Customers!

Increased foreign competition in company's domestic market. A company may also find that its customer base in its domestic market is dwindling because foreign competitors have moved in. For example, in the latter part of the twentieth century, Mars, Inc., a U.S.-based chocolate candy manufacturer, began to move into a variety of world markets, including the United Kingdom. Because it offered a variety of new products, Mars became quite successful in the U.K., hurting the sales of local candy manufacturer, Cadbury Schweppes. Cadbury then decided to regain its solid customer base by moving into international markets, including the United States, the home turf of Mars. Today, both candy companies are highly successful in both the U.S. and U.K. markets.

Now that you know why companies enter global markets, let's look at how they enter them. When a company does decide to enter a new foreign market, it selects a market entry strategy, the mode of ownership and operations in this new market. A company's market entry strategy may vary according to the politics, culture, market size, location, geography, and transportation infrastructure of that country.

As the company continues to operate in the market, it develops its market operating strategy, a modified mode of ownership and operations in this market. A company may use the same market entry and operating strategies or, after entering the market with one strategy, it may find that a different strategy is more beneficial to continue operation in that market.

Five examples of market entry and operating strategies are:

- *Indirect exporting.* This strategy occurs when a company uses an independent intermediary to export its product. A representative of the company may actually never even set foot in the target country! Compared to the next four strategies, this market entry strategy requires the least cost and risk for the company, but also typically produces the lowest levels of profit overall. For example, in a small country or a new, untested market, a company may choose to use indirect exporting to "test the waters" to see how its product will do in that new market before placing any of its valuable financial assets or resources there.

- **_Direct exporting._** When a company decides to export its products on its own to the desired foreign market, it engages in the somewhat riskier and potentially more profitable market entry strategy of direct exporting. When engaging in direct exporting, a company may use: a domestic-based export division, an overseas sales branch or subsidiary, traveling export sales representatives, or foreign-based distributors or agents. Companies with large, expensive products often use direct exporting for smaller and newer markets. In these situations, a company might find it too expensive to set up extensive production or distribution operations but would benefit from having highly knowledgeable sales reps to market and represent the company's products in these markets.

- **_Licensing._** If a company decides to grant a license to another firm so that it may produce the original company's product, use its production processes, or use its brand name, it engages in the market entry strategy of licensing. With licensing comes low cost and low risk, but the main company (the licensor) often has little control over strategy, marketing, and manufacturing. It also cannot benefit from experience curve effects or location economies.

- **_Joint venture._** A joint venture occurs when two or more otherwise independent companies join to form a new company, sharing knowledge, cost, risk, and profits. Joint ventures with local partners often ease a company's entry into foreign markets, providing political advantage and access to local market knowledge. Large consumer goods companies that need to produce a large volume of products and get them to customers in a new market often use this strategy. For example, both The Coca-Cola Company and PepsiCo frequently form joint ventures with local enterprises when entering new foreign markets. Although the companies import some ingredients, soft drink bottling is far more cost effective when done as close to the customer as possible. Therefore, both companies must set up full-scale bottling plants when entering a new market. Partnering with a local enterprise for a joint venture helps them defray cost, minimize risk, and get immediate knowledge of the local market.

WHERE IN THE WORLD IS THIS?

Figure 9.2 - Thanks to joint ventures with local partners, the production and bottling of popular soft drinks occurs worldwide!

- **_Wholly owned subsidiary._** If a company sets up an operation in a foreign country and owns 100% of the stock, it is a wholly owned subsidiary. The company may set up a new operation or it may purchase an existing operation to produce and/or promote its product. With wholly owned subsidiaries, companies have complete control over strategy, marketing, and manufacturing. Although the wholly owned subsidiary strategy presents a company with the highest cost and greatest risk of all market entry and operating strategies, it also provides the potential to reap the greatest profits.

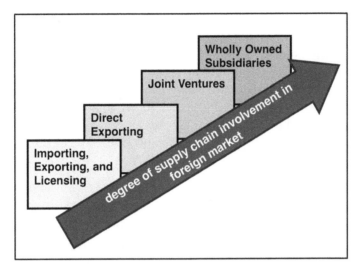

Figure 9.3 - The Relationship Between Market Strategy and Supply Chain Involvement

The nature and complexity of a company's supply chain within a foreign market is related to the market entry and operations strategy of that company. For companies that are less directly involved with a foreign market (such as those with exporting and licensing strategies), their supply chains are shorter and logistics operation simpler. For companies that are more directly involved with a foreign market (such as those with joint venture and wholly owned subsidiary strategies), their supply chains are longer and their logistics operation more complex.

TRADE AGREEMENTS AROUND THE WORLD

To promote and protect international commercial trade, countries set up trade agreements with other countries around the world. A trade agreement is a contractual agreement concerning the trade relationship between nations. Trade agreements may be bilateral, i.e., between two nations, or multilateral, i.e., between more than two nations.

Bilateral and multilateral trade agreements often establish areas of trade covered under the agreement. A free trade area (FTA) is a set group of countries that have agreed to eliminate or minimize tariffs (such as customs duties), product quotas, and other restriction for goods traveling across the FTA countries' borders. NAFTA and the European Union are examples of FTAs. A trade bloc is a large free trade area that is formed by formal trade, tariff, and tax agreements between its countries. Again, NAFTA and the EU are examples of trade blocs.

A regional trade agreement (RTA) is a term used by the World Trade Organization (WTO) when two or more of its members enter into a regional trade arrangement presenting more favorable trade conditions (such as minimization or elimination of tariffs, quotas, and other restrictions) to each other than to other WTO members. The sea of politics and economics gets a bit murky here because the terms free trade area, trade bloc, and regional trade agreement often mean the same thing or apply to the same relationships. It all really depends on the agreement and whom you ask!

According to its website **www.wto.itn**, the World Trade Organization (WTO) is: "the only international organization dealing with the global rules of trade between nations. Its main function is to ensure that trade flows as smoothly, predictably and freely as possible." As of January 2013, the WTO reported that there are currently more than 350 ***regional trade agreements (RTAs)*** with possibly 200 more to be added. What all RTAs in the WTO have in common is that they are reciprocal trade agreements between two or more partners. More information on existing and possible future RTAs is available in the WTO RTA Database at **http://rtais.wto.org/?lang=1**.

Some of the more widely known RTAs include:

- **the European Communities (EC)**, whose members include Austria, Belgium, Bulgaria, Cyprus, the Czech Republic, Denmark, Estonia, Finland, France, Germany, Greece, Hungary, Ireland, Italy, Latvia, Lithuania, Luxembourg, Malta, Poland, Portugal, Romania, the Slovak Republic, Slovenia, Spain, Sweden, The Netherlands, and the United Kingdom;

- **the North American Free Trade Agreement (NAFTA)**, whose members include Canada, Mexico, and the United States;

- **the Southern Common Market (MERCOSUR)**, whose members include Argentina, Brazil, Paraguay, and Uruguay;

- **the Association of Southeast Asian Nations (ASEAN)**, whose members include Brunei, Darussalam, Cambodia, Indonesia, Laos, Malaysia, Myanmar, the Philippines, Singapore, Thailand, and Vietnam; and

- **the Common Market of Eastern and Southern Africa (COMESA)**, whose members include Angola, Burundi, Comoros, the Democratic Republic of Congo, Djibouti, Egypt, Eritrea, Ethiopia, Kenya, Madagascar, Malawi, Mauritius, Namibia, Rwanda, Seychelles, Sudan, Swaziland, Uganda, Zambia, and Zimbabwe.

The ***North American Free Trade Agreement (NAFTA)*** between the United States, Canada, and Mexico, which came into effect on January 1, 1994, has definite implications for logistics and supply chain management. NAFTA's goal is to remove trade barriers, allowing companies to easily conduct cross-border business. It is phasing out trade tariffs between its members. However, because it is still in its early days, NAFTA poses many challenges to the logistics environment, including: packaging and labeling laws (three countries with three national languages and different cultural preferences), a poor transportation infrastructure in Mexico, and different levels of information technology infrastructures.

Another international trade factor with implications for logistics in the U.S. are the growth of maquiladoras in Mexico and, more recently, other parts of Latin America. A ***maquiladora*** is a foreign factory in Mexico that imports materials and equipment (duty-free and tariff-free), assembles or manufactures goods, and then exports them, typically back to the company's home country. Most Mexican maquiladora factories are owned by U.S companies representing a wide variety of industries, including transportation, electronics, textiles, and machinery. Maquiladoras may be 100% foreign-owned, but they may also be a joint venture between both foreign and local companies.

Figure 9.4 - The Road to Maquiladoras in Mexico and the Gateway to Free Trade Zones in China. Completed in 2003, la Entrada al Pacifico or "the corridor to the Pacific" (pictured left), runs through Texas and northern Mexico and ends at a port on the Pacific Ocean. Many maquiladoras are located along this highway, which was constructed jointly by the United States and Mexico. Across the Pacific Ocean, Shanghai, China (pictured right) is traditionally known for its history of commerce and is now active in the global market through its Waigaoqiao Free Trade Zone.

Finally, along with the RTA and the maquiladoras is the ***free trade zone (FTZ)***, also called an ***export processing zone (EPZ)***, an area within a country in which tariffs, quotas, and bureaucratic requirements have been eliminated or minimized to attract foreign companies by providing incentives for doing business there. FTZs are beneficial to the countries in which they are based because they generate employment opportunities and foster development of export-oriented industries. While the idea of free trade zones began in Latin America in the first half of the twentieth century, there are now more than 3000 FTZs in more than 100 countries worldwide producing a variety of goods, including electronics, clothes, shoes, and toys. Examples of FTZs are areas within Waigaoqiao FTZ in Shanghai, China and the Colón FTZ in Panama at the Atlantic gateway to the Panama Canal.

INTERNATIONAL TRADE DOCUMENTATION

As supply chains grow and span across more countries, increasing amounts of paperwork are required. In the world of international trade, such documentation is a necessity. Without accurate and timely paperwork, companies would not be permitted to trade outside their own countries. Exporters, importers, shipping companies, freight forwarders, banks, insurance companies, the regulating authorities of the countries both importing and exporting the goods, consular offices, chambers of commerce, and a massive battery of attorneys are all involved in ensuring that a global supply chain's complex network of documentation is completed.

While there are thousands of different trade documentation forms that vary from country to country and from company to company, there are six primary categories of trade documentation. Some forms of documentation may span two or more of these categories when used by multiple parties for multiple functions. In addition, the amount of documentation required may vary according to the nature of the goods and the regulations of the countries importing and exporting the goods.

The six categories of trade documentation are:

- **Transaction documents.** Also found in domestic trade, transaction documents are those documents exchanged between a buyer and a seller as part of the agreement to sell and/or purchase goods. Examples of transaction documents include: RFPs (Request for Proposal), proposals, purchase orders, sales contracts, and commercial invoices.

- **Export documents.** Documents required by the export authority of a country are called export documents. When completed and approved, these documents allow goods to leave a country. Export documentation varies according to the country of export and the goods involved. Examples of export documents include: export licenses and permits, Bill of Lading, export declaration and inspection certificates, and Certificate of Origin.

LOGISTICS LINGO

Bill of Lading

A **Bill of Lading** (also referred to as **BOL** or **B/L**) is a document issued by a carrier.

It acknowledges that specific, listed goods have been received as cargo for conveyance to a specific, listed place for delivery to an identified consignee.

- **Carrier documents.** Carrier documents are those documents issued and used by a carrier or transportation provider such as a barge or shipping line, a railroad, an airline, an international trucking company, a freight forwarder, or a 3PLP. Examples of carrier documents include: Bill of Lading and insurance and inspection certificates.

- **Import documents.** Those documents required by the import authorities of a country are called import documents. When completed and approved, these documents allow goods to enter a country. Import documentation varies according to the country of import and the goods involved. Examples of import documents include: import licenses and permits, commercial invoices, Bill of Lading, Certificate of Origin Import Declaration, and inspection certificates.

- **Banking documents.** Banking documents are those documents required by the banks participating in international transactions. The types and degree of banking documentation required is influenced by the regulations and banking practices of the importing and

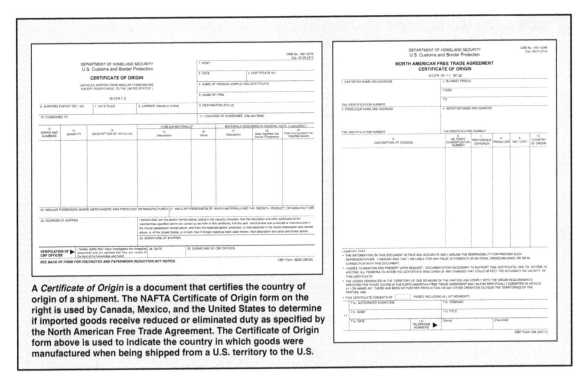

Figure 9.5 - Examples of Certificate of Origin Forms

exporting countries involved. Examples of banking documents include all documents associated with company credit issues.

- **Goods-specific documents.** Finally, goods-specific documents are those documents required for import and/or export based on special requirements for the nature of the items being trades. Goods-specific documents are typically required for international trade of goods including: arms and ammunition, radioactive materials, animals, and food products.

In exploring the world of international trade documentation, we must also discuss ***INCOTERMS***. International Commercial Terms, or INCOTERMS, are standardized international trade terms that describe the obligations of both the buyers and the sellers under the contract of sale. Specifically, INCOTERMS are a set of eleven terms created and published by the International Chamber of Commerce (ICC) that clearly outline and allocate the costs, risk, customs, and insurance responsibilities of each the buyer and the seller in the international transaction. They are accepted by governments and other legal entities worldwide for terms used in international trade. By themselves, INCOTERMS are not contractually or legally binding, but they are regularly included in buyer and seller contracts around the world.

Each of the eleven INCOTERMS is referred to by a three-letter abbreviation. According to their most recent update in 2012, the complete list of INCOTERMS, along with a brief explanation of each, is:

- **EXW or Ex Works.** The exporter must make the goods available for collection from his premises by the importer or the importer's agent. The goods are generally packed ready for shipment.

- **FCA or Free Carrier.** The exporter will transport the goods to an Inland Clearance Depot (ICD), where they will be consolidated into a larger consignment ready for shipment by an intermodal carrier.

- **FAS or Free Alongside Ship** (waterway transport only). The exporter delivers the goods alongside the ship that will carry the goods overseas. This is where the responsibility of the exporter ends. The Purchaser bears all costs and risks from this point on.

- **FOB or Free on Board** (waterway transport only). The goods are delivered by the exporter to the port of export, where they then become the responsibility of the importer as soon as they are loaded over the ship' side rail. The Purchaser bears the loss if the goods should fall and become damaged just after being loaded onto the ship.

- **CFR or Cost and Freight** (waterway transport only). The seller must pay the costs and freight as far as the port of destination, but the risk passes to the Purchaser as the goods cross the ship's rail in the port of shipment.

- **CIF or Cost, Insurance and Freight** (waterway transport only). The seller is in the same position as in CFR but must also provide marine insurance during the carriage. The risk passes to the Purchaser as the goods cross the ship's rails, but the insurance policy covers the Purchaser's risk.

- **CPT or Carriage Paid to**. The seller pays the freight and the risk passes to the Purchaser once the goods are delivered to the first carrier, regardless of the type of transportation used.

- **CIP or Carriage and Insurance Paid to**. The terms are the same as in CPT, but the seller also has to insure the goods for all modes of transportation to the Purchaser's destination. The risk transfers to the Purchaser when the goods are given into the custody of the first carrier, after which point the risk is covered by the insurance policy.

- **DAT or Delivered at Terminal**. The seller pays for delivery to the terminal, not including import clearance costs, and assumes all risk until the goods are unloaded at the terminal.

- **DAP or Delivered at Place**. The seller pays for delivery to the named place or destination, not including import clearance costs, and assumes all risk until the goods are ready to be unloaded by the buyer.

- **DDP or Delivered Duty Paid**. This represents a maximum commitment from the seller and a minimum one from the Purchaser. The seller delivers to the Purchaser after paying the import duty to the country of destination.

THE INTERNATIONAL SUPPLY CHAIN ENVIRONMENT

In the world of global logistics, companies typically deal with countries and cultures quite different from their own. When a company expands its operations from domestic to global, it faces many new challenges, including country-to-country differences in: culture and language; politics, economics, and currencies; business practices and norms (Bribery may be the norm!); time zones and attitudes toward time; required documentation and contracts; and security and types of legal recourse when infractions occur. Even between two countries that have relatively similar cultures and who speak the same language, words, demeanor, tone of voice, and body language can send confusing and conflicting messages. For example, English-speaking logistics managers in both the United States and England sometimes use very different words to describe the same thing, as in the case of "18-wheeled tractor-trailer" (US) versus "articulated lorry" (UK).

Therefore, before engaging in international supply chain relationships, it is important to learn as much as you can about the many countries and regions through which your supply chain passes. It is then important to consider the ways in which these countries and regions might have an impact on your company's logistics and supply chain management. While logistics and supply chain management may be influenced by the wide variety of practices, procedures, customs, and capabilities in each country, these context-based (i.e., country specific) influences typically fall within one of three categories: *political/legal*; *economic*; and *social/cultural*.

Examples of **political/legal factors** that might influence the management of global supply chains include a country's:

- **Political climate.** When a country is in political turmoil, this wreaks obvious havoc on supply chains. After the dissolution of the Soviet Union in 1991, for example, many Russian-foreign joint ventures quickly formed and folded because of the difficulty of getting goods to customers largely because the foreign partners did not understand the nature and location of political power within Russia at the time.

- **Attitude toward foreign trade.** Countries with more positive attitudes toward foreign trade are generally much easier on international companies with local supply chain operations because these countries have considerable economic support, often from the IMF (International Monetary Fund) and other economic communities. Countries with less positive attitudes don't have this economic support and often impose restrictions on foreign companies, including license requirements, tariffs, taxes, quotas, complicated customs procedures, and discriminatory government and private procurement policies, all of which make supply chains far more expensive and challenging to operate.

- **Government stability.** The stability and reliability of a country's election process and the consistency and predictability of its policies and practices (e.g., regarding taxes, profits, and ownership rights) can also influence international supply chains. For example, in a 1996 study of the domestic and international operations of Hungarian businesses published in the *International Journal of Physical Distribution and Logistics Management*, Atilla Chikan found that Hungary's embargo against Yugoslavia cost the nation $50 million (US) in distribution channel and supply chain management costs.

- **Legal system.** A country's legal factors that can influence international supply chain management include: legal understanding and accountability, protection of patents and trademarks, freedom in market competition, recourse for dispute adjudication, and adherence to international laws. One of the most commonly cited legal factors affecting international logistics management in many emerging and less-developed economies around the world is corruption and the lack of legal recourse of companies to counteract it. In these countries, companies' distribution channels are competing against an array of informal vendors. These informal vendors, often selling smuggled goods, can make consumer demand almost impossible to estimate. They also pose particular problems for strategic planning, alliances, and corporate control of global brands and pricing. In these markets, the same global brands can be competing alongside one another, with only their means of distribution, traditional distribution or smuggling, separating them. (I.e., a Snickers bar that was marketed and distributed by Mars, Inc. might be competing side-by-side in an Uzbekistan market stall against a Snickers bar that "fell off the back of a truck" in Russia and was smuggled into Uzbekistan.)

Figure 9.6 - Informal vendors with small market stalls are prevalent in developing and less developed economies.

Examples of **economic factors** that might influence the management of global supply chains include a country's:

- **Economic orientation.** Often, the degree to which a country embraces a capitalist economic orientation has a significant influence on supply chain operations in that country. People in many of the world's developing, transitioning, and less-developed economies are more worried about product availability and less accustomed to streamlined logistics management practices, such as Just-In-Time. As a result, companies in these countries sometimes use hoarding as a means of assuring supply, resulting in production delays due to material shortages, which then means longer lead times and late deliveries.

- **Geography.** A country's physical barriers and geographic distances can also influence the speed and cost of its supply chains. For example, the cost and speed of getting goods manufactured in Japan to a remote village in the Himalayas would be far greater than getting the same goods to a port city in India, although the distances to the two locations would be the same.

- **Location and concentration of buying power.** The goal of a supply chain is to get goods to customers. When many customers are located in or near the same place, companies can achieve an economy of scale and supply chain costs can decrease. (As a fun little experiment, start in a large metropolitan area and note the price of a gallon of milk. Then, take a drive further and further from the city into a remote area. Stop at store every thirty miles or so and notice how the price of milk increases.)

Because global businesses are now so heavily reliant on information technology systems for day-to-day operations, the reliability of a nation's energy infrastructure plays a significant role in a company's decision to place critical logistics operations there.

Figure 9.7- The Importance of a Nation's Energy Infrastructure

- **Infrastructure.** A country's energy, communications, and transportation systems form its infrastructure, the backbone that allows businesses and individuals to operate as quickly, conveniently, and easily as they do. International supply chains are largely at the mercy of the infrastructures of the countries in which they operate. Countries with poor or outdated telecommunications networks, road systems in disrepair, and frequent power outages all cause significant supply chain delays and increased costs.

Finally, examples of **social/economic factors** that might influence the management of global supply chains include a country's:

- **Language differences.** Language difference is one of the most obvious external influences on international business. Companies are also finding that it is a barrier to effective international logistics management. For example, there are three different languages spoken within NAFTA's three countries. These language differences along with NAFTA's labeling requirements have posed many challenges to the logistics management of North American companies, from communicating effectively with the logistics-related workforce to ensuring that all product labeling is both correct in all three languages and NAFTA-compliant.

Figure 9.8 - Accepting a Business Card or Cultural Insult?

- **Values and customs.** Differences between a company's home- and host-country values and customs often pose complex problems for effective logistics and supply chain management. Even something as simple as a business card can confound logistics managers when working abroad. For example, an American logistics manager, who typically travels with approximately 20 business cards in his/her wallet, may unknowingly insult Chinese suppliers when accepting their business cards in the normal American fashion (grasping the center or center edge of the business card between the thumb and edge of the forefinger) instead of the customary Chinese fashion (grasping each of the two bottom corners of the business card using the tips of the thumb and forefinger).

- **Personnel preparedness.** The degree to which a country's workforce is educated and prepared for logistics tasks can substantially influence the effectiveness of logistics and supply chain management in that country. Most global companies rely on hiring local mid-level to lower-level logistics managers because of their understanding of the local workforce, infrastructure, and economy. It is easier for these companies to achieve more immediate supply chain success when their locally savvy logistics managers also understand the concepts and practice of logistics and supply chain management.

In the increasingly vast and complex global marketplace, companies are reducing the learning curve of understanding a local host-country by relying on a variety of service providers to help them get their products to customers and end consumers. In the previous chapter, we explored transportation carriers (third parties that provide the mode and means of transportation). In a global supply chain, there are additional third party logistics service providers, known as 3PLPs, that also provide services critical to effective global transportation and supply chain management. These 3PLPs include:

- ***International freight forwarders***, who use their expertise and knowledge in the international shipping arena to assist companies in arranging shipments and preparing the correct documentation and packaging.

- ***Shipping brokers***, who facilitate communication and agreements between a ship owner and those chartering the shipment.

- ***Shipping agents***, who represent the ship and facilitate its arrival, clearance, unloading, and financial obligations at a port.

- ***Nonvessel Operating Common Carriers (NVOCC)***, who consolidate goods coming from a variety of companies and/or locations into container-loads for ocean or air freight.

- ***Export packers***, who provide packaging services to companies sending their products overseas. While some companies perform their own packaging function, others rely on export packers to ensure that they are in compliance with the various packaging regulations from country to country and from product to product.

- ***Customs brokers***, who similarly handle compliance issues for companies distributing their goods overseas. They ensure that a company completes the correct documentation and submits to the appropriate authorities within the correct timeframes according to the customs regulating authorities of both the exporting and importing countries. Customs regulations vary widely from country to country.

Whether or not a 3PLP is used, it is important for a logistics manager to understand the complexities of the countries in which its logistics and supply chains operate. An understanding or lack of understanding of a local operating environment can "make or break" a supply chain.

CHAPTER 9 REVIEW QUESTIONS

1. Why is it important for a logistics manager to understand the global market environment?

2. What is the difference between direct exporting and indirect exporting? Which market entry strategy would be more desirable for a company to use in a country undergoing significant turmoil and political upheaval?

3. In what types of situation would a wholly owned subsidiary be more beneficial than a joint venture market strategy? In what types of situations might the reverse be true?

4. What is a regional trade agreement? What benefits does it bring businesses operating in its member countries? Which well-known RTA includes the United States as one of its three members?

5. What is a free trade zone? How is this different from a free trade area?

6. What are import documents and export documents? How are they different and how are they similar? What are some examples of each?

7. What are some types of political/legal factors that might influence a global supply chain? What is an example of a political/legal factor in your country that might influence an international company's logistics and supply chain management?

8. What are some types of economic factors that might influence a global supply chain? What is an example of an economic factor in your country that might influence an international company's logistics and supply chain management?

9. What are some types of social/cultural factors that might influence a global supply chain? What is an example of a social/cultural factor in your country that might influence an international company's logistics and supply chain management?

10. What is the role of a customs broker in an international supply chain?

CHAPTER 9 CASE STUDY

CASE STUDY

The Race to Indonesia

Indonesia, a small island nation in southeast Asia, has recently caught the eye of a few of the world's large economies. Unnoticed or perhaps avoided for many years because of a national financial crisis in the late 1990s, Indonesia has become a very attractive market for foreign businesses. The country is politically stable, continues to experience a 6% annual growth, and has more that 30,000 people in its growing middle class. It is also southeast Asia's largest economy, due in large part to its role as the world's largest supplier of coal and palm oil. Indonesia is poised for economic development, with its burgeoning middle class clamoring to purchase a range of consumer goods previously unavailable to them.

Both China and the United States are currently trying to curry favor with this newly discovered gem of southeast Asia. In an April 2011 visit to Indonesia, Chinese premier Wen Jiabao offered the country $9 billion in loans for infrastructure development and a trade delegation accompanying him signed commercial agreements for $10 billion. Many signs indicate that China could be a suitable trade partner for Indonesia. It is located much closer; it may better understand the country's infrastructure needs, political challenges, and low-wage manufacturing industry; and it is free of regulatory measures imposed by countries such as the United States.

Despite its apparent plusses, China may not be an ideal trade partner for Indonesia. Although almost 20% of their country's goods come from China, many Indonesians are concerned with China's $4.7 billion trade surplus and its historic lack of investment. The market entry strategy for Chinese firms in Indonesia has been direct and indirect exporting, resulting in very little investment of local employees or the local economy. The market entry strategy for U.S. firms, however, tends to be joint venture agreements with local companies. As a result, in 2010, American companies invested $930 million in Indonesia while their Chinese counterparts invested only $170 million. Furthermore, when China has invested in Indonesia, it has been most interested in operations with low-wage factory workers. Conversely, the United States has displayed greater interest in the oil and gas, mining, and information technology sectors, all of which need a more highly skilled and educated workforce. To help Indonesia develop its workforce, the U.S. has established many educational exchanges with American universities.

China also faces long-term market entry challenges due to the very aspect that made it initially so successful in Indonesia: low prices. Initially, Chinese goods of inferior quality but very low prices were welcomed in the Indonesian market because that was what the consumers could afford. Now that the growing middle class can afford higher quality goods at higher prices, China has become synonymous with poor quality. Many Indonesian business people fear entering into business agreements with Chinese companies because of the history of quality problems and the need to renegotiate deals when things go wrong.

Interestingly, although China and Indonesia are both Asian nations, the United States may have an advantage in developing trade relationships with Indonesia because Indonesian business partners feel closer to their American counterparts socially. U.S. President Barack Obama is much beloved in Indonesia because he spent many of his formative years living there. U.S. business partners have also shown a willingness to work with local business partners to develop local employees and build long-term deals. Finally, many of Indonesia's upper class have spent time or been educated in the United States. Although China got a head start and occupies 20% of the consumer goods market, it remains to be seen who will end up as Indonesia's dominant trade partner.

References

Gordin, A. (2011, May 5) Beyond borders, the key to survival. *Business Finance.* Retrieved from http://businessfinancemag.com/article/beyond-borders-key-survival-0511.

Johnson, J. and Tellis, G. (2008, May) Drivers of success for market entry into China and India. *Journal of Marketing,* vol. 72.

Schonhardt, S. (2011, May 6) U.S., China vie for influence among Indonesian circles. *Asia Times Online.* Retrieved from http://www.atimes.com/atimes/Southeast_Asia/ME06Ae02.html.

Case Study Questions

1. What market entry strategies did companies from each China and the United States use to enter Indonesia's market? Why might different strategies have been used for companies from the two different countries?

2. What political/legal,economic, and social/cultural advantages or disadvantages do each China and the United States offer as a major trade partner for Indonesia?

3. What supply chain implications might each country and its political/legal,economic, and social/cultural factors have for operations in Indonesia?

Chapter 10

Customer Service in the World of Logistics

The big game is coming up in two weeks. Your hometown is competing in the national championship and everything is aflutter! You decide to have a huge party so that you and twenty of your closest friends can watch the game together. Deciding to dip in to your life savings, you go to the big box electronics store and select the biggest flat screen television they have. The sales person notes there are none in stock in their regional distribution center, but that it will only take a week for the television to arrive from the next closest distribution center. You plunk down a hefty 50% deposit onto the counter and schedule a delivery date exact one week before the big game.

Next, confident that the TV will be in place for the big event, you send out party invitations to your twenty closest friends, all of whom RSVP that they would be delighted to come! To prepare for the party, you begin to buy all the supplies you will need, including fifteen bags of tortilla chips from your local grocery store so you can make your "Artichoke Nacho Mountain" that everyone loves so much. You are very careful with the nacho bags and place them safely in your cupboard at home, knowing that crushed chips would ruin the aesthetically breathtaking effect of your nacho mountain.

A week before the big game, tragedy strikes. You wait all day for your 71" flat-screen television and no one shows up. When you call the store's customer service department at the end of the day, they are surprised to hear that your TV did not arrive, but they tell you that their delivery department is now closed and they will not be able to check on the status of your delivery until tomorrow. Early the next morning, you call the customer service department, who then checks with the delivery department who cannot locate your delivery records.

Five hours later, the customer service department calls you back to let you know that they have located your order and your television. They report that, unfortunately, the television was sent to the wrong store. The customer service employee then whispers conspiratorially under her breath that this happens all the time. She says that she will be happy to arrange a new delivery date for you next week. You tell her that you need the television this week because you bought it especially for the big game, which is only six days away on Sunday.

The customer service employee apologizes that there is no way to make this delivery on time because the trucks that run between the distribution center from which the television was incorrectly sent only run to this store on Mondays and, although today is a Monday, the truck has already left. When you ask about canceling my order and returning the $15,000 television to get my 50% deposit refunded, the customer service employee says that this will be no problem, but that you will have to pay a 10% restocking fee, equaling $1,500. When you then begin to scream and rant into the phone, she transfers you to the manager, who conveys the same information to you in a less polite tone. You then decide to accept the situation and accept the late delivery.

Trying to make the best of a bad situation, you charge ahead with the party plans, believing that you and your twenty friends can have just as much fun watching the game on your 29" television. You get all the ingredients needed to make your famous Artichoke Nacho Mountain. An hour before your party, you open the fifteen bags of tortilla chips to begin to construct your nacho mountain, only to find that every single bag has been crushed, leaving you with only thirteen chips still intact. You know that grocery store would gladly exchange the crushed chips for new bags, but there's just no time. Twenty guests will begin arriving in less than 60 minutes to watch the biggest game of your lives on a mediocre, undersized television while eating pulverized nachos!

Although your team won the game and party winded up being a huge success, you were very upset by the unnecessary stress you were forced to endure at the hands of the electronics and grocery stores. You immediately wrote complaint letters to the customer service departments of both. Although your contact to each company was through its customer service department, was this department the root of the problem? Although the electronics store could have provided better customer service to help you after the problems occurred, what really caused the problems of a late television and crushed tortilla chips? The root of your problems can be summed up in three words: poor logistics management.

The problems began when the product (the television) marketed within the store and selected by the customer (you) was not held in stock. Further logistics-related problems the distribution system broke down by delivering to the wrong location and not informing the customer. The existing physical distribution system and the customer service department did not work together to allow extra deliveries to be made between distribution centers off-schedule when problems arise. Finally, logistics-related problems topped off your day by causing the Terror of Nacho Mountain, i.e., fifteen bags of crushed tortilla chips. The crushed chips were the result of poor packaging, packing, and shipment, all of which could have been addressed with better logistics management practices.

Although it may not be immediately apparent, the worlds of customer service and logistics are inextricably linked. Many of the logistics management decisions a company makes directly influence the service the customer receives. This chapter will explore the relationship between logistics and customer service and how a logistics manager can measure and analyze logistics performance to improve customer service.

Before You Continue Reading, Consider...

What could the tortilla chip manufacturer and electronics superstore have done to change their logistics operations and management to create a better customer service experience?

UNDERSTANDING CUSTOMER SERVICE

Before we look at how logistics and customer service are related, let's explore what we mean by the terms *customer* and *customer service*. A **customer** is a party who receives a product or service from another party. Although we usually think of customers as people, customers may also be organizations. For example, Walmart is one of Coca-Cola's many customers. When looking at customer service, organizations must consider the service they provide to both individual people and other organizations.

Customers are also either *external* or *internal* to the organization providing the product or service. When we think of customers, we typically think of **external customers**, i.e., those who receive a product or service who are private individual end users or organizations other than the company providing the product or service. For example, when you buy a bag of tortilla chips from a grocery store or when the Taco House Restaurant chain buys the same chips from the tortilla chip manufacturer, you are both external customers.

Internal customers are those individuals or departments within an organization who receive goods or services from within their same organization. For example, at the tortilla chip production facility, the production department creates, fries, and salts the chips, which are then sent to the production department's internal customer: the packaging department. After the packaging department places the chip into bags and seals them, it sends the bags of chips to its internal customer: the finished goods warehouse. This process of sending goods from internal customer to internal customer continues until the product reaches the external customer and, eventually, the end user.

Therefore, when developing customer service policies and standards, companies must have a clear understanding of exactly who their customers are. Many companies create great global customer service policies for their external customers, but fail to address their own internal customers. Companies with exceptional customer service not only have external customer service policies, but their functional departments also have policies and procedures for their individual internal customers. Had the physical distribution department of our electronics store at the beginning of this chapter established customer service policies and procedures with its internal customer, the individual stores' customer service desks, much of the resulting stress and confusion to you, the end user, could have been minimized.

Regardless of whether its customers are internal or external, an organization that provides goods or services must focus on the concept of customer service to achieve financial success. But what exactly does the term **customer service** mean? According to its website glossary, the Institute of Customer Service defines customer service as "the sum total of what an organization does to meet its customer expectations and produce customer satisfaction."

The Institute adds that, although just one person may take the leading role in delivering and coordinating customer service, "it normally involves actions by a number of people in a team or in several different [departments or] organizations." Customer service, then, is the responsibility of customer service managers and staff, all departments within an organization, and other third-party service providers who play a role in getting an organization's goods or services through all the players in its supply chain to the external customer or ultimate end user.

A BIT OF EXTRA LINGO FROM THE WORLD OF CUSTOMER SERVICE

For a basic understanding of customer service, there are a few more words to know…

customer relationship management

Customer Relationship Management, also known as **CRM**, is a department within or an approach used by an organization that addresses meeting the needs of the customer before, during, and after the sales transaction. The primary functions of CRM are marketing (pre-transaction), sales (transaction), and service (post transaction).

customer service and support

Customer Service and Support, also known as **CSS**, is the department or function within an organization to whom customers turn for immediate help with a product or service after delivery. Typically, Contact Centers or Help Desks are part of CSS. Marketing, Sales, and CSS are often the three primary branches of a Customer Relationship Management department.

customer service policy

A **customer service policy** is a written statement concerning how an organization or department will treat its external or internal customers and what customers can expect from the relationship. Many organizations post their customer service policy in the location visible to the customer during the sales transaction.

customer service procedures

Customer service procedures are the actual physical routines and detailed steps an organization or department uses to provide customer service to its external or internal customers. Many organizations develop these procedures as situations arise and do not put them in writing. Far more effective companies, however, record their customer service procedures in writing and make them available to all who provide or have an impact on the organization's customer service. This allows for consistent customer service with all parties working toward the same customer service goals.

CUSTOMER SERVICE AND LOGISTICS MANAGEMENT

According to our definition above, the goal of customer service is to meet customer expectations and produce customer satisfaction, which are both related to the concept of *utility*. (Remember this from way back in Chapter 2?) **Utility** is an economics term referring to the satisfaction or happiness customers experience when they consume an organization's goods or services. The four primary types of utility are: *form*, *time*, *place*, and *possession*.

Form utility is the value added to products as their form changes, for example, as raw materials are transformed or manufactured into finished goods. ***Place utility*** is the vale added to products when they are at the right place within the supply chain, from the receipt of raw materials from suppliers to distribution of finished goods to external customers, i.e., when they are where both internal and external customers want them. ***Time utility*** is the value added to products when they are available at the time (i.e., *when*) both internal and external customers desire them. ***Possession utility*** is the value added to products when a desire to possess them has been created in the minds of the consumers.

In the relationship between a customer and an organization providing a product or service, the organization attempts to add value to the customer using all four types of utility. First, when the company produces the product, its manufacturing or production department works to ensure that the product will be of a good quality and meet the customers' expectations of the product and its performance. This stage creates *form utility*.

Next, the logistics or physical distribution department works to ensure that the product is available where and when the customer wants it. This task ranges from ensuring that a delivery van is loaded on time and arrives at the end user's home at the correct time to using marketing forecasts of customer demand to ensure that the right quantity of goods is readily available through warehouses, distribution centers, or JIT systems at any given time of the year. This logistics-driven stage creates both *time* and *place utility*.

Finally, the marketing department is hard at work before the customer even places an order for the product by creating a desire for the product. The customer is educated in both what the product does and in the company's customer service policy regarding the product, its delivery, and its corresponding service. If this stage, which creates *possession utility*, is done correctly, the customer will then evaluate whether or not the company and product have lived up to expectations after the product is delivered. This provides the basis upon which the customer then forms an evaluative judgment about whether or not they have received satisfactory customer service.

In many companies, the marketing department (and its customer service arm) then calls, mails, or e-mails customers to find out if the customer is indeed satisfied with the product and each of the four types of utility the company has attempted to provide. Think about the last time you took your car to a large dealership's department for a routine service. Chances are, you received a follow-up telephone call a few days later asking you questions about your degree of customer satisfaction.

Some companies opt to get immediate feedback from customers while customer service judgments are still fresh in their minds. For one furniture company in Alaska, immediate customer feedback is standard procedure. Immediately after Furniture Enterprises delivers and sets up a piece of furniture, its delivery crew provides a feedback section on the delivery bill, which must be signed by the customer. It contains a few brief questions asking customers questions about their degree of satisfaction with the furniture delivery and setup process. Regardless of how and when customer feedback on the organization's utility provided is obtained, it is valuable knowledge that all departments within an organization should use to continue to improve their levels of both external and internal customer service.

We saw in the example earlier that all four types of utility are needed to achieve the primary goals of customer service. However, a whopping half of them – *time utility* and *place utility* – are added by logistics and supply chain management activities! Therefore, the relationship between logistics management and an organization's customer service is a very important one.

Logistics management also plays a critical role in all three stages of the customer service process. The ***customer service process*** has three primary phases that cover the entirety of the relationship between the customer and the organization supplying the desired goods or services. The phases are: *pre-transaction*, *transaction*, and *post-transaction*. Logistics management and operations play a significant role in providing effective customer service during all three of these phases.

Figure 10.1 - The Customer Service Process

The ***pre-transaction phase*** of a customer service relationship between a customer and a supplier takes place before the sale has occurred, often before the customer has gone anywhere near the supplier. During this initial phase, companies establish their customer service policies and procedures, working closely with their physical distribution department or third party providers to ensure that these policies and procedures are realistic and can be consistently delivered to customers. For example, you might initially attract customers with a customer service policy that states "We promise to deliver your order to you less than one hour after you have placed it," but this is likely to be impossible for your physical distribution department to carry out, leaving you some very unhappy, unsatisfied customers.

During the pre-transaction phase, companies also ensure that they are ready for upcoming potential sales by forecasting customer demand and maintaining enough stock (or ready access to enough stock) to fill future orders. Companies also ensure that all of their information technology and communication systems are in place and in working order for upcoming sales so that products can easily be found and tracked as orders are filled and products are delivered to customers. In today's age of immediate gratification and rapid advances in information technology, a critical element of customer service is ***inventory visibility***, the ability of organization and its customers to know exactly where a specific product is in the supply chain at any time as it is being delivered to the customer.

The ***transaction phase*** of the customer service relationship is the actual sales transaction: the customer placing an order for a product or service and the company delivering that product or service to the customer. When a customer places an order for goods with an organization, it is essentially that organization's logistics-related departments that fill the order. The order is picked from the warehouse, packaged for delivery, and transported to the customer. Although an organization's marketing department typically makes the sale, it is the warehousing and physical distribution departments that do all the grunt-work during this phase.

Figure 10.2 - With inventory visibility, companies know exactly where their products are during the distribution process. This allows them to inform customers of delays and early deliveries.

Finally, the ***post-transaction phase*** of a customer service relationship between a customer and a supplier takes place after the sale has occurred and the product or service has been delivered. This phase is largely the domain of a Customer Service and Support department, who handles customer complaints, returns, recalls, customer satisfaction surveys, and post-sales service, such as warranties and repairs. However, logistics-related departments such as physical distribution and warehousing also play a significant role during this phase, especially in dealing with the reverse logistics aspects and physical handling of goods in product returns and recalls. ***Reverse logistics*** is a specialized area of logistics that is concerned with the backwards or reverse flow of goods up the supply chain, i.e., moving goods from the customer back to the supplier as a result of product returns and safety or quality recalls.

THE MARKETING-LOGISTICS RELATIONSHIP

Back in Chapter 5, we learned that an organization's marketing department determines the nature and structure of its product's ***distribution channel*** (the marketing term for the flow of goods from the company to its customer) and the level of customer service the organization will provide throughout. Its marketing department selects and designs the distribution channel, such as when, where, and to whom goods will be delivered. It is then the mission of the organization's logistics operations departments (such as warehousing, physical distribution, and transportation) to carry out the marketing department's plans and strategy by physically moving goods through the distribution channel established, ensuring that all of marketing's distribution channel goals and promises to customers are met. In simpler terms, marketing makes the customer service promises and logistics must keep them.

Marketing departments often establish their organization's customer service goals and promises based on the marketing mix. A term commonly used by marketing academics and professionals, the ***marketing mix*** is the mix of variable factors that a company controls and adjusts to achieve its desired level of sales and customer service while maintaining the desired level of profitability.

The most commonly used classification of variable factors within the marketing mix is known as the ***Four Ps of marketing***: *product*, *price*, *place*, and *promotion*. Companies make adjustments to their own decisions and levels of effort within each of these 4P categories to maximize sales, service, and profitability simultaneously.

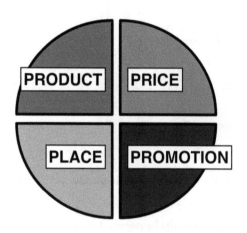

The ***product*** factor of the 4Ps focuses on getting the exact product customers want. The ***price*** factor focuses on setting a price that is both good for the customer and good for the company's bottom line. The ***place*** factor concerns getting the product where it is needed when it is needed. Finally, the ***promotion*** factor of the 4Ps focuses on educating consumers about: the product and all of its wonderful qualities; existing incentives to purchase the product; and how and where they can buy this amazing product. Many professionals in the worlds of marketing and logistics believe that logistics management plays a role primarily in the place factor of the 4Ps, focusing on how to get goods where they are needed when they are needed in the most efficient

manner possible. While logistics management is heavily involved in the *place* factor, it plays a significant role in all four factors of the marketing mix.

The **product** factor of the 4P mix is concerned with decisions regarding the product itself, such as *is this the product customers want* and *is its construction both of sufficient quality and profitable*? While this is largely the domain of the manufacturing or production department of an organization, logistics management also has an impact on the product factor in the following ways:

- **product availability.** Logistics managers must ensure that the products customers want will be available when they want them, either by forecasting demand and keeping products in stock or by keeping product readily available through Just-in-Time systems.

- **product quality.** All of those in warehousing, physical distribution, and transportation must ensure that the finished products are kept safe and packaged and held securely during storage, handling, and transportation. It is this attention to product quality throughout the supply chain that keeps our fragile tortilla chips intact!

- **order accuracy.** Logistics managers must also ensure that customers get the exact products they want by paying close attention to the product picking stage of the logistics chain. If mistakes are made in the order picking stage and customers receive the wrong product, such as 100 cases of yellow corn tortilla chips instead of 100 cases of blue corn tortilla chips, not only are customers unhappy and unlikely to become repeat customers, but the tortilla chip company must also incur the added reverse logistics expense of collecting the wrong product and redelivering the right one.

The **price** factor of the 4P mix focuses, naturally, on setting the right price for the product, generally a price that will be acceptable for the cost-conscious customer and the profit-focused supplier. While an organization's marketing department is the major player in setting product prices, the organization's logistics costs have a significant impact on the prices set. For example, streamlined and efficient logistics processes reduce operational costs (flashback to Chapter 8), which allows the marketing department to set lower product prices. Furthermore, logistics inefficiencies and errors can significantly increase product prices. For example, if the customer's order is filled incorrectly, filled incompletely, delivered late, or contains items damaged in transit, additional logistics costs will be incurred in correcting the order and handling returns.

As we discussed earlier, the **place** factor of the 4P mix is the responsibility of the logistics management of an organization. This factor focuses on getting products to customers *where* and *when* they are needed. The logistics functions of an organization, such as warehousing, order picking, physical materials handling, and physical distribution all work in concert to ensure a correct, on-time delivery and working overall to reduce the company's *order cycle time*. The ***order cycle time*** is the time it takes for a company to fill an order, from the time the order is placed by the customer to the time the customer receives shipment of the product. Because we live in a world of instant gratification, the shorter the order cycle time, the greater the levels of customer satisfaction.

Finally, the **promotion** factor of the 4P marketing mix, which is handled primarily by an organization's marketing department, focuses on creating a desire for the product in the consumer market and selling it to customers. Although the role of logistics may be less obvious in this part of the marketing mix, the logistics team plays a significant role in the informal promotion of a company's product to potential repeat customers. Often when customers orders a product, they do not actually meet anyone from the company selling the product until it is delivered onto their home or goods-in bay doorstep. The company's physical distribution employees, their professionalism and courtesy, and the accuracy and timeliness with which they fill the order are all part of a company's product promotion efforts. When physical distribution is handled well, customers feel more inclined to purchase products this company again. If physical distribution is handled poorly through late deliveries or impolite employees, customers are likely to look elsewhere when purchasing similar products in the future.

Now that we understand the role logistics management plays in marketing and customer service, let's look at a few very basic, bare-bones rules logistics managers follow to help their organization provide exceptional customer service. While most of these may seem obvious, they sometimes get forgotten or neglected as managers become occupied with immediate tasks and putting out fires in their day-to-day operations.

The basic rules for exceptional logistics management customer service are:

- **Fill the order correctly.** It is essential to deliver the customer what they want in the right quality and of the right quantity when and where they want it. Performing this first step correctly keeps customers happy and avoids costly reverse logistics corrections.

- **Address mistakes immediately and professionally.** No matter how well you follow the first rule, mistakes do happen. When they do, the logistics management of a company must address them immediately and professionally while keeping the customer informed in the process. When considering your company for repeat business, customers are more likely to remember how well a mistake was addressed rather than remember the mistake itself.

- **Consider how to provide added value and service.** Good logistics teams are always on the lookout for how to improve what they offer the customer. For example, companies may find ways to decrease delivery times, provide additional packaging to minimize product damage, or keep customers informed of product location by e-mail while in transit.

- **Perform customer service audits.** Logistics managers can gain much insightful information on how to improve customer service through customer service audits. In these audits, both external and internal customers are questioned about their degree of satisfaction with specific logistics-related elements of the transaction in ordering and receiving the product

- **Develop repeat customers.** Above all, logistics managers and staff must remember that their primary goal is not simply to fill an order and deliver it. Their goal is also to provide an exceptionally good experience for the customer, which will make them want to do business with the company again.

MEASURING LOGISTICS PERFORMANCE IN CUSTOMER SERVICE

Throughout this chapter, we have established that logistics plays a significant role in customer service. To maintain and increase customer service levels, logistics managers isolate each of the elements of logistics that have an impact on customer service. Logistics managers then measure and analyze these elements based on preset standards to see if their department's contribution towards the company's overall picture of customer service is sufficient.

Let's look now at how logistics managers measure and analyze the elements of their company's logistics performance that is needed to maintain acceptable levels of customer service. As shown in the table on the following page, these elements of logistics performance can be categorized and sorted into each of the three stages of customer service. Once sorted into their customer service phase, these logistics elements are then measured by logistics managers and their staff. These measurements are analyzed and compared to preset standards, based on what the company believes is acceptable to achieve the desired level of customer service.

For example, in the pre-transaction phase of customer service, logistics managers are concerned with assessing the logistics element of product availability. These managers want to be certain that they are prepared for customers' orders by holding or having ready access to enough product to meet customer demand and thus provide an adequate level of customer service. They can use product demand forecasts to set a desired level of stock to be held in order to meet potential customer needs. Logistics managers can then periodically measure the actual percentage of stock held to see if it matches the preset level desired.

The table on the following page looks at eleven elements of logistics, such as product availability, that have an impact on customer service across each of its three phases. It then provides questions logistics managers ask about each logistics element related to customer service and how the performance of this element can be measured.

Phase of Customer Service		LOGISTICS	OVERVIEW	PERFORMANCE MEASURE
Pre-Transaction		PRODUCT AVAILABILITY	Will the product be ready and available, even before the customer's order has been placed? Demand forecasts are used to determine the stock levels of products that should be held. The product availability is the percentage of product currently held compared to these predetermined levels.	% of product available compared to predetermined level desired
		INFORMATION AND COMMUNICATION SYSTEMS	Are the information technology and communication systems adequately prepared for future transactions? Can the systems get accurate and timely information to customers?	1. % of systems functioning correctly 2. Tests and spot checks of systems for speed and accuracy of information transfer
		CUSTOMER SERVICE POLICY CONSISTENCY	Do the current customer service policy and standards set by the organization match its logistics capabilities?	Comparison of company customer service policy with realistic order picking and distribution standards
Transaction		STOCK LEVELS	Is enough stock available to fill a customer's order?	% or amount of desired product in stock
		ORDER CYCLE TIME	How long does it take to fill a customer's order from the time the order is placed until the customer receives the goods? Was the delivery early, on time, or late?	Speed and historical consistency of both the entire order cycle and its individual segments
		DAMAGED SHIPMENTS	Are the goods damaged during order picking, packaging, or in transit?	% or number of goods damaged in shipment to the customer
		ORDER ACCURACY	Is the order sent to and received by the customer accurate? Have the correct types, quantities, and qualities of the item been received?	1. % or amount of current order filled correctly 2. Number of mistakes in order filled
		ORDER INFORMATION AVAILABILITY	Is product information readily available to the organization, such as in-stock availability? Is delivery information such as inventory visibility readily available to both the organization and the customer?	1. Number of occurrences of unavailable information per transaction 2. Customer evaluation of quality and content of information available
Post-Transaction		POST-SALES SUPPORT	How quickly and professionally are customer complaints handled by the logistics department? How quickly are product returns picked up?	1. Response time to customer complaints 2. Customer evaluation of quality of response to complaints
		POST-SALES SERVICE	How quickly and professionally are warranty and repair service matters handled by the logistics department? Are customers satisfied with the quality of reverse logistics service they receive?	1. Response time and quality in handling warranty service and repairs 2. Customer evaluation of quality of post-sales service
		RECALLS	Are product recalls handled rapidly and professionally? Are all product owners reached?	1. Recall scope & response time 2. Customer evaluation of recall process

Figure 10.3 - Measuring Logistics Performance in the Customer Service Process

As long as a company has a customer service policy and corresponding procedures, understands the role of logistics in customer service, and understands how to better understand the impact of logistics performance, nothing else can go wrong for a logistics manager wanting to provide exceptional (or even adequate) customer service to the company's valued customers ... right? Wrong! No matter how well a company and its managers understand the impact logistics management has on customer service and how to measure and assess logistics performance, something can still get in the way: human behavior. In the next chapter, we will explore how to address the unique, unpredictable, and sometimes-disruptive human side of the logistics-customer service interface.

CHAPTER 10 REVIEW QUESTIONS

1. What is the difference between an internal customer and an external customer?

2. What is customer service? Who is responsible for the customer service provided to an organization's external customers?

3. What is the role of Customer Relationship Management in an organization? What is the connection between CRM and CSS?

4. What are the four types of utility? What do they have to do with customer service?

5. What is the first phase of the customer service process? What role does logistics play in this phase?

6. What are some examples of reverse logistics? During which phase of the customer service process do they occur?

7. What is the most commonly used classification of the marketing mix? What do each of the four letters represent?

8. What role does logistics play in one of the letters of the marketing mix?

9. Why do logistics managers perform customer service audits?

10. How is order cycle time used as a performance measure of the transaction phase of customer service?

CHAPTER 10 CASE STUDY

Logistics and the Skyrocketing Success of Zappos.com

Successful companies have understood the connection between logistics and customer service for decades. Some, however, have been been the stuff of supply chain legends. One company that has leveraged the logistics-customer service connection to almost epic proportions of success is Zappos.com, a once little known online shoe retailer led by a young man who, himself, owned only two pairs of shoes. When young internet millionaire Tony Hseih invested in the company and became its CEO in the late 1990s, Zappos' annual gross sales were $1.6 million. When the online shoe retailer was sold to Amazon in 2009 (with an agreement to keep Tony Hseih at the helm and retain its business and customer service model), Zappos was worth an astounding $1.2 billion!

Although its sales have grown astronomically in the past ten plus years, Zappos invests very little money in marketing. For example, you're not likely to ever seen a Zappos magazine ad or TV commercial. Instead, the online retailer has focused its efforts of creating an exceptional customer experience. As a result, an overwhelming majority of its sales continue to be to repeat customers. Most of the remaining customers are ones that have found Zappos by word-of-mouth from highly satisfied friends, family, neighbors, and coworkers. Zappos has also responded to customers' requests to carry other categories of goods, such as clothing and kitchenware, just because customers would prefer to do more of their regular shopping with Zappos for as many goods as possible.

In 2005, Zappos instituted a customer service training camp required of all its employees, regardless of whether or not they worked directly with external customers. Know as the Zappos "boot camp," the required training grew from a one-week session to a five-week experience that includes two weeks of phone center training (even for those who don't work in the customer call center), one week of training at the Kentucky distribution center (even for employees who don't work in Kentucky or with the order fulfillment side of Zappos), and intensive training on Zappos' history and culture, public speaking, "Tribal Leadership," "Science of Happiness 101," and "Delivering Happiness."

Although this intensive and lengthy training of all employees is costly, it brings a multitude of benefits including increased employee retention and a cross-trained workforce that is able to substitute for departments that are short-staffed during the busy November and December holiday season. This intensive training also helps employees become fully entrenched in the company's culture and core values, which embraces a no-hold-barred approach to customer satisfaction. There are no scripts or time limits for call center employees. Zappos recently made customer service history on December 8, 2012, when a single customer service call lasted 10 hours and 29 minutes. Rather than be reprimanded, the call center employee was praised for embracing Zappos' commitment to the customer experience. This mammoth call resulted in the sale of a pair of Ugg boots and scads of free advertising through main stream media coverage, all in the middle of the busy holiday shopping season.

Along with focusing on the customer call center experience, Zappos has also focused on customer satisfaction in the order fulfillment and returns process. When Zappos was purchased by Tony Hseih in 1999, the online retailer relied on a "drop shipment" model, in which Zappos would take the orders, but the shoe manufacturer would fill the order and send the shoes directly to the consumer. With this drop shipment model, Zappos had little control over the levels of customer service provided and its shoe suppliers sometimes sent late or incorrect shipments to customers. Hseih decided to switch from the drop shipment model to an inventory model and invested in an 86-acre distribution facility in Kentucky. Zappos now stocks all the shoes it sells online and handles the entire order fulfillment process in house. It's distribution center and customer service call center are also open 24/7 so that customers' orders can be filled as quickly as possible.

In 2008, Zappos decided to take its logistics-customer service connection to an even higher level by investing in 72 Kiva robots for order picking. Although the initial cost of a robotic system is approximately 10 to 20% more than a traditional conveyor bely system, orders can be filled up to four times faster. Overall, the Kiva robot system doubled the productivity of Zappos' pickers and cut the distribution center's utility costs in half because the robot-operated sections of the facility didn't need the same level of heating or air conditioning as the human-operated sections. The company also did not have to lay off any workers who might have been supplanted by robots. They were instead trained in the advanced technology system and were kept on to meet the growing needs of Zappos continuous rapid increase in orders.

In addition to improving order picking, Zappos also focuses on its inbound supply chain by developing collaborative and transparent partnerships with its suppliers, allowing for inventory visibility at all times. At the other end of the supply chain, Zappos provides inventory visibility to its customers in both order fulfillment and returns, thanks to its close relationship with UPS. Zappos uses UPS as its preferred shipper and the two companies have coordinated their information systems so that inventory being shipped and returned is always visible and trackable by both companies and their customers. Part of Zappos' strategy in delivering an exceptional customer experience is providing free and hassle-free returns. A supply chain partnership with UPS has allowed Zappos to achieve this goal, which is a key component of the company's rapid growth and high levels of customer satisfaction.

References

Brohan, M. (2006, January 11) Zappos implements a customer service boot camp. *InternetRetailer.com*. Retrieved from http://www.internetretailer.com/2006/01/11/zappos-implements-customer-service-boot-camp/.

Huffington Post. (2012, December 21) Zappos' 10-Hour Long Customer Service Call Sets Record. *The Huffington Post*. Retrieved from http://www.huffingtonpost.com/2012/12/21/zappos-10-hour-call.

Nie, W. and Lennox, B. (2011, February 16) Case study: Zappos. *FinancialTimes.com*. Retrieved from http://www.ft.com/cms/s/98240e90-39fc-11e0-a441-00144feabd.

Scanlon, J. (2009, April 15) How Kiva Robots Help Zappos and Walgreens. *Bloomberg Business Week*. Retrieved from http://www.businessweek.com/innovate/content/apr2009/id200.

UPS.com. (2013) UPS reverse logistics results in a 75% repeat customer rate. *UPS: The New Logistics*. Retrieved from http://thenewlogistics.ups.com/customers/reverse-logistics/.

Case Study Questions

1. For employees at the Zappos distribution center, who are their internal and external customers?

2. Zappos places its primary strategic focus upon which two types of utility? Please explain your answer.

3. Describe the pre-transaction phase of customer service at Zappos.

4. Describe how Zappos addresses the marketing mix (the four Ps of marketing). Is this a successful or unsuccessful approach?

Chapter 11

The Human Side of Customer Service

Even if you have never worked in the logistics field, after having read the first ten chapters of this book, you now have a pretty good idea of what logistics management and supply chains are. Thus, when we think of supply chains, we generally think of a flow of goods. We think of a flow initiated by a user's need, moving seamlessly from raw materials suppliers to factories to warehouses to distribution centers, finally reaching the eventual retailer or end user. We think of physical goods, transportation equipment, and advanced IT systems.

When most of us think of supply chains, often overlooked are the tens, sometimes hundreds, or even thousands of *people* involved in the supply chain. There are the *people* who place the orders, the *people* who receive the goods, the *people* who check the order after it is received, the *people* who store and issue the goods, the *people* who set the prices, the *people* who keep the information system running, the *people* who make the big corporate decisions, and so on almost ad infinitum! But isn't a *supply chain* really about the physical *supply*? Why mention all of these people?

People, in their various roles (such as purchasing, warehousing, and customer), are the links of the supply chain. Their relationships are the essential solder of the supply chain's links. If even one is weak, the entire chain can fail. This chapter will focus on how to keep the solder in those links strong by developing exemplary interpersonal customer service skills. When members of the supply chain don't focus on developing their interpersonal skills for open and friendly communications with their internal and external customers, even the smallest differences of opinion can erupt into larger conflict which can stop a supply chain dead in its tracks.

WHO IS THE CUSTOMER?

For most products, the supply chain from raw materials through to the end consumer is made up by a number of companies. These companies are either those supplying goods and services or customers receiving the goods and services. Many of the organizations in the supply chain are likely to be the customers of one company and the suppliers of another. For example, the supply chain of Frannie's Fabulous Fish Fingers runs from the raw materials, haddock swimming happily in the ocean, to the end consumer, children eating fish fingers at Pirate Pete's family restaurants. Frannie's has multiple suppliers, including its packaging, breading, and fish suppliers. The fish supplier, the North Atlantic Fishing Consortium, also has suppliers, including a wide range of independent fishermen. Frannie's also has multiple customers, including national grocery chains, fast food wholesalers, and family restaurants, such as the Pirate Pete's chain. Pirate Pete's then has its customers, the individual restaurant consumers.

How many customers and suppliers were involved in getting these fish sticks to your dinner table?

Figure 11.1 - How Many Customers and Suppliers Are in a Fish Finger Supply Chain?

The entire supply chain of Frannie's Fabulous Fish Fingers, from the fisherman reeling in the haddock to the kiddies sitting down to eat shark-shaped fish fingers at Pirate Pete's, is made up of a series of suppliers and customers. All of these suppliers and customers are engaged in a series of independent, interpersonal interactions between individuals. How well you handle these interactions as a supplier can have an impact on both your company and the entire supply chain.

For example, imagine that the management of individual Pirate Pete's restaurants became sloppy and inattentive, not noticing that dishes were not washed properly and that the wait staff was more concerned with socializing with each other than with serving customers. Even if the managers weren't noticing these flagrant flaws, the customers certainly were! Eventually, Pirate Pete's would become known for poor customer service and lose a substantial portion of its repeat-customers. As a result, Pirate Pete's would suffer financially and be forced to close half of their restaurants. Frannie's Fabulous Fish Fingers and the North Atlantic Fishing Consortium would also suffer from this loss of sales, all due to Pirate Pete's poor management of customer service.

Therefore, for anyone who works for a company that supplies goods or services to customers, harnessing the individual skills needed for the human side of customer service is an absolute

Would you be a repeat customer at Pirate Pete's if you knew this was happening in the kitchen?

Figure 11.2 - The Importance of Customer Service

necessity. As we explore this human side of customer service, let's first look at exactly who the customer is and what their role is in the interaction.

As we mentioned in the previous chapter, a ***customer*** is a party who receives a product or service from another party. Everyone within the supply chain has customers, including both ***external customers*** (those who receive a product or service who are private individual end users or organizations other than the company providing the product or service) and ***internal customers*** (those individuals or departments within an organization who receive goods or services from within their same organization). Wherever you are in the supply chain or whoever your customers may be, you must try to understand who your customer is and what they mean to you. So, what is the first thing you know about your customer?

The customer is always right. If you have ever worked in the service industry, you've certainly heard this old gem. But is it true? Is the customer *really* always right? For example, a new customer might call to complain that the shipment they just received from your company was only 900 palletized crates of fish fingers instead of 1000, making it 100 crates short. You check your records and find that, in the purchase contract, the customer had only ordered 900 crates of fish fingers, not 1000 as they claim.

In many instances such as this, the customer may not be right, but is it your job to point out your customer's mistake and mock their flaws in a game of "I Was Right - You Were Wrong," leading to a belittled and unhappy customer who is unlikely to do business with you again? Or, with the *customer is always right* philosophy in mind, is it your job to tell that customer that they were indeed correct (even though they weren't) and send the 100 crates of fish fingers out immediately at no cost to the customer, leaving your company with the loss of the cost and potential profit of an entire 100 crates of fish fingers? Neither solution is correct. You must instead perform the balancing act of customer service, keeping both your customer and your company happy with the solution. Much of keeping your customer happy will depend on your interpersonal skills and how well you treat your customer. In later sections of this chapter, we will focus on the interpersonal skills needed to handle the delicate balancing acts of customer service.

Although the customer may not always be right, it is absolutely critical to remember the importance of the customer to both you and your organization. In the relationship between a supplier and a customer, a customer has needs for specific goods or services. In a market economy, there are likely to be many suppliers vying to be the one selected by customers. When a customer selects your company, you must be appreciative of the customer and understand that, at any moment, the customer could become dissatisfied with your company and its service, change their minds, and take their business elsewhere. A loss of multiple customers or even a single large customer can result in significant loss of profit or even closure of your company altogether. For example, during the 1990s and early 2000s, a fair number of medium-sized manufacturers grew exponentially when they added Walmart and other large big box retailers to their customer base. Many of these companies became too heavily dependent on their new customers, often for up to 90% of their sales. When some could not meet the large retailers' customer-centered pricing, they were dropped as suppliers.

On a more personal level, if a customer becomes dissatisfied with the service you are providing as an individual, the customer might complain about you to your company's upper level managers. As a result, you might decrease your chances for a future promotion, face demotion, or even lose your job! Therefore, the customer often holds the key to your job security, at both the personal level, in the influence they have over your individual employment status, and at the corporate level, in the influence their continued business has in your company's ability to stay financially afloat. Therefore, instead of *the customer is always right*, a better and more accurate mantra to remember might be: *the customer may not always be right, but they do pay your paycheck!*

Despite their power and influence over your continued employment, customers are not evil, malicious, omnipotent beings. They are instead individuals and organizations with needs for specific goods and expectations for the customer service accompanying these goods. They will include a diverse range of people with different perspectives. They will all react differently when faced with the same situation. As a member of the supplier's team in customer service interactions, it is your job to understand your company's variety of customers and their needs while using interpersonal skills to provide them with a positive, open interaction. To do this, you must first identify and understand your role in the customer service interaction.

YOUR ROLE AS SUPPLIER IN CUSTOMER SERVICE

In the previous section of this chapter, we discussed the role and power of the customer. Let's now turn to the *supplier*. What are the roles and responsibilities of the individual people representing the supplier in customer service interactions?

The **supplier**, also known as the **vendor**, is the company that supplies goods or services to a customer. Goods supplied may be finished products supplied for resale; raw materials and in-process goods used in the manufacturing process to produce a finished product; and maintenance, repair, and operating (MRO) supplies, i.e., goods essential to the operations of an organization but not used to become part of the finished product. As we discussed in Chapter 10, the role of the supplier is to fill the customer's order by keeping the promises made by the sales and marketing departments to deliver the right quantity of goods of the right quality at the right time to the right place. Although the overall, big-picture role of the supplier is to fill the order, there are specific implied roles and responsibilities of the many individuals representing the supplier in the human side of the company's customer-supplier interactions.

There are many individuals that work for the supplier who are involved in customer-supplier interactions. All individuals working for or on behalf of the supplier who have face-to-face, telephone, or e-mail contact with the customer are engaged in the human side of customer-supplier interactions. For example, the sales person taking the customer's sales call by telephone, the warehouse manager who e-mails the customer to clarify a packing request, and the physical distribution employees who bring and the unload the goods into the customer's warehouse are all engaged in customer-supplier interactions.

All of these individuals must understand, first and foremost, that they represent the supplier, i.e., they are the supplier in human form. Therefore, it is important for suppliers' representatives to have a thorough understanding of: **their company** and **how to present themselves**.

If you are representing a company, you must understand what you are representing and what that company means to its customers. You can understand what your company stands for and what its goals are by reading its company mission statement and its corporate goals and objectives. Your customers may have also read your mission statement, goals and objectives and expect you to stay true to them. Even if your customers haven't read them, they almost certainly will have heard your corporate slogan or jingle. If nothing else, it is absolutely imperative that you know how your company is marketing itself with slogans, logos, and jingles and that you ensure the customer service you provide matches all of what the marketing department's clever turn-of-a-phrase promises. For example, the slogan of the Avis car rental company, "We Try Harder," sticks in the heads of many car rental customers. Therefore, when selecting Avis, a customer expects to see all Avis employees as more diligent, hardworking, and customer-focused than its competitors.

You must also fully understand and stay true to your company's customer service policies and procedures. Even if you do not interact with customers on a regular basis, it is still very important that you stay current with all of your company's customer service policies so that you can provide service consistent with the rest of your company, even if your input is fairly infrequent. It is also important to be consistent, stay true to your company's customer service policies, and make sure that your employees are empowered to follow these policies. Repeat customers are likely to know these policies and may come to depend on them or even see them as an added value that makes them keep coming back to you.

For example, L.L. Bean, an American catalogue and retail chain selling outdoor clothing and equipment headquartered in Freeport, Maine, is well known for its exceptional product return policy. L.L. Bean will accept returns on defective or broken products, no matter when they were purchased or what condition they are in. The authors of this book were once in the Customer Returns line at the original L.L. Bean store in Freeport standing behind a customer holding a dirty, scruffy, almost threadbare backpack that looked as if it gone to two world wars and back. When the customer approached the Customer Returns desk to complain of a broken strap fastener, we thought to ourselves that there was no way this 30 year-old item could ever be accepted for a return. To our surprise and the customer's delight, the customer service representative explained to the customer that they no longer carried this backpack, but that the customer could pick one of a similar design in the same size from the retail floor for an exchange!

Figure 11.3 - The original L.L. Bean customer service policy posted in the Freeport store by L.L. Bean himself in 1916 (left) and the current L.L. Bean customer service policy posted on the company's website (right)

We later saw the same very satisfied customer in the check-out line, with a cart full at least $700 in winter coats and sleeping bags. Staying true to L.L. Bean's customer service and returns policy may be costly for the company in the short term, but it reaps the company far more benefits in happy, repeat customers, willing to make larger future purchases because they know that, should anything go wrong, the returns process is hassle-free.

In addition to understanding your company, it is important to select the most appropriate way to present yourself as your company's representative. In your interactions with customers, you make a series of choices in how you present yourself in person, on the telephone, and in writing. If your choices are subconscious ones or you feel that you are not actually making choices, but instead just "being yourself," you must become aware of the choices you do make and consciously select whether these choices represent your company in the best light possible. We'll now look at the three common customer-supplier interaction venues (**face-to-face**, **telephone**, and **e-mail**) and explore how the ways in which supplier's representatives should present themselves.

Meeting with a customer in person, especially for the first time, often forms their most indelible impression of you. Although we all learned in kindergarten that, "You should never judge a book by its cover," this lovely idea is just not a part of human nature, especially when we are in shopping mode. Imagine that you are buying a box of oatmeal. The first box you pick up is significantly dented in one of its upper corners. Most of us are likely to put the box back and select the perfect, un-dented box in the second row, even though there is no way the oatmeal in the first box could have been damaged. Because we are paying our hard-earned money for goods, such as our oatmeal, we opt for the brightest, freshest, and most perfectly packaged products.

Imagine now, that your organization regularly purchases ball bearings from the Bert's Big Ball Bearing Company. Following Bert's customer service policy, a customer service representative meets face-to-face with you after every large order to make sure that you are satisfied. On paper, this may seem like a great policy, but the Bert's representative that is assigned to your company has a lower standard of grooming and cleanliness than you do. His clothes are always disheveled, his hair is rarely combed, he smells as if he has never used deodorant, and it is obvious that he has not brushed his teeth in about fifteen years! He is very nice and personable, but you have a hard time breathing when you are around him. Most of us would not want to hurt his feelings, get him in trouble, or even become involved in a possible confrontation by complaining to him or his boss about his grooming and hygiene. Some of us may even think that Bert's values our business so little that they send us the "smelly guy." Unfortunately for Bert's, one of the easier ways out of the situation is simply to find another ball bearing supplier.

Figure 11.4 - Which gentleman would you select as your fast food supplier?

Think now about your interactions with your customers. Are you the "smelly guy" or "smelly gal" they try to avoid? Although your hygiene may not be as bad as the poor fellow in our example, are there things about your appearance or behavior that your customers might find disagreeable? For *face-to-face* interactions with customers, you must always be aware of the following three characteristics of yourself:

- **Grooming.** Do you bathe or shower every day? Brush your teeth at least twice a day? Consistently wear deodorant? Are you clean-shaven or is your beard or mustache neatly trimmed? Is your hair clean and neatly cut? Is your make-up well applied and appropriate for your work situation? Do you check for bad breath before meeting with customers? Regular coffee-breath or cigarette-breath in even the otherwise cleanest person can make a customer cringe.

- **Dress.** Are your clothes clean? Are you dressed neatly and modestly? Are all the buttons buttoned that should be buttoned? Does your style of dress meet the expectations and standards of both your employer and your customer? For example, many business etiquette books and seminars will focus on selecting the appropriate suit, but a suit is not always the most appropriate form of dress when working with customers. For example, a representative from a company that manufactures tractors and other farming equipment may choose to dress in a clean, new, well-ironed pair of jeans and a button-down flannel shirt when meeting with their farming customers in eastern Tennessee, who are more likely to trust and communicate openly with someone in jeans than with someone in a suit.

- **Behavior.** Are you polite and courteous when dealing with your customers? Do you arrive for your appointments on time? Do you shake hands and maintain eye contact when speaking to your customers? Do you allow your customer a personal buffer space of about 3 feet? Do you hold the door open for your customers? Do you provide a neat and clean business card? Do you maintain appropriate small talk and avoid off-color jokes and remarks?

We've just discussed the first of our three common customer-supplier interaction venues, in-person contact. Let's now look at the second venue, the telephone, and how you as a supplier's representative should present yourself. When speaking to customers over the telephone, you are at more of a disadvantage than when you have face-to-face meetings because you cannot read their body language. You must instead attempt to read their understanding, approval, or disapproval from their words and tone of voice alone.

How I do when making small talk with a customer?

Tune in to your customers by smiling, leaning forward, and maintaining eye contact.

DO talk about the weather, current events (without getting political), music, and sports.

DO NOT talk about your income, misfortunes, or personal health.

ABSOLUTELY DO NOT gossip, reveal intimate details of your life, or tell off-color jokes, even if your customer does!

For example, think about your own face-to-face interactions. When you are speaking to others, you can tell that they understand what you are saying because they nod their heads. You can similarly tell that they don't understand when they have a perplexed expression on their faces. Over the telephone, you can no longer see and interpret the nonverbal messages your customer may be sending. Therefore, you must remain particularly alert during *telephone interactions*, paying special attention to:

- **Telephone manners.** If you are the one making the call, do you first identify yourself clearly and ask if this is a good time to talk? Do you speak slowly and clearly? Do you allow your customers to speak without interrupting them? Do you smile when you are speaking? Do you avoid chewing gum, eating, or drinking? Do you end your conversations with polite closers, such as *Thanks for calling* or *It's been nice talking to you*? Do you wait until your customer hangs up first?

- **Tone of voice.** Are you listening to your customer's tone of voice to assess their approval and whether or not they understand what you are saying? Do you monitor your own tone of voice to ensure that you are not unintentionally sending a message of disapproval to your customers?

- **Organization and attentiveness.** Are you prepared for your conversation before you call your customer? Do you have a list of talking points to follow? Do you give your customers your full attention when speaking with them? Do you take and receive customers' calls in a quiet place with a minimum of distractions? Do you refrain from putting your customers on hold, no matter who is on the other line?

- **Leaving messages and returning calls.** If you call your customer and must leave a message, do you make sure to include your name, the name of your company, your phone number, the reason for your call, and the best time the customer can reach you? When a customer has left a telephone message for you, do you return the call immediately or within 24 hours?

The third of our three common customer-supplier interaction venues, *e-mail*, is perhaps the most treacherous and must be handled with extreme care. With face-to-face interactions, you can read and assess your customers' nonverbal communication and body language. With telephone interactions, you can read and assess your customers' tone of voice. E-mail interactions, however, are one-sided and do not allow you to immediately assess your customers' understanding or acceptance by reading body language or tone of voice. Even more challenging is the fact that e-mail communication, like any written communication, is indelible, permanent, and possibly indestructible (unless, of course, you lead a Mission Impossible lifestyle with message that self-destruct only moments after receipt). Your e-mail messages can also, unbeknownst to you, be forwarded very easily to a host of recipients.

To sail safely through the treacherous waters of *e-mail communications*, you must pay special attention to:

- **Spelling and grammar.** Even though e-mailing is perceived as a more informal method of communication, messages that are riddled with spelling and grammar errors make you and your company appear substandard in your customers' eyes. Therefore, do you reread your messages aloud before sending them to check for errors and typos? If your e-mailing software does not have spelling or grammar checkers, do you write your messages in a word processing document such as Microsoft Word first, then use its spelling and grammar check function to correct mistakes, and, finally, cut and paste your message text into an e-mail? E-mails that demonstrate attention to spelling and grammar sends the customer the message that you are serious about their business and that you will be attentive to their account and products or services ordered.

- **The content of your message.** Apart from succinct and pleasant greetings and closings, do your e-mails to customers stick to the core purpose of the message, containing only relevant facts, questions, and requests? Do you avoid placing jokes and revealing personal information in your e-mails to customers? Even if customers regularly forward you e-mails with jokes and other non-work-related items, do you avoid forwarding them similar e-mails? Even though customers may send you five jokes a day, even one joke from you may irritate or offend them.

- **The style of your message.** The style of all of your e-mail messages to customers should be warm, polite, and professional. E-mails should start with a friendly greeting that may be more or less formal, depending on your business relationship, such as *Dear Mr. Smithers* or *Hi Ned*. E-mail messages should also start and end with succinct and pleasant statements such as *I hope all is well in Cleveland* or *I look forward to seeing you at our upcoming meeting*. Also, at all costs, you should avoid using the informal style of writing that is now sweeping the internet world. Many people use an abbreviated form of written communication in e-mails and chat rooms so they can write almost at the speed of speech. This abbreviated style includes: writing entirely in lower case letters; using acronyms for phrases and sentences, such as *LOL* for *laugh out loud*; and using symbols, called **emoticons**, to convey emotions and facial expressions, such as a colon and right parenthesis to convey a smile :) or a semicolon and a right parenthesis to convey a wink ;) . Using this informal style in your e-mails may either completely confuse your customers or send the message that you are immature in your business dealings.

UNDERSTANDING YOUR CUSTOMER AND YOURSELF

You understand your customer's role and you understand your role as the supplier. Is that enough knowledge to master the human side of the customer-supplier interaction? Not by a long shot! In any human interaction, including those focused on customer service, to communicate effectively, you must understand yourself and the person with whom you are speaking. You need to develop a type of intelligence that helps you understand the spoken and unspoken messages of communication through understanding the context in which both you and your customers are operating, exploring why you say what you say and how you say it, and empathizing with your customers so they are encouraged to communicate more openly. The type of intelligence needed is known as *emotional intelligence*.

Throughout our first eighteen years or more, most of are measured according to academic success and our IQ. How well we perform in elementary school determines our course placement in secondary school. How well we perform in our secondary school courses and on our college placement tests then has an impact on which colleges or universities will accept us as students. Finally, the reputation of the college we attend and how we perform academically at that college has an enormous impact on which companies will hire us and how much they will pay us. Although this focus on academic performance and IQ has been the predominant model in the United States and other countries for many years, companies are now finding that emotional intelligence (or *EQ*), not IQ, is a better predictor of employment, management, and customer service success.

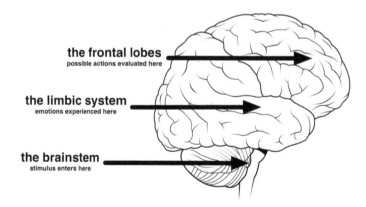

Figure 11.5 - Three Regions and Functions of the Human Brain

Before we explore the notion of emotional intelligence and EQ, let's take a quick look at the human brain. When our body experiences something through one of the five senses, information about this sensation (such as the pain experienced when we hit ourselves on the thumb with a hammer or the wonderful smell of fresh bread baking) travels to our brain by way of our nerves, up the spinal column, to the brain stem the base of the brain. The brainstem is the brain's intermediary, which receives and sends messages to the rest of the body. Information travels immediately from the brain stem through the brain's limbic system, the region in which we experience our emotions. Only after traveling through this emotional center does the information finally reach the outer layers of the brain, including the frontal lobes of the cerebral cortex, which assists in our rational thinking by evaluating whether our potential actions and reactions may be good or bad and perceived by others as socially acceptable or unacceptable.

Therefore, when we hit our thumb with a hammer, we first experience the emotion of extreme, blinding pain before we experience the rational thought that, although we might want to scream in pain nonstop for thirty minutes, we must instead go to the hospital because our thumb looks broken. In a more pleasurable experience, when we smell fresh bread baking, we first have happy feelings and experience pangs of hunger before we experience that rational thought that, although we want to rip the bread from the oven and eat the entire loaf immediately, we just ate, we are not hungry, and the bread must be saved for dinner to be shared among the entire family. But what does all of this brain anatomy have to do with success in the customer service? Everything!

During the past thirty years, computers have increasingly been doing much of the "grunt work" of the cognitive thinking process for us. (Think about how different filing your taxes is now, thanks to software programs like TurboTax.) The human population and the average workplace, however, have grown increasingly full of people. Therefore, much of the time in our day must now be devoted to getting along with the people with whom we must interact. Where we could once sit quietly in our closed-door offices performing our small, insular tasks, we now must sit in cubicles, side-by-side with our coworkers, with whom we must frequently interact to solicit information and opinions in order get our jobs done. Those of us engaged in interactions with customers face the added pressure of these additional critically important social interactions.

Therefore, we must now have good "people skills," which puts our frontal lobes into overdrive as we try to regulate our emotions so that we don't yell at our coworkers or run screaming from the building when things go wrong. For many employers, our ability to regulate our emotions in order to get along and work with others, such as our coworkers and our customers, is becoming a more highly valued commodity than pure cognitive intelligence alone. In contrast to IQ, this ability is called our **EQ** or our ***emotional intelligence***.

Although the idea of emotional intelligence has been around since the mid-1980s, it has been popularized more recently in the works of author Daniel Goleman. In his book *Emotional Intelligence*, Goleman describes our emotional intelligence as the combination of our personal competence (how self-aware we are and how well we manage ourselves) and our social competence (how socially aware we are and how well we manage relationships with others).

In order to develop greater emotional intelligence, we must first look inward to become aware of who we are, what we are, and the decisions we make that affect our own lives. Once we have looked inward, we must then look outward to become aware of social dynamics and the decisions we make and actions we take in our interpersonal interactions. Two concepts that can lead to greater emotional intelligence by understanding others and ourselves are *paradigm* and *personality type theory*.

At the beginning of this chapter, we said that the solder of a supply chain's links are people and their ***interpersonal relationships***, i.e., the social associations, connections, or affiliations between two or more people. Interpersonal relationships vary in different levels of intimacy and sharing and they are typically centered on something shared or in common. Those within interpersonal relationships within supply chains, such as the relationships between customers and suppliers, may sometimes have nothing in common other than the need for the supply chain transaction. Customers and suppliers in supply chain relationships will have a variety of differences, including the companies or departments for whom they work, their work methods and goals, or even their perception of the relationship and work to be done.

Successful relationships, in both supply chains and the world at large, often depend on our perceptions of reality or paradigms. A ***paradigm*** is the set of experiences, beliefs, and values that affect the way an individual perceives reality and responds to these perceptions. It is the way we see the world, not literally and visually, but within the realm of perception, understanding, and interpretation.

In the best-selling management guide *The Seven Habits of Highly Effective People*, author Stephen Covey asserts that our paradigms are a powerful influence in our lives and in our ability to be effective individuals. He describes paradigms as the maps in our heads of "the way things are" (our realities) and "the way things should be" (our values). Covey states that we assume that the way we "see" things is the way that they are or should be, i.e., we see the world not as it is, but as we are conditioned to see it. He further adds that, "Our paradigms, correct or incorrect, are the source of our attitudes and behaviors, and ultimately, our relationships with others."

Conventional wisdom and the idea of conditioning might lead us to believe that the maps in our heads, our paradigms, are based on our experiences. (The paradigm of Pavlov's dog, for example, is that every time a bell rings, I get a treat.) Contemporary personality theory research, however, reveals that paradigms are also related to our innate *personality types*. Therefore, how we see the world depends partially on the personality we were born with.

As used by psychology, management, and education professionals, ***personality type*** refers to a personality preference typology first outlined in psychologist Carl Jung's *Psychological Types* (1921) and later developed further by mother and daughter personality researchers, Katherine Briggs and Isabel Briggs Myers. According to ***personality type theory,*** we are capable of acting according to any of the personality characteristics outlined, but we have an innate preference for specific characteristics and most often behave according to those preferences. Just as we can use both of our hands, but are born with a preference for our right or left hand, we can use all the personality types, but are born with specific preferences.

In 1942, Briggs Myers and Briggs developed a psychological personality inventory, ***the Myers Briggs Type Indicator (MBTI)***, to help individuals sort their preferences and determine their unique personality type. In the MBTI, there are four categories in which you are sorted into one of two preferences. Each of these preferences is designated by a single letter. After you have been sorted according to all four categories, you will have been assigned four separate letters. These four letters combined will reveal your personality type. There are sixteen different combinations of letters and, correspondingly, sixteen different distinct personality types.

The first of the four preference categories sorts people according to how they gain energy. If you become more energized from the outside world, you have a preference for **Extraversion** and are given the letter **E** as the first letter of your four-letter personality type. If you become more energized from your own inner resources, you have a preference for **Introversion** and are given the letter **I** as the first letter of your four-letter personality type.

The second of the four preference categories sorts people according to how they take in information. If you prefer to deal with individual, specific facts, you have a preference for **Sensing** and are given the letter **S** as the second letter of your four-letter personality type. If you prefer to deal with the "big picture," you have a preference for **Intuition** and are given the letter N as the second letter of your four-letter personality type. Intuition is given **N** instead of I to avoid confusion because I has already been assigned to Introversion.)

The third of the four preference categories sorts people according to how they make decisions. If you more often make decisions using logic and critical analysis, you have a preference for **Thinking** and are given the letter **T** as the third letter of your four-letter personality type. If you more often make decisions based on your values and by taking other people into account, you have a preference for **Feeling** and are given the letter **F** as the third letter of your four-letter personality type.

The fourth and final of the four preference categories sorts people according to how they approach life. If you prefer order and structure, you have a preference for **Judging** and are given the letter **J** as the final letter of your four-letter personality type. If you prefer flexibility and spontaneity, you have a preference for **Perceiving** and are given the letter **P** as the final letter of your four-letter personality type.

Extraversion (E) versus Introversion (I)

How we gain energy: from the outside world (E) or from within (I)

Sensing (S) versus Intuition (N)

How we take in information: in specific facts (S) or in a "big picture" (N)

Thinking (T) versus Feeling (F)

How we make decisions: deferring first to logic (T) or values and relative worth (F)

Judging (J) versus Perceiving (P)

How we approach life: preferring order & structure (J) or flexibility & spontaneity (P)

After you have been sorted in each of the four preference categories, you will be left with four letters. When written together, these four letters represent your **MBTI personality type**. As show in the type table to the right, there are sixteen possible MBTI types. Each of these sixteen types is unique and has unique means of communicating, learning, handling conflict, working with others and relaxing. Typically, people of one given type will have an easier time communicating with and understanding people of the same or similar types and a more difficult time with those of very different types. According to personality type theory, we cannot change our innate personality preferences to match those of others with whom we interact, such as our customers. By learning about the personality type preferences of ourselves and others, however, we can improve communication and enhance understanding.

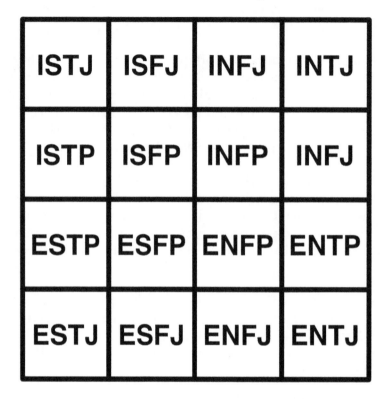

Figure 11.6 - The MBTI Personality Type Table with the Sixteen Possible MBTI Types

For example, a 2006 case study of Southwest Airlines conducted by CPP revealed that MBTI-centered (i.e., personality type) leadership and employee training has had significant positive impacts on team building, conflict resolution, leadership, and trust:

> *Southwest employed the MBTI tool as a method for understanding each other's differences, enabling the leaders to understand how their coworkers could approach the same challenge from a completely different perspective. The MBTI tool helped these leaders understand the "why" behind their coworkers' behaviors, which helped in building trust and empathy within the department. "In these, classes we saw a lot of 'a-ha!' moments," said Bryant. "Behaviors that might have once caused misunderstanding and frustration were now viewed through a different filter."*

Therefore, in your understanding of other people, such as your customers, you may not be able to change the personality type you are born with, but you can adjust your *paradigm* (remember: the map in your head) to better understand and communicate with them. Knowing about personality type theory allows you to better understand your own paradigm, the paradigms of others, and how these maps in our heads influence our actions.

Since 1942, the MBTI and personality type theory have been studied and tested multiple times. Throughout the past fifty years, hundreds of studies have shown that differences in personality type relate to differences in: how we respond to conflict; work and learning styles; decision making and problem solving; team processes; communication; and conflict resolution techniques. There are many resources available to help you better understand personality types, their differences, and their impact on customer service relationships. A great place to start is the fun and informative book, *The Art of Speed-Reading People* by Paul Tieger and Barbara Barron-Tieger, and the website of the Center for Applications of Psychological Type, www.capt.org.

INTERPERSONAL SKILLS FOR DIFFICULT INTERACTIONS

After reading the first fifteen pages of this chapter, you might understand who your customers are and why they are important to your organization. You might also explore your role as the supplier's representative and focus your responsibility for creating more positive and open customer-supplier interactions. You might even work toward developing greater emotional intelligence by understanding the paradigms and personality types of your customers and yourself. Will all of this hard work always result in perfect, hassle-free customer service relationships?

DIFFICULT CUSTOMERS... REVEALED!

The Overly Demanding Customer

These customers may place an inordinate number of demands on you and still never appear satisfied. Demanding customers may simply have high expectations or they may have had unpleasant customer service experiences in the past and always expect the worst.

The Indecisive Customer

These customers may actually be pleasant, happy people, but be extremely reluctant to commit to any decisions. They may consume lots of the supplier's time, filled with promises of "I'll get back to you." Indecisive customers may be commitment-phobic or they may be uncertain of their own position and power within their company and are afraid to commit to decisions.

The Super-Sensitive Customer

These customers may overanalyze everything you say and write. They may find offense at even the most seemingly innocuous statements. These customers may be having a bad day, they may be particularly sensitive due to life experiences, or they may simply just not trust you. It's important to be aware that a significant portion of the American population just doesn't trust sales people!

The Unhappy or Angry Customer

Regardless of what you say or do, these customers appear ready for combat when they meet you. They may be experiencing a particular problem with you, your company, your product, or your service that you don't know about. They may be in physical pain or having a bad day. Or, worst of all, they just may not like you because you remind them of someone else they don't like!

Unfortunately, all of this hard work may not be enough if you encounter a difficult customer. Some customers may have paradigms or recent life events that make them a little more challenging to interact with than other customers. Furthermore, a perfectly happy and affable customer one day could unexpectedly behave as a difficult customer the next day, perhaps due to physical illness or simply just a rotten day. If you are not careful, your interactions with difficult customers could easily and rapidly escalate into conflicts. Left unchecked, these conflicts could cause customers to seek their business elsewhere, even if they were initially in the wrong.

With a difficult customer, using a few simple communication techniques could go a long way in preventing a challenging interaction escalating into a nail-biting and unnecessary conflict. Being careful of your word choices and respecting their emotions or frustrations allows your customer to vent and explain what is wrong. This then allows for more open subsequent communication. Some of the communication techniques that you can use to prevent conflict with difficult (and even not-so-difficult) customers are:

- **Understanding & Addressing Body Language.** Sometimes you know when your customers will be difficult ones before they even open their mouths just by reading their body language. For example, when customers frown and stand with their arms crossed, you can take this as a clear signal that something is wrong. When customers tap their feet and repeatedly look at their watch, you can tell that they are in a hurry and may not have long to meet with you. When customers yawn and look at you with an expressionless face, you can guess that they are taking the time to speak with you but don't see the purpose or value of your meeting.

When you read a customer's body language or tone of voice and notice that they are upset or may not be open to communication, it is best if you acknowledge it and address it immediately. For example, to the customer with the frown and crossed arms, you might say, "I've noticed that you seem a bit upset. Is anything wrong?"

What does his body language say to you?

Addressing negative body language provides an invitation for the customer to explain what might be bothering them. Once they have explained the problem, you can rectify or address it and get back to the business at hand. The problem may not even be about you. The customer may be upset about something else and not even be aware of their own body language or agitated state of mind. Expressing your concern or allowing customers to vent shows that this business interaction is important to you and that you value them as customers.

- **Making "I" Statements.** When dealing with excessively sensitive, demanding, and angry customers, a particular turn-of-phrase can appear insensitive or aggressive, providing a spark to ignite conflict with these powder-keg customers. This dangerous language is the *"You" statement*. When you are speaking with difficult customers (and non-difficult customers,

She might be making a "you" statement!

too), avoid starting possibly contentious statements with the word "you," which sounds accusatory and set you up for an immediate conflict. Instead, take ownership of your statements by starting them with the word "I" and expressing what you have felt or noticed.

For example, if a customer is complaining but does not know that they are wrong, it would be counterproductive to make them angrier by pointing out their mistake with a "You" statement, such as, "You've got it all wrong. Look at these figures here." A less combative way to make the same statement would be to use an "I" statement, such as, "I noticed that the figures in our paperwork are different from the ones you mentioned."

- **Using Anticipatory Statements.** When you want to make a suggestion to difficult customers that you suspect they might react negatively to, using ***anticipatory statements*** is a useful technique that steers clear of conflict and even gets the customer to consider your suggestion. With this technique, you anticipate your customer's negative reaction to your suggestion and incorporate it into your statement to them.

For example, a customer erroneously receives a Model XJ tractor instead of a Model HY tractor, but you believe the Model HY might be better suited for their needs. You want to suggest that the customer consider the possibility of keeping the Model HY tractor instead but know that you'll be met with immediate resistance. If you anticipate and mention the customer's concerns yourself before making the suggestion, the customer might be open to listening to you suggestion because you have demonstrated that you have considered their concerns and point of view in your suggestion. A possible anticipatory statement for this scenario could be, "I know that you didn't order the Model HY tractor and are not especially pleased with its color, but I'd like to suggest a few reason why the Model HY might be more suited to your particular needs."

- **Listening and Paraphrasing.** A final technique useful in dealing with difficult customers (and all other customers, too) is careful listening followed by paraphrasing your customers' points to check for understanding. When customers know that you have taken the time to fully understand their point of view, their anger or frustration is more likely to be diffused.

Remember to listen and paraphrase!

To listen effectively, you lean in, maintain eye contact, and nod periodically to show that you are interested in what your customer is saying. You do not interrupt, but instead let them finish what they have to say. You then check to ensure that you have fully understood them by paraphrasing their main points. To ***paraphrase*** effectively, you restate their main ideas in your own words, using a neutral tone of voice that conveys neither approval nor disapproval of their message. The purpose of paraphrasing is to make sure that you have understood your customer because the difficulty between the two could be the result of a simple misunderstanding.

While it is difficult to keep these techniques forever at the forefront of your mind, it can be achieved by focusing on one technique at a time until they become a natural and automatic part of your customer service behavior. We can't change overnight, but we can keep the **Platinum Rule** in mind. We are all familiar with the Golden Rule: *Do unto others as you would have them do unto you.* Therefore, if I like to receive hugs from business acquaintances, should I give them great big bear hugs whenever I see them? Unless all of your business acquaintances are similarly physically demonstrative, most will avoid you when they see you coming for the fear of your bone-crushingly close bear hugs. When dealing with customers and coworkers, a better rule to keep in mind is the empathetic and more emotionally intelligent Platinum Rule: *Do unto others as they would like to have done unto them.*

In every customer-supplier interaction, both the customer and supplier have needs that must be met. As a supplier's representative, it is your job to provide exceptional customer service by performing the delicate balancing act between the needs of your customer and the needs of your company. Paying attention to how you present yourself, increasing your emotional intelligence, and knowing how to handle difficult customers are all invaluable customer service skills that can take you a long way in achieving mutually beneficial customer-supplier interactions.

CHAPTER 11 REVIEW QUESTIONS

1. Why are people and their interactions an important part of the supply chain?

2. Is the customer really always right?

3. If you work for a supplier, why is it important to understand your company's mission statement and customer service policies?

4. In face-to-face meetings with a customer, is it a good idea to engage in small talk? If so, which subjects should be discussed and which should be off limits?

5. Why are e-mails a dangerous ground for customer-supplier relationships?

6. What is emotional intelligence? Why is important for effective customer service?

7. Looking at the personality preference categories, which four letters do you believe would represent your personality type? Why?

8. Explain how you would use one of the four communication techniques when dealing with an angry customer.

CHAPTER 11 CASE STUDY

CASE
STUDY

A Closer Look at the Myers Briggs Type Indicator

One of the many life lessons offered by *The Godfather* came from the lips of Al Pacino's Michael Corleone: "It's not personal, Sonny. It's strictly business." As much as we may want to believe this, all business *is* personal because all business involves *people.* Each of the people involved in a business transaction, for example, is likely to have a very different personality and corresponding behavioral traits. With so many different personalities involved in even the simplest of business transactions, conflicts can easily erupt when people don't understand personality differences and how to interact effectively with people of different personality types.

One tool that people can use to understand their own personality and the personalities of others is the Myers Briggs Type Indicator, or MBTI. Successful businesses are aware that people are the heartbeat of a business and a majority of Fortune 500 companies use the MBTI for customer service training, team building, and leadership development. The MBTI is a multiple choice assessment used to sort a person into one of sixteen possible personality types. Taking the assessment is followed by a session with a psychologist or a workshop with a management training expert (who is qualified to administer and interpret the MBTI) to help you confirm and understand your results.

Taking the MBTI can be a valuable and eye-opening experience, but if you do not have the opportunity or funds to do so, do not despair! If you understand the MBTI labels and preference pairs, you can quickly determine your own personality type and use a variety of free online resources to help you better understand all sixteen types.

There are sixteen different four-letter personality types, but you will have one four-letter *preferred* type. This means that you may have to adjust your behavior to act like any of the sixteen personality types depending on where you are, who you're with, and what you're doing. Although you might sometimes behave like all sixteen types, your one preferred type is the type that takes you no extra effort. It is the type you are when you are relaxed and being your true self. During those times in life when you put yourself on autopilot, you are probably acting according to this preferred type.

Your preferred personality type is made up of four letters. Each letter comes from a different preference pairs. Because the MBTI personality type is made up of four different letters, there are, unsurprisingly, four different preference pairs. Each of these four preference pairs reflect a different aspect of your personality.

The first preference pair is the **Extraversion-Introversion** pair. People with a preference for Introversion gain their energy from within and generally prefer quiet settings. They are reflective and sometimes deep thinkers. They will often think before they speak. Sometimes they will think so much that they may not want to speak at all! They might feel uncomfortable in crowds or large social gatherings, perhaps standing to the side at a large party talking only to one or two close friends all night. On the flip side, people with a preference for Extraversion gain their energy from other people and external experiences. They often act before they speak, sometime resulting in foot-in-mouth syndrome! They are likely to feel comfortable in crowds but highly uncomfortable if they have to sit in silence for too long. If there are pauses in a conversation, they may feel the need to say something. Those with a preference for Introversion are assigned the letter "I" and those with a preference for Extraversion are assigned the letter "E."

The second preference pair is the **Sensing-Intuition** pair. This preference pair is all about how we take in information. People with a preference for Sensing see specific parts and pieces when they look at something. For example, if you put a piece of artwork in front of them and asked them to rattle off the first few things that popped into their head, they would likely list literal pieces of the art, such as green, sky, flowers, or table. They also don't mind getting into the detail and nitty-gritty of a task. When assembling furniture, they are likely to count all the pieces and read the instructions. They are sometimes thought of as "the practical types." Conversely, people with a preference for Intuition see the big picture or other relationships when they look at something. For example, if you put a piece of artwork in front of them and asked them to rattle off the first few things that popped into their head, they would likely list concepts related to the art or other things the art has reminded them of, such as desolation, ecoterrorism, or what they had for dinner last night. The also look at the big picture when tackling a task. When assembling furniture, they are likely to throw away the instructions and rely on a picture or memory for assembly. They are sometimes thought of as the dreamers and "the creative types." Those with a preference for Sensing are assigned the letter "S" and those with a preference for Intuition are assigned the letter "N."

The third preference pair is the **Thinking-Feeling** pair. This preference pair is all about how we make decisions. People with a preference for Thinking are more comfortable with logic and analysis and make decisions with their heads. They tend to critique before giving compliments, if they even give a compliment at all! Many Thinkers believe that, "It is better to be right than to be liked." People with a preference for Feeling are more comfortable considering relationships and harmony and make decisions with their hearts. They tend to easily give compliments but may find it difficult to critique others. Many Feelers believe that, "It is better to be liked than to be right." Those with a preference for Thinking are assigned the letter "T" and those with a preference for Feeling are assigned the letter "F."

The fourth and final preference pair is the **Judging-Perceiving** pair. This preference pair is all about our outlook on life. People with a preference for Judging like a planned and orderly lifestyle. They like clear limits and will often make lists. They are very comfortable making decisions but uncomfortable with chaos or last minute changes. When given an assignment, they are likely to plan it out and begin as soon as possible. People with a preference for Perceiving like a flexible and spontaneous lifestyle. They enjoy being curious and love to explore without limits. They are comfortable with chaos and change but can become uncomfortable when they have to commit to a decision. When given an assignment, they are likely to let things mull over gradually in their heads before making any formal plans and then formally starting the task at the last minute. Those with a preference for Judging are assigned the letter "J" and those with a preference for Perceiving are assigned the letter "P."

When all four preferred letters from these four different preference pairs are combined, you have your MBTI personality type! Armed with these four letters, you can find a wealth of resources online simply by Googling the letters or by consulting MBTI-specific websites, such as www.capt.org or www.oddlydevelopedtypes.com.

Case Study Questions

1. Based on the information in the article, what is *your* personality type? Give an example of how your behavior demonstrates each of the four letters.

2. Select a family member, friend, or coworker with whom you have a close relationship. Based on their usual behavior, what is *their* personality type? Are your personality types the same? Have you had any conflicts with this personal based on the difference or similarity of your personalities?

3. Studies have shown that introverted (I) sensing (S) types are overrepresented in finance and accounting departments. Why might IS types be drawn to these occupations?

4. Studies have shown that extraverted (E) intuitive (N) types are overrepresented in marketing and sales departments. Why might EN types be drawn to these occupations?

Chapter 12

Logistics in the 21st Century

With an ever-growing world population, rapid advances in information technology, and more of the world opening up to a global market economy, the twenty-first century is likely to bring many changes to the world of logistics management. Throughout this chapter, we will explore the future of logistics management, focusing on growing changes in the supply chain and in each the **inbound**, **internal**, and **outbound** processes of logistics management.

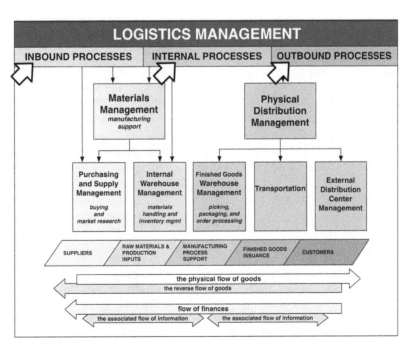

Figure 12.1 - Inbound, Internal, and Outbound Process of Logistics Management

FUTURE TRENDS IN SUPPLY CHAIN MANAGEMENT

Twenty-first century customers are already accustomed to almost immediate gratification and having some control over the speed at which we receive our products. We are used to shopping for what we need online, having a wide range of vendors vying for our business, comparing their prices and delivery times, and then tracking our purchase as it is en route to our doorstep. What has prompted this shift to create a more powerful and demanding customer? Information technology!

The past three decades have seen exponential advances in information technology hardware and software systems. As the power of information technology and communications systems grew, their cost decreased and they became available to a wider and wider audience. Advances in information technology had many direct applications to logistics. As we saw in Chapter 7, advanced software applications, such as ERP, EDI, EPOS, MRP, DRP, and VMI, became an integral part of the supply chain. Advances in hardware applications, such as bar coding, RFID, and voice recognition technologies, are beginning to become standard practice in the world of logistics management.

As we move further into the twenty-first century, information technology and communication systems will continue to provide advanced applications for the supply chain. As prices of IT-based hardware fall, more organizations, including medium-sized ones, will begin to use RFID systems to track inventory throughout the supply chain. These RFID systems will be linked to inventory software systems in greater numbers of companies, providing greater *inventory visibility* for both suppliers and customers throughout a product's supply chain.

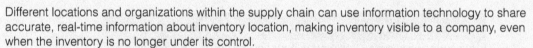

How Can Companies Locate Inventory in Complex Supply Chains?

Different locations and organizations within the supply chain can use information technology to share accurate, real-time information about inventory location, making inventory visible to a company, even when the inventory is no longer under its control.

This **inventory visibility** helps reduce cost by allowing an organization to move more to Just-in-Time operations and hold less "just-in-case" inventory. It also enhances customer service because it helps an organization control the process of getting the right quantity and quality of finished goods to the exact time and place a customer desires.

Inventory visibility has become possible only through advances in information technology, including: computerized inventory information systems; bar code printing and scanning; RFID (radio frequency identification) technology; GPS (Global Positioning System) technology; and wireless connectivity.

All of these advances in information technology now make it possible for all members of a supply chain to instantly and easily share information. Information that once could travel only as fast as a courier could carry it or as fast as someone could convey it by telephone can now travel instantly in the blink of an eye. This now opens up a wide range of possibilities in information-sharing between a customer and its suppliers and even its suppliers' suppliers to create even greater supply chain efficiency and effectiveness.

Although supply chain information technology systems may be ready for such information-sharing, the humans within the supply chain may not be. It is still a part of the psyche of those within a competitive market economy to view knowledge as power. People within individual companies may be reluctant to share information with their suppliers and customers for fear of relinquishing some of their power base. Their companies, however, will need the speed and efficiency resulting from open and immediate communication between all members of the supply chain to remain viable in an increasingly competitive global market. Therefore, twenty-first century supply chains will begin to place a heavier reliance on openness and trust in supply chain relationships.

Most logistics managers today have education and experience in how to make a supply chain more efficient and effective through a series of "best practices" in logistics management. They are often less experienced in or comfortable with the "softer side" of business, including how to create openness and trust and build relationships with supply chain partners. These soft skills will become essential, however, as information-sharing and trust among members of the supply chain become common practice. The world of **logistics management** will move increasingly to the more broadly focused world of **supply chain management**, which includes working more closely with suppliers and customers through supplier relationship management (SRM) and customer relationship management (CRM) respectively. Those logistics managers with human resources skills and training in negotiations, partnering, relationship-building, customer service, and conflict resolution will be well armed for the changing twenty-first century supply chain.

Besides information technology, another factor that will have a significant have an impact on logistics management in the twenty-first century is **globalization**. As we saw in Chapter 9, more than $10 trillion of goods are exported annually from countries around the world. As the world's population grows and its developing nations become more reliant on goods provided by the global market economy, more goods will need to be transported to more locations across the globe. Furthermore, to reduce costs, companies will increasingly look to a variety of global suppliers or even to *offshoring*, i.e., moving their own production operations overseas to be closer to suppliers or customers, operate in countries with more favorable trade regulations, and/or reap the benefits of reduced labor costs.

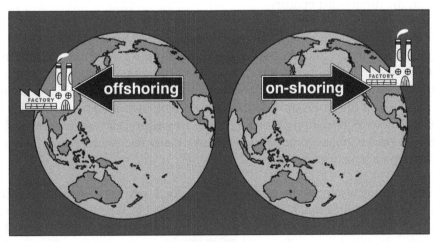

Figure 12.2 - Offshoring and On-shoring from a North American Perspective

With supply chains appearing to be hurtling nonstop toward globalization, the beginning of the twenty-first century has also presented an unanticipated wrinkle that may also have an impact on global logistics management: dramatic rises in fuel costs. While globalization and offshoring are on the lips of most logistics managers today, twenty-first century managers will also have to begin to consider **on-shoring**, i.e., moving a company's production operations from overseas back to its home country, such as the U.S., to offset the increases in transportation costs and the increased risk of operating overseas. In the twenty-first century, offshoring will no longer be the obvious choice. Companies will instead be faced with strategic decision-making for sourcing and production that takes into account not only production costs, but also: transportation costs and possible further fuel cost increases; lead times; and the political, economic, security, and weather-based risks of overseas operations.

LOOKING FORWARD: INBOUND LOGISTICS MANAGEMENT

Just as advances in information technology and increasing globalization will change the overall supply chain in the twenty-first century, they will also have a significant influence on purchasing, one of the core activities of inbound logistics management. For example, information technology is allowing purchasing to become a computer-based, online activity.

As we mentioned earlier in the chapter, most of us are becoming increasingly accustomed to internet shopping. We place our orders for books, clothes, and even food, pay for them, and then track their delivery all online and all at whatever time is most convenient for us. We are becoming a world of internet shoppers, with vast arrays of competing suppliers and product information available at our fingertips.

In the twenty-first century, customers will expect similar convenience and service from their workplace purchasing process. Many businesses have moved to e-commerce and **B2B (business to business)** IT-based systems, which directly connect customers and suppliers. Because it is becoming standard practice in the personal consumer's purchasing process, the availability of internet-based purchasing will become an important element of a company's core customer service strategy in the twenty-first century.

Increased internet-based purchasing will influence logistics management, especially in the areas of globalization, customer service, and alternative purchasing venues. For example, internet purchasing systems, which run 24 hours a day, will allow a customer to consider a variety of global competitors, despite differences in time zones and language barriers. Exposure to many new vendors from around the world provides purchasers with increased power as they use information-based knowledge to shop according to best price, product availability, and delivery times. This internet-driven global competition will force many twentieth century leading suppliers to reconsider their price structure and service.

Internet-based purchasing also provides customers the added service of inventory visibility, allowing them to see if and how much of the product is available, where the inventory is, and how long it will take to get to them - all before the order is even placed! When using 3PLPs for product distribution, such as Lynden, Inc. and Carlile Transportation Systems or small package carriers such as FedEx, DHL, and UPS, customers can track shipments online in real time.

Internet-based purchasing also provides added accessibility and convenience throughout the purchasing process. For example, through well-developed company websites, customers can research the company's product, read product reviews, and check on product availability. This can all be done immediately at any time of the day without having to listen to excruciating elevator music while on hold or without having to wait for a return call and then get it returned at a time that is less than convenient for you!

Finally, internet-based purchasing will open up a world of alternatives to standard procurement methods, such as internet auctioning. Just ten years ago, when we heard the word "auction," it conjured up images of groups of people in fur coats or tweed jackets with numbered paddle in hand competing over antique highboys or long-lost Picassos with a fast-talking auctioneer banging down a hammer to declare a sale. Say the word "auction" today, however, and immediately we picture someone sitting at a computer anxiously pressing keys as they bid on any range of items from a new house in the Bahamas to a thirty-year-old *Welcome Back Kotter* lunchbox. Because so many of us have been exposed to online auction sites such as E-Bay, purchasing from internet auctions will become a more accepted alternative means of procurement in the twenty-first century, especially when goods are hard to find or cost is a consideration.

LOOKING FORWARD: INTERNAL LOGISTICS MANAGEMENT

As we move further into the twenty-first century, rapid advanced in technology and information technology will have an impact on internal logistics management, especially within the world of warehousing. Advances in automation technology in conjunction with advances in warehouse and inventory management software are changing the shape, location, and organization of warehouses.

During the few decades, significant advances have been made in automation technologies, many of which are finding their way into some of today's larger warehouses. For example, Automatic Guided Vehicles (AGVs), automated carousels, robotic picking arms, voice controlled technology, and Automated Storage Retrieval Systems (AS/RS) are becoming increasingly popular in warehouses around the world.

Although all forms of warehouse automation are likely to increase in the twenty-first century, the most significant impact on warehouses of the future will most likely come from **Automated Storage Retrieval Systems (AS/RS)**. With an AS/RS, goods are stored in a racking system, which can reach as high as 100 feet. Palletized or individual goods are stored and issued using automated equipment typically tied to an organization's computerized inventory and warehouse management systems.

Although initial setup costs are somewhat expensive, twenty-first century organizations will turn increasingly to AS/RS systems because of the many benefits they offer, including decreased labor cost, better space utilization, and increased security. With AS/RS, inventory can be stored and orders can be picked much quicker and with far greater accuracy than with the traditional manpower-based system. Labor costs also decrease because a single person can monitor multiple pieces of equipment picking multiple orders, a job that may have previously taken ten or more people.

AS/RS is also likely to become a reality of this new century because of the improved space utilization it now provides. AS/RS equipment uses narrower warehouse aisles than traditionally needed for lift trucks and much taller racking systems, resulting in a dramatic increase in per-foot storage capacity of a warehouse. These narrower warehouse aisle and taller racking systems also provide the added bonus of increased warehouse security. Warehouse employees and other opportunity thieves are less likely to contemplate stealing goods if they must squeeze between narrow aisles with automated equipment in operation or climb fifty feet to retrieve their booty.

Because of their many advantages, AS/RS is likely to become a feature of twenty-first century warehouses, resulting in facilities that are likely to become much taller, more secure, and more densely packed with goods.

Westfalia AS/RS systems can use satellite technology to retrieve loads stored deep within high-density storage systems.

Figure 12.3 - An AS/RS System Paired with Satellite Technology

Toward the end of the twentieth century, Just-in-Time appeared to be one of the prevailing philosophies in logistics and supply chain management. Logistics managers sought to decrease the amount of inventory held, creating leaner supply chains. Although Just-in-Time systems will be considered as a part of strategic decision-making, it will not be the panacea of twenty-first century supply chain management. Dramatic increases in fuel and transportation costs may leave logistics managers once again relying on warehouses and the practice of holding inventory. One solution may instead lie in larger regional warehouses or distribution centers engaged in extensive cross-docking.

As we learned way back in Chapter 5, when warehouses or distribution centers use **cross-docking**, goods from a variety of suppliers or locations are received at one end of the facility, immediately sorted, and then immediately placed into trucks or containers at the other end of the facility for shipping. Thanks to advances in automation technology and advanced software systems, large scale cross-docking is becoming increasingly efficient and effective and will continue to become more of a standard logistics management practice in the twenty-first century.

LOOKING FORWARD: OUTBOUND LOGISTICS MANAGEMENT

When considering recent developments in the world of logistics management, the future of outbound logistics management and transportation may be the most difficult one to predict. Like the areas of purchasing and warehousing, transportation is also likely to benefit from advances in technology and information technology in the twenty-first century. For example, the twenty-first century has seen the creation of bigger and better forms of transportation, such as the Airbus 330-200F and the Boeing 747-8, two of the world's largest freight aircrafts, and Denmark's newest Maersk container ships, able to hold 18,000 TEUs (20-foot equivalent unit). This new century has also seen advances in transportation-based information technology systems, such as **transportation management system (TMS)** software, which provides solutions for shipping unit management, shipment scheduling, carrier selection, benchmarking, rate management, load optimization, documentation, and 3PLP coordination.

Despite these technology-related advances, transportation in the twenty-first century will also be fraught with many challenges posed by the global business environment, such as rising fuel costs, increasing congestion, a greater focus on port security, stricter emissions standards, and global warming. For example, as oil costs rise and roads become increasingly congested, logistics managers may have to consider switching traditionally road-based transport routes to rail-based ones. In the twenty-first century, more energy efficient trucks and materials handling equipment will become the norm. For example, Toyota is currently developing hydrogen fueled lift trucks and a joint effort between the Department of Energy's Oak Ridge National Laboratory, Schrader Trucking, Michelin, and the National Transportation Research Center is currently conducting a yearlong mission to collect data which will be made available to the automobile industry to develop more energy efficient trucks.

Two topics found frequently in twenty-first century headlines, border security and global warming, will also have an impact on transportation in the supply chain. Border security requirements, such as the relatively new U.S. Department of Homeland Security's Transportation Worker Identification Credential (TWIC) program, will require that all employees at U.S. ports will have to undergo background checks and be issued a TWIC Smart Card before they can obtain unescorted access to secure areas of maritime facilities and shipping vessels. As a result, hiring transportation workers who regularly come into contact with U.S. ports will become a more time-intensive process as potential employees are fully vetted and screened.

Global warming will also have an impact on transportation within the supply chain throughout the twenty-first century. All the current primary forms of cargo transportation (truck, rail, cargo ship, and cargo plane) are significant emitters of carbon dioxide. Those in the transportation industry may be encouraged and perhaps eventually mandated to reduce their CO_2 emissions and modify their transportation routes. For example, scientists are now finding that the condensation trails, or **contrails**, left by airplanes flying at higher altitudes form a heat-trapping web that can raise air temperatures. In the coming days of the twenty-first century, national legislation of various governments may require airplanes to fly at lower altitudes, which would increase both flight times and fuel costs.

Global warming has also presented a rather odd bright spot in transportation world. The rapidly melting polar ice cap in the Arctic Ocean is beginning to create new northern shipping lanes through areas that were once impenetrable. Rather than traverse the long, expensive, and crowded shipping lanes between Europe and ports in north east Asia, cargo ships will soon be able to take regular short cuts across the Arctic Ocean for approximately a third of the total cost.

Whether the changes the twenty-first century brings to logistics and supply chain management will be largely positive or negative has yet to be determined. We can be certain, however, that there will be change, especially in the more externally focused world of transportation. To keep up with the rapid and drastic changes in the transportation environment, logistics managers will need to be ever-vigilant of changes in the technology and the global economy.

ARMING YOURSELF FOR A WORLD OF CHANGE

To confront, tackle, and gain the greatest competitive advantage from a rapidly changing present and future in logistics and supply chain management, good logistics managers arm themselves with the most potent weapon available: knowledge!

To keep abreast of advances in logistics and supply chain management, managers and their companies stay informed using the resources of core professional organizations. These organizations typically hold annual conferences and issue both trade and academic publications covering the latest theoretical and practical advances in their fields. Their websites also provide a wealth of up-to-date information and useful links related to their fields. Many also offer a variety of free e-learning opportunities.

Core professional organizations utilized by logistics and supply chain managers and practitioners include:

- **CSCMP (www.cscmp.org).** The Council of Supply Chain Management Professionals (CSCMP) is the largest professional organization in the United States whose members represent those working and studying within the field of supply chain management. CSCMP's annual conferences and academic periodical, the *Journal of Business Logistics*, supply warehousing, inventory management, and other supply chain professionals with information on the most recent research, practices, and technologies available across the supply chain.

- **ISM (www.ism.ws).** The Institute for Supply Management (ISM) is a professional organization devoted to supply management and its related standards of excellence, research, promotional activities, and education. ISM publishes *Inside Supply Management*, a trade publication which has become an industry standard. ISM's website also contains a variety f research, education, and professional development resources.

- **WERC (www.werc.org).** The Warehousing Education and Research Council (WERC) is a professional organization devoted to warehouse management and its relationship to the supply chain. WERC publishes a wide variety of research papers and trade materials for its members and also includes member searches for both suppliers and employers.

- **MHIA (www.mhia.org).** The Material Handling Industry of America (MHIA) is a professional association for those who provide materials handling and logistics services. The MHIA website contains a variety of free online educational resources for those who want to learn more about current practices in materials handling.

- **ATA (www.truckline.com).** The American Trucking Associations (ATA) is a professional organization devoted to promoting truckers and trucking issues in the legislative, judicial, and press arenas. ATA also serves as a knowledge center to those in the trucking industry through its publications, meetings, and conventions.

- **APICS (www.apics.org).** The Association for Operations Management is a professional association for those interested in operations management, which includes the fields of production, inventory management and control, supply chain management, materials management, purchasing, and logistics. Along with information on recent research and trade publications, the APICS website also provides useful information on professional certifications within a variety of fields of operations management.

- **RFID Update (www.rfidupdate.com).** RFID Update was established in 2004 as an organization that published free daily briefings about RFID (radio frequency identification) technology news from around the world. *RFID Journal* acquired RFID Update in 2009 and it is now a comprehensive source on all things RFID for supply chain management professionals, offering a bimonthly journal, free newsletters, daily online updates, face-to-face events, and certificate-based training.

There are also a variety of government resources upon which logistics and supply chain managers rely. An especially important one is the U.S. Department of Homeland Security. The attacks on September 11, 2001 brought drastic and continuously changing security measures to global supply chain management. To keep up with the most recent changes, logistics professionals use resources such as the Transportation Security section of the **U.S. Department of Homeland Security website (www.dhs.gov/topic/transportation-security)**, which includes up-to-date information on aviation security and cargo screening.

A final change in the world of supply chain management for which logistics and supply chain professionals must be prepared is the way in which the world itself it changing! As the polar ice caps are melting, new routes for cargo ships are opening in the Arctic, allowing for faster transit times while posing a slew of new border challenges. The case study at the end of this chapter explores this exciting new topic.

To you future managers of logistics and supply chain management, thank you for taking a look at logistics with us and welcome to the brave new world of global supply chain management!

CHAPTER 12 REVIEW QUESTIONS

1. What has made today's customer a more powerful and demanding one? Please explain.

2. What is inventory visibility? What role will it play in the future of logistics management?

3. Why will "soft skills" become increasingly important to logistics managers in the twenty-first century?

4. What is the difference between off-shoring and on-shoring? What role will they play in strategic decision-making in supply chain management?

5. What are some of the advantages of internet-based purchasing?

6. What is AS/RS? What role will it play in the warehouse of the future?

7. Is Just-in-Time an obvious strategy choice for twenty-first century supply chains?

8. What impact will global warming have on the future of transportation within logistics and supply chain management?

CHAPTER 12 CASE STUDY

Melting Polar Ice and the Changing Future of Global Trade Routes

When we think of the effects of global climate change, we often picture rising seas covering cities, cataclysmic climate events, droughts and accompanying famine, and all around doom and gloom. One potential result of climate change, however, has many global supply chain managers sitting on the edge of their seats with bated breath, excitedly waiting for the change to occur: the melting of polar sea ice.

The Arctic Ocean covers approximately 5.4 million miles and is largely inaccessible because it is covered in permanent sea ice, part of which is known as the Polar Ice Cap. A 2012 study by scientists at UCLA found that the overall temperature increase by the year 2050 will be 3.6 to 6.2 degrees, with up to a 10.8 degree increase in the winter. These scientist predict that, with this increase in temperatures, polar sea ice will continue to melt at a steady rate, making it possible for ordinary, non-icebreaking ships to navigate across Arctic waters before 2040 to 2050. An ice-free shipping route in the Arctic would have an enormous impact on global supply chain management.

Currently, goods shipped from Asia to Europe or the eastern United States follow sea routes down and around through the Suez or Panama Canals. The most direct route would be through the Arctic Ocean, but it is currently impassable most of the time because of once-permanent polar sea ice. Beginning with their first observations in 1979, scientists have documented a significant shrinking of the volume of polar ice. Only in the past few years, however, has the melting been substantial enough to allow for ships' passage.

Beginning in 2007, two Arctic passages have been temporarily ice-free during the final weeks of summer. This has allowed cargo ships and freighters to begin to take tentative steps toward using the Northern Sea Route (NSR), the route along the Arctic Ocean skirting Russia's border, long considered only the domain of ice breakers and their daring captains. In 2011, the first supertanker, a mammoth 160,000 ton beast of a ship, successfully followed the NSR. This shortcut from Europe to Asia is currently only passable for two months a year with the assistance of ice breaking vessels, which allowed 46 ships to make the trip during the summer of 2012.

On the other side of the Arctic Ocean lies the Northwest Passage, the icier route that borders the United States and Canada. This route is currently navigable with icebreakers only one out of every seven years. Should Arctic scientists' predictions about the melting polar ice hold water, regularly used international shipping lanes may become available in the Northern Sea Route, Northwest Passage, and even across the North Pole itself!

New Arctic shipping lanes would have an enormous impact on supply chain distances, delivery times, and costs. For example, Humpert and Raspotnik of the Arctic Institute Center for Circumpolar Studies posit that a ship traveling from Murmansk to Tokyo, which is currently routed through the Suez Canal, would decrease its traveling distance by an astounding 40% if shipped along a polar route. Obviously, traveling at normal shipping speeds would result in dramatic fuel cost savings and provide faster service. This decreased distance would also allow for ships to engage in super-slow sailing, with our Murmansk ship arriving at Tokyo at the same time but burning only half as much fuel and with drastically reduced carbon emissions.

As the polar ice continues to melt, there will be geopolitical implications for the development of new shipping lanes. The Arctic Ocean is controlled by Russia, Denmark, Norway, Canada, and the United States and the area around the North Pole is considered international waters. New international shipping routes would need international regulation and an established infrastructure and network of ports to address fueling, supply, and safety issues.

The Arctic Council, made up of the countries that have Arctic territory (the United States, Canada, Russia, Norway, Sweden, Finland, Denmark, and Iceland), have been meeting regularly to discuss the next steps forward as the use of Arctic shipping lanes is become more feasible over the next few decades. Not only are Arctic nations beginning to take action, however. Larger non-Arctic Asian countries understand the importance of polar shipping lanes to international trade and are themselves beginning to plan. In recent years, China has established a research station in the Svalbard Archipelago and increased its economic cooperation with the tiny island nation of Iceland and the even tinier Danish Faroe Islands. India has also established an Arctic research station and South Korea has declared its interest in the area by establishing a series of Arctic policies and regulations.

References

Cayias, J. (2013, April 22) As the U.S. pivots east; Russia pivots north. *International Affairs Review*. Retrieved from http://www.iar-gwu.org/node/483.

Humpert, M. (2011, September 15) The future of the northern sea route - a "golden waterway" or a niche trade route. *The Arctic Institute Center for Circumpolar Studies* website. Retrieved from http://www.thearcticinstitute.org/2011/10/future-of-northern-sea-route-golden_13.html?m=1.

Humpert, M. and Raspotnik, A. (2012, October 11) The future of Arctic shipping. *The Arctic Institute Center for Circumpolar Studies* website. Retrieved from http://www.thearcticinstitute.org/2012/10/the-future-of-arctic-shipping.html?m=1.

Ross, P. (2013, March 5) Global warming affects polar ice caps: new shipping routes to be created as melting continues. *International Science Times*. Retrieved from http://www.isciencetimes.com/articles/4629/20130305/global-warming-polar-ice-caps-melting-shipping.htm.

Case Study Questions

1. What myriad of challenges might ships face along this new polar route?

2. In your opinion, would the reduced shipping distance, time, and cost offered by new polar routes be worth dealing with the many challenges you have described in your answer to question 1?

3. Find a map of the Arctic Ocean from a polar perspective (with the North Pole at the center of the map). Which countries appear to have the largest borders along the Arctic Ocean and possible new polar shipping routes?

4. If the U.S. were to become actively involved in the Arctic shipping routes as polar ice begins to melt, what infrastructure development would be needed? In which areas of the U.S. should this infrastructure development be focused?

Index

About the Authors

Philip M. Price, Ph.D., is a Professor and Chair of the Logistics Department at the University of Alaska Anchorage. Dr. Price has over thirty years of experience in university instruction and professional training in management and supply chain management settings. Before joining the University of Alaska Anchorage, Dr. Price was Professor of Logistics and MBA Director at the Kazakhstan Institute of Management, Economics, and Strategic Planning as part of a European Union initiative to develop an MBA program in post-Soviet Central Asia. Throughout his career, he has also provided training and consultancy services to a wide range of private and public sector customers, including Shell Oil, the Bureau of Engraving and Printing, the U.S. State Department, and the U.K. Ministry of Defense.

Dr. Price has co-authored a series of handbooks through Liverpool Academic Press, including *Stores and Distribution Management* and *Integrated Materials Management*. His research in supply chain management has appeared in the *Journal of Business Logistics*, *Journal of Marketing Channels*, and the *Central Asia Journal of Management*. His current areas of research include supply chain management in post-Soviet economies and the role of personality type within the logistics chain.

Natalie J. Harrison, M.Ed., is the owner of Access Education, a publication, training, and research firm focusing on issues within business management and logistics. She is also an Adjunct Professor at Kenai Peninsula College and has been involved with corporate communications and training for almost twenty years, delivering programs to a wide range of government and commercial clients, including the Bureau of Engraving and Printing, the U.S. Department of State, the National Institutes of Health, the U.S. Peace Corps, U.S. Forest Service, U.S. Bureau od Land Management, Arctic Slope Regional Corporation Energy Services, Federal Management Systems, Alaska Communications, Carlile Transportation, and the State of Alaska Division of Public Health. For the past ten years, she has worked extensively with the Myers-Briggs Type Indicator and is certified to administer and interpret the MBTI, the MBTI Step II, and the MMTIC.

Dr. Price and Ms. Harrison have additionally co-authored *Warehouse Management & Inventory Control* and co-edited *Fundamentals of Purchasing and Supply Management*. They are currently developing an instructional model of supply chain education for secondary school classrooms and are conducting research on the role of personality type within the supply chain.

CPSIA information can be obtained
at www.ICGtesting.com
Printed in the USA
LVHW011916050921
697025LV00008B/463